GEORGE ELIOT
and the Landscape of Time

Studies in Religion

Charles H. Long, *Editor*
The University of North Carolina at Chapel Hill

EDITORIAL BOARD

Giles B. Gunn
The University of North Carolina at Chapel Hill

Van A. Harvey
Stanford University

Wendy Doniger O'Flaherty
The University of Chicago

Ninian Smart
University of California at Santa Barbara
and the University of Lancaster

Mary Wilson Carpenter

GEORGE ELIOT
and the Landscape of Time

Narrative Form and Protestant Apocalyptic History

The University of North Carolina Press
CHAPEL HILL   LONDON

© 1986 The University of North Carolina Press
All rights reserved
Manufactured in the United States of America

Library of Congress Cataloging in Publication Data
Carpenter, Mary Wilson, 1937–
  George Eliot and the landscape of time.

  (Studies in religion)
  Bibliography: p.
  Includes index.
  1. Eliot, George, 1818–1880—Religion.
2. Apocalyptic literature—History and criticism.
3. Protestantism in literature. 4. History in
literature. 5. Time in literature. 6. Narration
(Rhetoric) I. Title. II. Series: Studies in religion
(Chapel Hill, N.C.)
PR4692.R4C37   1986   823'.8   85-31831
ISBN 0-8078-1681-7

Chapter 5 was published in somewhat different form as "The Apocalypse of the Old Testament: *Daniel Deronda* and the Interpretation of Interpretation" in *PMLA* (January 1984).

Some material from Chapters 1 and 3 was published under the title "Ambiguous Revelations: The Apocalypse and Victorian Literature" by Mary Wilson Carpenter and George P. Landow, in *The Apocalypse in English Renaissance Thought and Literature*, edited by C. A. Patrides and Joseph A. Wittreich, Jr., copyright © 1984 by Manchester University Press. Reprinted with permission of Manchester University Press.

Design by Dariel Mayer

For Cynthia, Deborah, and Grace

Contents

Preface ix

Acknowledgments xiii

CHAPTER 1 George Eliot and
the School of the Prophets 3

CHAPTER 2 History and Hermeneutics
in *Adam Bede* 30

CHAPTER 3 The Scheme of the Apocalypse 54

CHAPTER 4 Transposing the Apocalypse
in *Middlemarch* 104

CHAPTER 5 The Apocalypse
of the Old Testament 131

CHAPTER 6 Revising *The Christian Year* 154

Notes 191

Bibliography 223

Index 241

Preface

> He was absorbed in mastering all those painstaking interpretations of the Book of Daniel, which are by this time well gone to the limbo of mistaken criticism . . . —*Felix Holt*

It is sometimes more productive to investigate those sources an author disclaims than those openly avowed. According to Jacques Lacan, the *epos* by which the individual "brings back into the present the origins of his own person" often includes a "discourse of earlier days in its own archaic, even foreign language."[1] We may not think it important that the interpretive discourse George Eliot here hastens to assure us was "well gone to the limbo of mistaken criticism" in fact was flourishing in the mid-Victorian era, as it continues to do in the late twentieth century.[2] But certainly more important than her deliberate underestimate of its popularity is her veiled admission of a personal knowledge of "those painstaking interpretations," for what is recognized as "mistaken" does not vanish into some welcome limbo but continues to construct our recognition of what we believe is *not* mistaken. The "archaic" discourse George Eliot consigns to limbo is actually one she employs extensively in her construction of personal and historical origins—and ends.

Like Rufus Lyon, the young Mary Ann Evans was for a time absorbed in the intricacies of apocalyptic "continuous historical" interpretation centering on the Books of Daniel and Revelation. My investigation therefore at first sought to recover an understanding of this traditionally Protestant interpretation of biblical prophecy in order to better understand George Eliot's "creation" as a historian. I wanted to know how this exegetical tradition presupposed "history" in narrative, what particular designs and strategies it might have furnished a Victorian novel-writer, how it constructed beginnings, ends, and middles. I have noted in my text that a passion for structure characterizes Victorian "continuous historical" exegesis: the significant difference between typology and the "prophetic history" over which Rufus Lyon labors may be the desire for an all-inclusive narrative of history.

As Patrick Fairbairn (a Victorian scholar of both typology and prophecy) commented, "the evidence of prophecy is essentially of a connected and cumulative nature. It does not consist so much in the verifications given to a few remarkable predictions, as in the establishment of an entire series, closely related to each other, and forming a united and comprehensive whole."[3] Not only was the connection between prophecy and history "close and pervading," but "the testimony of prophecy, therefore, like the testimony of history, is a chain composed of many links, each running into others before and after it." The "end" of prophetic exegesis was to construct a narrative of historical coherence, or as Fairbairn put it, God "informs the minds of his people in respect to the end, that they may come also to know better than they could otherwise have done, the beginning and the middle."

The exegetical weaving together of evidential "links" into a "chain" of prophetic history obviously resembles the tasks of both novel-writer and novel-reader. Its greater capacity to satisfy a desire for narrative coherence as well as the common belief in its essential historical validity may account for its greater popularity in the nineteenth century than typology, which Fairbairn describes as "one of the most neglected departments of theological science."[4] As Fairbairn explained, typology had never "altogether escaped from the region of doubt and uncertainty," while prophetic exegesis—despite the embarrassment of many conflicting interpretations of individual prophecies—affirmed a single "great plan" in scripture, stretching from "the fall of man to the final consummation of all things in glory."[5] Fairbairn's description clarifies not only Rufus Lyon's but Mary Ann Evans's interest in mastering such interpretations. As exegetes believed "prophecy" could not be distinguished from "history," so neither of these discourses can be separated from the monumental development of the realistic novel that took place in the nineteenth century. All three enterprises depended on a belief in narrative as the medium that could create beginning and end, thus conferring significance on the "middle."[6]

But to an even greater extent than George Eliot's "creation" in history, I found myself drawn to a consideration of the effects of her inevitable "fall" from history when she broke with the church and began to question all of its teachings. Such a "fall," I came to realize, must provoke the recognition that every history maps the landscape of time by imposing an imaginary line on an otherwise inchoate mass, and that every history is therefore a fiction. A "fall" from "continuous historical" exposition necessarily exposed the diversity and plurality of history in a way that indoctrination in the most advanced German historical theory might not. From such considerations emerged the hypothesis that George Eliot's narratives construct multiple "fictions" of history through reference to various formal and symbolic systems of codification.

Probably the most startling corollary of this thesis for my readers will be the proposal that George Eliot often manipulated numerological symbolism, even implicating chapter numbers in her extensive plays on Victorian "continuous historical" exegesis. Readers recognize her pervasive reference to biblical texts, yet often neglect the fact that such references are never to biblical texts transparently apprehended but always to interpretations of them. I have tried to read such references as George Eliot's response to a specifically Victorian hermeneutics—as part of a dialogue between the author and a now invisible interpretive body. That she no longer venerated that body as "truth" or "reality" but saw it as the construct of certain very human expositors suggests even more, I believe, that she could ironize or parody it, or even convert it into comedy, the more pleasurable for its less public puns bubbling beneath the public wit that every reader enjoys.

It is my thesis that the body of "mistaken criticism" over which Rufus Lyon labors thus forms the basis for many of George Eliot's constructions and deconstructions of illusions of coherence. The knowledge that the "landscape of time" was a fiction seems only to have facilitated her production of new apocalyptic "histories."

Acknowledgments

I am most indebted to Roger B. Henkle and George P. Landow, under whose guidance I originally began my work on narrative form and biblical hermeneutics. But I would also especially like to thank Joseph A. Wittreich, Jr., and Barbara Kiefer Lewalski, whose scholarship and teaching, though not in the field of Victorian literature, was invaluable to my study of an exegetical tradition that proved to be as important to George Eliot as to Milton, despite their different genres and genders. Lastly, I also thank Claire Rosenfield, who encouraged my work on George Eliot's "subversive hermeneutics."

Fellowships from both the Danforth and the Charlotte W. Newcombe foundations supported my work while at Brown University. I am indebted for support of another kind from the members of the Pembroke Research Seminar at Brown University, whose rigorous critical discourse informed and stimulated my attempts to analyze George Eliot's rapprochement with a hermeneutical discourse of a very different order. I am especially grateful to both Elizabeth Weed and Joan Scott, whose searching analysis of historical and interpretive problems in the seminar did much to revise my assumptions and open new possibilities.

U. C. Knoepflmacher's reading and criticism of the manuscript led to many revisions. He is not responsible for any remaining mistakes, but certainly is for some of the improvements made between the final version and earlier ones.

A group known as ID 450 has greatly fostered my involvement not only with George Eliot but with women's writing "in the plural." Finally, I would like to thank my mother, who first read to me, and my husband, who stayed with me throughout the years of my "adult" education and who has contributed more than he recognizes to this book. To my three daughters, who mothered both the text and its author, this book is dedicated.

GEORGE ELIOT
and the Landscape of Time

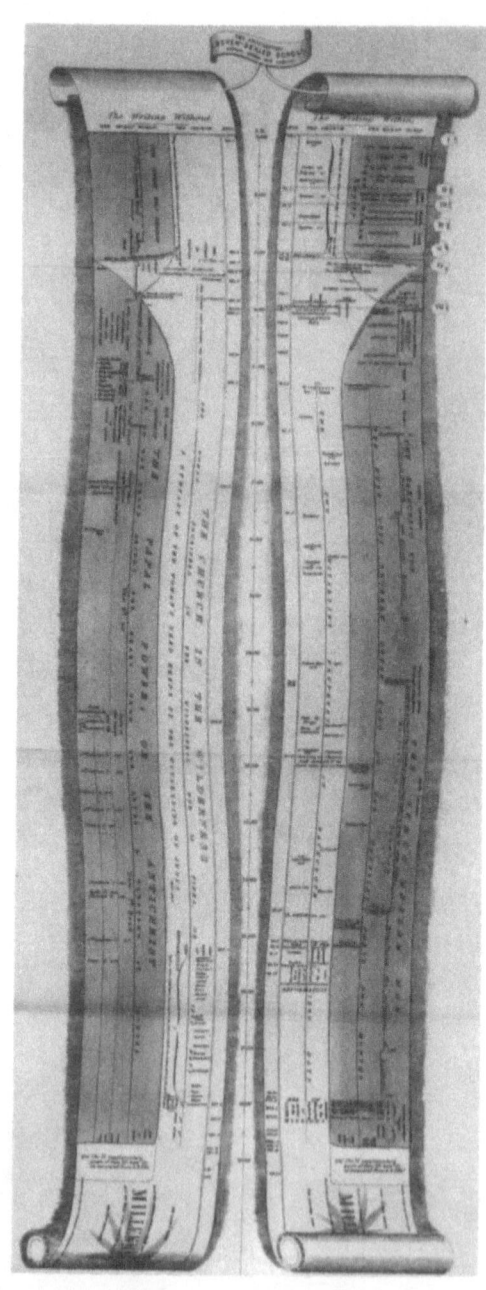

"The Apocalyptic Seven-Sealed Scroll Written Within and Without." From E. B. Elliott, Horae Apocalypticae (1862).

CHAPTER 1

George Eliot and the School of the Prophets

Although scholars have repeatedly scrutinized George Eliot's religious beliefs, her youthful interest in prophecy "fulfilled and unfulfilled" has gone largely unremarked.[1] Yet her first conception of history seems to have taken shape in the school of "continuous historical" exposition of the Book of Revelation. This clerical, millenarian tradition—a prominent aspect of British exegesis since the Reformation—reached new heights of scholarly development, as well as popular interest, during the Victorian era.[2] Readers approached the Apocalypse of St. John as a mirror of "continuous" history, its mystic scheme believed to signify the history of the Western world from the beginning of the Christian era to the end of time. Enthusiasm for this school of apocalyptics was fed not only by continuing reevaluations of the French Revolution but by conservative responses to what were seen as major nineteenth-century "revolutions": the Greek uprising against the Turks; the Catholic Emancipation Bill, Jewish Civil Disabilities Bill, and Reform Act in Great Britain; the Napoleonic Wars; and most importantly, the Revolution of 1848. British expositors of the prophecies interpreted these events as the fulfillment of the third and last septenary of the Apocalypse—the seven Vials, whose outpourings of disaster heralded the near approach of the Second Advent.

But it was not only revolutionary events that fueled the "continuous historical" expositors, but the very spirit of the age itself. As John Stuart Mill observed, the nineteenth century was obsessed with history as no previous age had ever been.[3] Nineteenth-century apocalyptic expositors exhibit this fascination with the past even more than with the future: their explications of apocalyptic imagery take the form of lengthy discussions of historical minutiae, and often conclude with detailed charts and diagrams that attempt to encompass every important event from the first century A.D., or even from thousands of years before Christ, to the nineteenth century. In their works the landscape of history gradually took on a new shape, exhibiting an increasingly formal order even as it became more heavily weighted with historical data. Unwittingly, the "continuous historical" expositors created a literary hybrid: though all agreed the Apocalypse was a "poem," their commentaries interpreted it as a chronology of history, a work of utmost "realism." Yet despite their lengthy historical annotations, the Apocalypse remained the poetry of history or, as one well-known expositor put it, "God's philosophy of history!"[4]

George Eliot's early letters not only reveal her powerful attraction to the study of prophecy, but document her detailed knowledge of the "continuous historical" school of interpretation. By the time she became a writer of historical fiction she had long since rejected belief in the supernatural inspiration of the prophecies, yet I will propose that the apocalyptic structure of time became a "fiction" of time for George Eliot—a "fiction" of time that not only provided an elaborate narrative scheme for *Romola* but informed the narrative and metaphoric patterns of other novels. In 1860, *Essays and Reviews* brought to the forefront the long-simmering confrontation between German "higher criticism" and the English love for reading the Apocalypse as an inspired map of time. George Eliot's decision to write a "historical romance" based on the life of the apocalyptic prophet Girolamo Savonarola should be explored in the context of that confrontation and of her own past experience with "continuous historical" exegesis. The genesis of *Romola* is thus to be sought first in the apocalyptics of George Eliot's youth.

But George Eliot's early education in the "School of the Prophets" seems to have furnished her with much more than narrative schemes and metaphoric networks. Her entire canon of prose narratives, from *Scenes of Clerical Life* to *Daniel Deronda*, exhibits a continuing fascination with "ecclesiastical history," and at least one volume of poetry appears based on the liturgical interpretation of that history. It was ecclesiastical history that first opened the door to the poetry of history for the young Mary Ann Evans, a door that the German higher criticism must then have seemed to slam shut. The fall from orthodox Christianity in the Victorian era was also inevitably a fall from "history." But like its original it was a fortunate fall, for it opened the way to a perception of the duplicity of both history and narrative. As George Eliot wrote in her first full-length novel, *Adam Bede*, "No story is the same to us after a lapse of time; or rather, we who read it are no longer the same interpreters."[5] George Eliot learned early that history does not exist, only historians. But we may uncover a central key to her representation of history—a representation always resistant to a single interpretation—in her schooling in "continuous historical" hermeneutics.

Side by side with the sober piety of Mary Ann Evans's early letters exists a strain of enthusiasm—an enthusiasm that she strove to distinguish from millenarian fanaticism. As she confided to Maria Lewis in November 1838, she was fond of "unfulfilled prophecy," yet she emphasized the need for sobriety and caution in such studies:

> Are you fond of the study of unfulfilled prophecy? The vagaries of the Irvingites and the blasphemies of Joanna Southcote together with the fanciful interpretations of more respectable names have been regarded as beacons, and have caused many persons to hold all diving into the future plans of Providence as the boldest presumption; but I do think that a sober and prayerful consideration of the mighty revolutions ere long to take place in our world would by God's blessing serve to make us less grovelling, more devoted and energetic in the service of God. Of course I mean only such study as pigmies like myself in intellect and acquirement are able to prosecute; the perusal and comparison of Scripture and the works of pious and judicious men on the subject.[6]

Despite her attempt at restraint, the sense of imminent apocalypse that appears in this letter is even more evident in an October 1840 letter:

> Events are now so momentous, and the elements of society in so chemically critical a state that a drop seems enough to change its whole form. After expending the imagination in questions as to the mode in which the great transmutation of the kingdoms of this world into the kingdoms of our Lord will be effected we are reduced to the state of pausa-

tion in which the inhabitants of heaven are described to be held, before the outpouring of the Vials. (*GEL*, 1:72)

This combination of enthusiastic apocalypticism with a conservative religious outlook characterizes early nineteenth-century evangelical Anglicanism, for millenarian beliefs had infiltrated the established church. Ernest R. Sandeen documents millenarianism as a substantial religious movement in both the United States and England during the nineteenth century.[7] (Millenarianism, as opposed to millennialism, is a belief in the literal return of Christ *before* the millennium.) In England, the most influential millenarians were members of either the Anglican or the Scottish national churches. Sandeen divides this movement into two major phases: 1800–1845 and 1845–78.

Various events have been suggested as instigation for the movement, such as the French Revolution and later political revolutions in Europe or the growth of the missionary movement in England.[8] But whatever its origins, the movement was from its beginning characterized by "a new passion for the interpretation of the prophetic scriptures."[9] This passion for prophecy was far removed from the teaching of such popular, self-educated millenarians as Joanna Southcott: the prophetic exegetes of the Anglican church were almost all university men who prided themselves not only on their sober restraint but on their "laborious" scholarly productions. Although the French Revolution had given their calculations of the millennial date a new excitement, they retained the Anglican respect for tradition. Their interpretations of the prophetic scriptures—particularly Daniel and Revelation—as symbolic history rested on an exegetical tradition going back to the time of the Reformation or, some said, even to Joachim of Fiore.[10] Believing that the "evidence" or proof of Christianity provided by the fulfillment of prophecy "increases in strength as time rolls on," nineteenth-century exegetes devoted themselves to discovering the vast new array of parallels between history and prophecy now made possible by the "science" of history.[11] More of the Apocalypse than ever before could be unveiled because more of history had taken place and fulfilled its mystic scroll.

That the young Mary Ann Evans shared this fascination for historico-prophetic investigations is demonstrated by her plans for an "Ecclesiastical Chart" that she intended to sell as a church benefit.[12] The chart, as she described it to Maria Lewis in March 1840, at first appears an unordered jumble of ecclesiastical and political history, but her comments reveal that it would actually have followed a coherent design of history based on the scheme of the Apocalypse:[13]

> The series of perpendicular columns will successively contain, the Roman Emperors with their dates, the political and religious state of the Jews, the bishops, remarkable men and events in the several churches, a column being devoted to each of the chief ones, the aspect of heathenism and Judaism toward Christianity, the chronology of the Apos[tolical] and Patristical writings, schisms and heresies, General Councils, eras of corruption, under which head the remarks would be general, and I thought possibly *an application of the Apocalyptic prophecies*, which would merely require a few figures and not take up room. (GEL, 1:44, my emphasis)

Her intention to include Apocalyptic prophecies in the form of "a few figures" only (numbers for chapter and verse) suggests she may have had in mind the kind of simple chronologic-prophetic chart included in Edward Bickersteth's *Scripture Help*. This volume was published in the Christian's Family Library, to which Mary Ann Evans subscribed in 1839.[14]

Bickersteth's chart, which he noted was based on Thomas Scott's interpretation, divides history into eleven periods beginning with the Creation (in 4004 B.C.) and ending with the Reformation. Historical events are correlated with apocalyptic prophecies from the end of the first century A.D. onward. Mary Ann Evans apparently planned a much more detailed construction of early Christian history only. As in the *Scripture Help* chart, however, the point she had selected for termination of her history is significant in apocalyptic exegesis:

> I think there must be a break in the chart after the establishment of Christianity as the religion of the Empire, and I have come to a determination not to carry it beyond the first acknowledgment of the supremacy of the Pope, by Phocas in 606 when Mahommedanism be-

> came a besom of destruction in the hand of the Lord, and completely altered the aspect of Ecclesiastical Hist[or]y. So much for this, at present, airy project, about which I hope never to teaze you more. (*GEL*, 1:44–45)

The confident assertion of the year 606 A.D. as a major division in history links Mary Ann Evans clearly to a stage in "continuous historical" interpretation that developed about a decade after the French Revolution, in 1805 or 1806. Both Archdeacon Woodhouse, in *The Apocalypse* (1805), and George Stanley Faber, in *Dissertations on the Prophecies . . . Relative to the Great Period of the 1260 Years* (1806), make the claim that the year 606 gave rise to the "double apostasy" of papal Rome and Mohammedanism, thus fulfilling the prophecies of Daniel's "little horn" and St. John's "reign of the beast" (Antichrist), or 1260 days.[15] ("Continuous historical" expositors utilized the year-day principle, or the belief that a "day" in prophecy symbolized a year in history.) Since Faber's entire work focuses on this point, he is generally credited—or attacked—for the interpretation by later expositors. Faber states that the year which marks the beginning of the 1260 days

> seems most probably to be the year, in which the Bishop of Rome was constituted supreme head of the Church with the proud title of Universal Bishop: for by such an act . . . the saints of the Most High . . . were formally given by the chief secular power, the head of the Roman Empire, into the hands of the encroaching little horn. This year was the year 606, when the reigning Emperor Phocas, the representative of the sixth head of the beast, declared Pope Boniface to be Universal Bishop: and the Roman church hath ever since shewn itself to be that little horn, into whose hands the saints were then delivered.[16]

The year 606, according to Faber, was also the beginning of "the contemporary eastern Apostacy of Mohammedanism," an interpretation that arose from the fact that "Mahomet" was believed to have retired to the Cave of Hera and there conceived his new religion in that year.

Faber's motive for devoting an entire work to the explication of the 1260 "days" illustrates a dominant concern of the nineteenth-century "continuous historical" expositors. Since the French Revolution, apocalyptic works such as James Bicheno's *Signs of the Times* (1794) had interpreted the years 529–33 A.D., or the reign of Justinian, as the beginning of the 1260 years. The era of the French Revolution, 1789–93, thus represented the end of the 1260 years. This interpretation not only emphasized the "positive" aspect of the French Revolution as the overthrow of the papacy, but implied that the millennium was to begin whenever the French Revolution could be construed as having ended. Faber's revival of Bishop Newton's discarded suggestion about the year 606 allowed him to postpone the date of the millennium to 1866 and to interpret the French Revolution as only the first in a series of blows that would eventually topple the papal "beast."[17] Faber's work thus exemplifies the characteristic nineteenth-century disillusionment with the French Revolution. As opposed to the more radical interpretations of expositors writing in the early years of the Revolution, later writers developed an increasingly reactionary attitude toward political and social revolution of any kind.

The interpretation of the 1260 years espoused by Mary Ann Evans in 1839 also illustrates another significant characteristic of the nineteenth-century "continuous historical" expositors: their extensive knowledge of, and reliance upon, previous exposition of the prophecies. As a commentator writing in the *Jewish Expositor* (the journal of the London Society for the Conversion of the Jews) put it,

> ... it cannot be doubted that for the right interpretation of the book [the Apocalypse], the previous knowledge of its general scheme and structure, is indispensable.... As the waters of many streams form at length the majestic river, which rolls its flood into the ocean, the operation of many minds is required for the enlargement of knowledge, and to render it accurate and perfect.[18]

The "continuous historical" expositors thought of themselves as a community of biblical scholars and students devoted to the pursuit of a common truth. As the century wore on, their works exhibited an ever larger amount of annotation and allusion to "facts" established by earlier commentators. Because of their emphasis on joint effort, the development of the apocalyptic scheme can be charted fairly precisely through various changes in exposition during the century. Mary Ann Evans's scheme, it would appear, was slightly behind the times.

Faber's interpretation of 606 A.D. was, as already mentioned, in conflict with those designating 529 A.D., or the Justinian Code, as the commencement of the 1260 years and the reign of the papal "beast." This latter interpretation was defended by James Hatley Frere and eventually by Edward Irving. Irving organized a series of prophetic conferences at Albury Park during the first week of Advent in the years 1826–28. One of the points agreed upon at these conferences was that the 1260 years were to be measured from the reign of Justinian to the French Revolution.[19] Whether Faber was shaken by this consensus is unknown, but in 1828 he published his *Sacred Calendar of Prophecy*, which he stated was to supersede his earlier work and in which he declared yet another date for the commencement of the 1260 years: 604 A.D.[20]

Edward Bickersteth's works on prophecy clearly reflect this change in the apocalyptic scheme of history. The chronological chart in *Scripture Help*, reprinted in the Christian's Family Library series before 1834, designates 606 A.D. as the year when "Boniface, the third Bishop of Rome, procures the title of Universal Bishop from the Emperor Phocas" and also notes that "about the same time Mahomet commences his imposture in the East." No reference to Justinian is made. But in his later *Practical Guide to the Prophecies*, the "Sacred Chronology" lists Justinian's Code in 533 and suggests 1792 as the close of the 1260 days, omitting the year 606 from the chart.[21] Moreover, Bickersteth explicitly comments that "the most modern opinion (that of Mr. Cuninghame, Mr. Gisborne, Mr. Frere, and Mr. Irving)" for the commencement of the 1260 years is "A.D. 533, the date of Justinian's Edict in favour of the Pope." Thus, although Mary Ann Evans began work on her chart in 1839, her 606 A.D. termination suggests she was acquainted only with prophetic exposition published in the early 1830s or before.

On the basis of this conclusion, it is possible to deduce that the particular "apocalyptic prophecies" included in her chart would have been the first six seals (Rev. 6), the "sealed nation" (Rev. 7), and the first four trumpets (Rev. 8). (The fifth or first woe trumpet, Rev. 9:1–12, was almost universally interpreted as Mahomet and represents the cutoff point in her chart.) Most interpreters, following in Mede's tradition, interpreted the first six seals as the history of the church under pagan Rome. The mysterious "sealed nation" of the seventh chapter, however, received varying interpretations. In a strictly "continuous historical" interpretation, it could be seen as the era of Constantine, when Christianity became the official religion, but only those believers holding to a spiritual doctrine were "sealed" by God. Because of the obvious similarity between this chapter and the fourteenth, which concludes with a divine "harvest of the earth," it was also interpreted as the antitype of the Hebrew harvest festival, or Feast of Tabernacles. A third interpretation reveals a chauvinistic character, for some saw the "sealed nation" of Apocalypse as England herself, destined to carry out the sacred mission of propagating Protestantism. The four first trumpets were usually interpreted—again, following Mede—as the barbaric invasions of the Roman Empire. Since her chart would not continue beyond 606 A.D., Mary Ann Evans avoided any near approach to the problematic date of the millennium. Nevertheless, her selection of 606 implies belief in a Second Advent in 1866.

Mary Ann Evans seems to have been unaware of the large number of prophetic charts already in existence at this time, but the announcement of her plans quickly led to this discovery. On the "nice miniature chart" sent her by Maria Lewis, she commented that he (Dr. Pearson) "at least has not realized my conceptions" (*GEL*, 1:44). Within a few days she also wrote Martha Jackson to state she was "delighted with the little compact chronological table, the more so that it trenches not on my ground. Who is its author or authoress? and whose is the scheme of prophetic interpretation?"[22] But in May, when news of yet another chart reached her, she wrote Maria Lewis she had decided to give up her own project because "Seeley and Burnside have just published a Chart of Ecclesiastical History" (*GEL*, 1:51). By such a hair, the future George Eliot escaped publication first as a historico-apocalyptic expositor rather than as a poet.

Her ignorance of the most recent apocalyptic interpretation, however, does not mean she was totally isolated from current debates about prophecy and its interpretation. The pages of the *Christian Observer*, in which she published her first poem in January 1840, reflect many of the developments in prophecy "fulfilled and unfulfilled" that took place during her childhood and adolescence.[23] In 1825, while she was still a child, two lengthy articles reviewed a dozen recent English works on prophecy, including John Davison's *Discourses on Prophecy* (1825), which traced the outline of history in biblical narrative from the Creation down to the present, and Edward Bickersteth's *Practical Remarks on the Prophecies*.[24] The latter work must be distinguished from Bickersteth's *Practical Guide to the Prophecies*, which reflects his changed views after becoming a millenarian in the early 1830s.[25]

The writer of the 1825 review remarks on "the present revivification" of the millennial question, a revival perhaps stimulated in part by the Greek revolt against the Turks—an event that many thought fulfilled Faber's prediction of the sixth vial as the "drying up" of the Turkish Empire. Another factor involved in the 1825 "revivification" was a renewal of interest in the conversion of the Jews. In 1815, Lewis Way had invested his fortune in the nearly bankrupt London Society for the Conversion of Jews. Thereafter he wrote articles for the *Jewish Expositor* under the pseudonym of Basilicus, arguing for the premillennial advent of Christ.[26] One of the works reviewed in the *Christian Observer* article is *Letters by Basilicus*, reprinted from the *Jewish Expositor* for 1820, 1821, and 1822, and a main thrust of the reviewer's essay is the failure of both early and modern expositors to definitively solve the problem of Christ's pre- or postmillennial advent. Placing his discussion in the context of two centuries of exegesis, the reviewer contrasts those writers who follow in the "allegorizing" tradition of Grotius, Vitringa, and Whitby, and consequently expect a spiritual millennium that may already have begun, with those who follow in the tradition of "the altogether stupendous Mede" and look for a literal appearance of Christ preceding an imminent millennium. It may perhaps be characteristic of this early date in the century that the reviewer is unwilling to take a stand in "this difficult controversy."

During the next five years, interest in prophecy clearly grew among the readers of the *Christian Observer*: many articles and letters appeared on such still-unsettled questions as the number of the beast, whether the seventh chapter of Revelation referred to a period in church history or to the spiritual "church triumphant," and, of course, the commencement of the 1260 years.²⁷ In March 1830, Henry Drummond contributed a "Popular Introduction to the Study of the Apocalypse" that presented a "continuous historical" interpretation identifying the seven seals with Christian history from the time of Constantine to the Reformation, the seven trumpets with the division of the Roman Empire and with the armies of Mahomet and the Turks, and the seven vials with the French Revolution. Drummond's interpretation also identifies the "sealed nation" of chapter seven in the Apocalypse as most probably England, because of its missionary labors and its antipapist stand.²⁸

In 1835, James Hatley Frere commented that the "inundation of prophetic writings with which the church has been deluged for the last 10 years" had in some measure passed away.²⁹ This "deluge" was probably occasioned by the Reform movement (1829–32), especially the Catholic Emancipation Act. As Owen Chadwick comments, "the Book of Revelation rose easily to the surface" during this chaotic period, with the move for Catholic emancipation especially inclined to stir up the antipapal expositors of the Apocalypse.³⁰ It was also during these years that Edward Irving began to preach in London and that members of his congregation were reported to speak "in tongues." In 1833, Irving was expelled from his Scottish Presbyterian ministry, but eight hundred members of his congregation joined him in the founding of the Catholic Apostolic church. Mary Ann Evans's reference to the "vagaries" of the Irvingites indicates her conservative disdain for such extremes of religious enthusiasm. Finally, it was during this period that cholera reached England from the continent—an event also interpreted in apocalyptic terms by many.³¹

But the lull in prophetic writings to which Frere referred was only temporary, for by 1839 the heat of the Millennial debate was reflected in *Christian Observer* articles on the missionary question. An acrimonious dispute centered on a Rev. Goode who had stated that he did not expect great results from missionary endeavors because these were *not* premillennial times but rather "the times of the Gentiles," when the church could expect persecution and diminishment.³² The conservative editors of the *Observer* did their best to damp down the resulting flames of controversy, noting that "in reply to several correspondents who take different views of the bearing of the Pre-Millenarian question upon Missionary Societies, we think enough has been said on both sides for the purposes of truth, and that more might not promote love."[33]

Missionary work was in fact central to the Millennial question, for to "millennialists," or those who did not expect the literal advent of Christ until after a millennium on earth, conversion of the heathen—particularly of the Jews—was essential to the creation of the Lord's kingdom. But to millenarians, or those who looked for a literal appearance of Christ and resurrection of the saints *before* the inauguration of the millennium, missionary work was no longer so crucial. On becoming a millenarian in the early 1830s, for example, Edward Bickersteth "renounced the opinion, that missionary agencies would secure the gradual conversion of the world," although he continued to believe "they were the plain duty, and one of the highest privileges of the Christian."[34]

In Ernest Tuveson's useful distinction, millenarianism, or premillennialism, is commonly associated with a politically conservative attitude.[35] Since the millennium is not to be brought in through human efforts at reform but will take place entirely through supernatural means, political reform is no longer of primary importance. Owen Chadwick has observed that, despite their visions of millennial glory, the Evangelicals were "prayer book men, establishment men, Tories." In their interpretation, "Reform was of the heart," not the institution.[36] Edward Bickersteth, for example, argued vehemently against the Jewish Civil Disabilities Bill of 1836, stating that "what is called the *liberal* course really is open disbelief and contempt of the truths of God's word" and that "faithfulness to Christ is then the very basis of which power ought to be entrusted by a Christian government to those ruling under it. . . . On this principle our whole constitution was formed. Our king is to be a Protestant."[37]

Despite the editors' attempts to avoid too specific predictions of the millennium, a sense of impending apocalypse permeates the *Observer* throughout the years of George Eliot's youth. When, in January 1840, she published a poem—"Knowing That Shortly I Must Put Off This Tabernacle"—in the *Observer*, it is not surprising her text is taken from 2 Peter, an apocalyptic text that, like the

Book of Revelation, had been explicated by Joseph Mede.[38] The poem is itself an example of a "sober and prayerful" sense of apocalypse.

Not very long after she gave up her intended chart of ecclesiastical history, Mary Ann Evans broke decisively with Evangelical Christianity. Gordon Haight has described her "Holy War" with her father, beginning with a letter to him stating her intention to cease churchgoing.[39] This letter was written in January 1842, when she was twenty-two years old. From this time on, she read and studied "higher criticism" of the Bible—criticism that, among other things, rejected the interpretation of the prophecies as a supernatural knowledge of the future, and instead saw the prophet as a human being circumscribed by his own historical context. It is perhaps indicative that, among the few English works of this type written before 1860, the nature of biblical prophecy is a prominent concern.[40] Charles Hennell's *An Inquiry Concerning the Origin of Christianity* (1838) is probably the earliest such work read by George Eliot.[41] Although Hennell proposes that the prophecies do not refer to Christ but relate only to the Jewish nation, he deals extensively with the significance of Old Testament prophecies, referring to English historical expositors as well as German critics.

In 1851, George Eliot reviewed Robert Mackay's *The Progress of the Intellect* (1850). She had by this time already translated Strauss's *Das Leben Jesu* and some of Spinoza's *Tractatus Theologico-Politicus*, and it is interesting that she considered Mackay's work not only the equal but the superior of German "higher criticism": "We believe Mr. Mackay's work is unique in its kind. England has been slow to use or to emulate the immense labours of Germany in the departments of mythology and biblical criticism; but when once she does so, the greater solidity and directness of the English mind ensure a superiority of treatment."[42] Mackay's work is a *Universalgeschichte*, or universal history of the education of the human race, in which the Greek and Hebrew traditions are the chief educators. It may be seen, in fact, as a secularized version of such English works as John Davison's *Discourses on Prophecy*, which traces the history of the human race as divided between Jews and Gentiles and mirrored in the scriptures. Mackay explicitly interprets the prophetic structures of time as *poetic* structures. He interprets the

"KNOWING THAT SHORTLY I MUST PUT OFF THIS TABERNACLE."

As o'er the fields by evening's light I stray,
I hear a still small whisper—" Come away!
Thou must to this bright lovely world soon say—
    Farewell!"

The mandate I obey—my lamp prepare,
Gird up my garments, give my soul to pray'r,
And say to earth and all that breathe earth's air—
    Farewell!

Thou sun, to whose parental beam I owe
The sight that gladden'd me while here below,
Moon, stars, and covenant-confirming bow—
    Farewell!

Ye verdant meads, fair blossoms stately trees,
Sweet songs of birds, and soothing hum of bees,
Refreshing odours wafted by the breeze—
    Farewell!

Ye patient servants of Creation's lord,
Whose mighty strength is govern'd by his word,
Who raiment, food, and help in toil, afford—
    Farewell!

Ye feebler, freer tribes that people air,
Ye gaudy insects, making buds your lair,
Ye that in water shine and frolic there—
    Farewell!

Books, that have been to me as chests of gold,
Which, miser-like, I secretly have told,
And for you love, health, friendship, peace, have sold—
    Farewell!

Blest tome, to thee, whose truth-writ page once known,
Fades not before heaven's sunshine or hell's moan,
I say not of God's earthly gifts alone,
    Farewell!

Dear kindred, whom the Lord to me has giv'n,
Must the strong tie that binds us now be riven?
No! say I—only till we meet in heaven—
    Farewell!

Then shall my new-born senses find new joy,
New sights, new sounds my eyes and ears employ,
Nor fear that word that here brings sad alloy,
    Farewell!   M. A. E.

*** We do not often add a note to a poem; but if St. John found no temple in the New Jerusalem, neither will there be any need of a Bible; for we shall not then see through a glass darkly,—through the veil of sacraments or the written word—but face to face. The Bible is God's gift, but not for heaven's use. Still, on the very verge of heaven we may cling to it, after we have bid farewell to every thing   rthly; and this perhaps is what M. A. E. means.

"Knowing That Shortly I Must Put Off This Tabernacle," poem by
Mary Anne Evans, as published in the Christian Observer, *January 1840*.

six days of creation, for example, as a symmetrical scheme divided into two parts, with each of the second three days complementing the first three.[43] Moreover, Mackay redefines the function of the prophet as that of breaking through prejudice and formalism in order to bring about moral reform: the prophet reforms ancient ritual and symbolism into a "higher spiritualism." George Eliot refers to this point herself in her admiring review, stating that Mackay delineates the origin of Christianity as "an expansion of the prophetic spiritualism."[44]

Despite these early English attempts at exegesis of the prophetic tradition as a literary and historical phenomenon, millenarianism and "continuous historical" exegesis of the Apocalypse entered a second phase of growth in the late 1840s. In 1844, Edward Bishop Elliott published the first edition of his massive commentary on the Apocalypse, *Horae Apocalypticae*. In its summing up and pronouncing on apocalyptics from all eras and in many different languages, *Horae Apocalypticae* seemed a monumental achievement to Evangelical readers. Following the second edition in 1846, the Rev. John Cumming gave a series of lectures in Exeter Hall, explicating the Book of Revelation chapter by chapter. In the first of these lectures, he candidly admitted he would borrow all he could from Elliott's work, which he considered "one of the ablest productions on this subject."[45] Cumming's lectures were in fact simply a condensed and more palatable version of Elliott's commentary. The lectures evidently played to packed halls, and when published in book form went through edition after edition. It was these lectures that George Eliot read when, in 1855, she decided to castigate "Evangelical Teaching" in the person of Dr. Cumming.[46]

E. B. Elliott not only based his exposition of the Apocalypse on an extensive knowledge of previous "continuous historical" interpretations, but attempted to pull those interpretations together into one coherent scheme. For example, he dealt with the conflicting dates for the commencement of the 1260 years by the concept of a *double* commencing era: the primary commencement was the promulgation of Justinian's Code, 529–33 A.D., culminating in the years of the French Revolution, 1789–93; the secondary commencing epoch was the four years associated with Phocas's decree,

604–8 A.D., and this would culminate in the Second Advent between 1864 and 1868 A.D.[47] In the final chapter of his fourth volume, however, Elliott states that the "full and complete commencement" synchronizes with the year 606 A.D., and the corresponding end with 1866, thus risking his entire interpretation on an extremely specific date despite his knowledge of the failure of earlier predictions.

But the most striking "innovation" (it was not really an innovation but a revival of an earlier scheme) in *Horae Apocalypticae* is the interpretation of the tenth chapter of Revelation, in which the prophet is commanded to "prophesy again," as the Reformation itself.[48] With this interpretation, Elliott not only reverted to a very early post-Reformation scheme, but made the Protestant Reformation central both to the Apocalypse and to the structure of history. The "two witnesses" symbolize Eastern and Western lines of "protestant" witnesses within the Catholic church before the Reformation, and much space is devoted to the history of individual witnesses such as Augustine and groups such as the Waldenses. Since the Reformation itself is depicted in the tenth chapter, near the center of the Apocalypse, all time is seen to revolve around it. The preceding chapters move toward the Reformation, and the succeeding chapters recapitulate the history of witnesses before the Reformation and then proceed to the seven vials (the French Revolution) and the approaching millennium.

Elliott states that Leo Juda, Henry Bullinger, Bishop Bale, and John Foxe all adopted this interpretation during the sixteenth century. Joseph Mede, however, and all those who followed in his train, such as Isaac Newton and Thomas Newton, did *not* identify the Reformation directly in the Apocalypse. The sole post-sixteenth-century commentator who did so, according to Elliott, was Charles Daubuz, a French Protestant who published his *Perpetual Commentary on the Revelation of St. John* (1720) after he had immigrated to England. Elliott's interpretation thus reached back to what had originally been a radical interpretation directed against established papal Christianity. In Victorian England, buttressed by more than two centuries of established Protestantism, it had become a profoundly conservative interpretation. Its rebirth in this new political orientation was occasioned (according to Elliott's preface) by the increasing popularity of "futurist" interpretation—an interpretation associated both with Roman Catholicism and with the Oxford Movement in the Anglican church.

The immense popularity of Cumming's lectures on the Apocalypse may have stemmed, in part, from his willingness to identify the "Puseyites" with the pre-Reformation "mystery of iniquity," or Antichrist. He explained that the great error of the fourth century A.D., when Christianity became the official religion, was the same as the great error of the Oxford Movement: a superstitious faith in the baptismal rite.[49] Cumming's lectures detail the symbolism of the Reformation, including the pre-Reformation "protestants," and vehemently attack the Tractarian assertion that the Catholic church before the Reformation was the true church. Cumming was thoroughly satisfied that "Tractarianism is the smoke from the bottomless pit," and the number of the beast, 666, was decoded as Latinus, or Latin man: "His prayers are Latin; his canons Latin; his missal Latin; his breviary Latin; the decrees of his councils, his bulls, are all Latin; he worships in Latin; he blesses in Latin; he curses in Latin; all is Latin."[50]

But Cumming's success may also have stemmed from the seeming fulfillment of his historical predictions. His lectures were delivered in 1847. At that time, he followed Elliott's interpretation of "Our Present Position in the Prophetic Calendar" as being that of the sixth vial, under which the Ottoman Empire was to be "dried up." This "vial" was held to have begun no later than 1822, when the Greeks declared independence, and the total destruction of the Turkish Empire was expected at any moment. The world was, then, on the verge of the outpouring of the seventh vial, or the battle of Armageddon, to be shortly followed by the Second Advent in 1864 or thereabouts.[51] (Cumming was less specific than Elliott here, preferring to emphasize the large number of expositors who hedged their bets by predicting the millennium sometime between 1864 and 1885.)

No sooner had Cumming finished his series of apocalyptic lectures than the Revolution of 1848 broke out. In a sermon entitled "1848: or, Prophecy Fulfilled," Cumming affirmed that what he had announced as prophecy in 1847 had by 1849 become "performance." This revolution was like no other—kings, prime ministers, laws, and institutions were being flung aside. The "immensity" of the Revolution of 1848 was much greater than that of 1789. Quoting newspaper reports that also used apocalyptic language, he concluded: "Now I ask you if ever, in the history of Europe or of the world, there was such an earthquake, and so great, or any that could be compared to it at all? . . . it is only a preparatory to the yet more terrible disorganization that precedes the coming of the Son of Man."[52] E. B. Elliott also questioned, in the 1851 edition of *Horae Apocalypticae*, "whether revolutionary outbreaks of 1848 did not singularly coincide with the expectations so stated . . . of the seventh vial?"[53]

Despite the failure of the Turkish Empire to dry up on schedule, it thus seems likely that the Revolution of 1848 contributed substantially to the popularity of Cumming's *Apocalyptic Sketches*, which by June 1850 had reached a twelfth edition. In 1854, Robert Mackay spoke of the current "crazy infatuation about the prophecies" in his second book, *The Rise and Progress of Christianity*.[54] In 1856, an anonymous American work, *The Time of the End*, reprinted the final chapter of *Horae Apocalypticae*, "Our Present Position in the Prophetic Calendar," and pointed out that the majority of prophetic interpreters expected the millennium sometime between 1830 and 1880 A.D., with the largest number of these expecting it in 1864–66.[55]

George Eliot's essay, "Evangelical Teaching: Dr. Cumming," printed in the October 1855 *Westminster Review*, criticizes him for his greater interest in "the visible advent of Christ in 1864" than in the kingdom of God within.[56] Commenting sarcastically on his attempt to "rival Moore's Almanack in the prediction of political events," she states that his "theory of prophecy" does not deserve to be considered either "biblical interpretation" or a "philosophy of history." Clearly, she was here inveighing against the very system of interpretation and "philosophy of history" that had captured her imagination as a young woman. But she does not attack prophetic interpretation itself so much as the "net moral effect" it produces. "Dr. Cumming's religion," she insists, "may demand a tribute of love, but it gives a charter to hatred; it may enjoin charity, but it fosters all uncharitableness." Her essay does not exclude a reading as an implied call for "prophetic interpretation" that would give a charter to charity, as well as a serious critique of "continuous historical" exposition and millenarian enthusiasm.

But her critique probably had very small impact on Dr. Cumming and his followers. Indeed, on November 9, 1859, the *Times* printed an article, "The School of the Prophets," which suggests that those of his persuasion were daily growing in number:

> There has arisen during the stirring years which still run their course a very widespread attention to the study of unfulfilled prophecy. Books on the subject are in great demand, and the supply apparently meets the demand. It is not unnatural to expect this. The last 10 years, dating their beginning at the great European convulsion of 1848, have, without doubt, witnessed so many national complications, social changes, and individual sufferings—event has so rapidly thundered on event, and scene flashed on scene—so altered have the face of Europe and the relations of Cabinets become, and so unsettled is the European sky at this hour, that intelligent and sober-minded men, with no spice of fanaticism in their nature, have begun to conclude that the sublime predictions uttered on the Mount 1800 years ago are being daily translated into modern history. Students of prophecy allege that they see the apocalyptic "vials" pouring out, and hear the "seven trumpets" uttering their voices and pealing in reverberations through Christendom.

The *Times* writer describes the three schools of prophetic exposition as those "very few and feeble" writers, known as the Praeterist school, who believed the prophecies in Daniel and Revelation had all been fulfilled in the distant past; a second class, "far more numerous, learned, and intelligent," who believed that none of the Apocalypse had yet been fulfilled and were accordingly called the "futurist" school; and a third "most able and laborious school," who explicated the Apocalypse as a "continuous prospective history of Christendom." The *Times* writer found the last so convincing the reader "is almost driven to accept the interpretation."

Those "very few and feeble" writers of the Praeterist school were in fact at this time largely German critics: Dean Alford, for example, lists Ewald, Lücke, De Wette and Düsterdieck as the most prominent exponents.[57] Only one English critic, Samuel Davidson, and one American, Moses Stuart, are also included. The latter, a postmillennialist, had published a *Commentary on the Apocalypse* (1845), based on a thorough knowledge of German criticism and including a translation of part of Herder's commentary. This "school," which R. H. Charles has termed the Contemporary-Historical school and which may properly be considered the advance guard of modern criticism, rejected direct supernatural inspiration of prophecy and concentrated on the analysis of the prophet's own historical context.[58] George Eliot undoubtedly accepted this approach as authoritative, and indeed she seems to have employed De Wette's *Commentary on the Old Testament* in her critique of Dr. Cumming.[59]

The more numerous group known as futurist expositors were traced to Catholic, specifically Jesuit, roots because they interpreted Antichrist as a power to appear in the future rather than as the pope. The oddly assorted proponents of this school of interpretation, however, included the Plymouth Brethren and the Tractarians, as well as S. R. Maitland, William Burgh, and J. H. Todd.[60]

But the school most ardently endorsed by the *Times* writer was still the school of "continuous historical" exposition. John Cumming and E. B. Elliott are both cited prominently in the article. Although George Eliot herself certainly regarded this interpretation as "mistaken criticism," we should not dismiss it as nothing more than a polemical genre of hermeneutics addressed to the identification of Antichrist with the pope.[61] As Bernard McGinn has suggested, the fundamental impulse underlying apocalyptics is the attempt to give meaningful form to history:

> The apocalypticist is one who seeks, in Frank Kermode's phrase, "to be related to a beginning and to an end." The structure and meaning of time, the meeting place of this age and eternity, are consistent concerns of the medieval apocalyptic visionaries and scribes. The desire to understand history—its unity, its structure, its goal, the future hope which it promises—is not a passing interest or a momentary whim, but a perennial human concern. A sense of belonging in time, as well as the need to understand the special significance of the present, is the anthropological root of apocalyptic systems of thought.[62]

The Victorian school of "continuous historical" exposition not only developed in response to the need to "understand the special significance of the present"—i.e., the French Revolution and subsequent threatened "dissolution of the social fabric" in all of Europe and Great Britain—but conferred a particular shape on the chaotic events of modern history.⁶³ Although George Eliot rejected Cumming's fundamentalist interpretation and millenarian politics, the scheme of history constructed by "continuous historical" expositors seems to have provided the web on which she could position beginnings and ends and work out "meaningful form" in her narratives.

E. B. Elliott's organization of history, not around the birth of Christ but around the Reformation, led to the reinterpretation of Mede's division of the Apocalypse into "two principal prophecies" as the division of history into pre- and post-Reformation eras. This interpretation characterized history as the periodic rigidification and decay of a tradition into a "higher," more spiritual mode. By this means the past could be recovered—seen as the origin of the reformed tradition rather than as unalleviated darkness and corruption. Unlike the Romantic poets, who resorted to an ahistorical apocalypse of the imagination to solve the problem of disillusionment with the past, the "continuous historical" expositors were able to reaffirm the continuity of history through the principle of prophetic or spiritual reformation.⁶⁴

Even the appalling violence of the French Revolution became a predicted part of the final "reformation" of mankind: it signified the beginning of divine judgments on the wickedness of men, and especially on the papal religion, that would soon climax in the supernatural creation of a new heaven and earth. While totally pessimistic about human efforts to reform society, the prophetic expositors were paradoxically optimistic about the course of history. History was "continuous" in the sense that, though characterized by growing human corruption, God would periodically reform it, with his prophets leading the way.

R. G. Collingwood has postulated that histories formed on Christian principles are universal, providential, apocalyptic, and periodized.⁶⁵ The Protestant school of "continuous historical" apocalyptics added to these the peculiar characteristic of a universal history that, because it is divided by the Reformation rather than the birth of Christ, describes history as divided between a "Roman" and a "Protestant" era. This in turn suggests a division of history between classical and Christian traditions, for the apocalyptic history of the Roman Empire was often seen as including not only pre-Christian Rome but also the Four Empires of Daniel: Rome, Greece, Medo-Persia, and Babylonia. The Apocalypse therefore seemed to mirror the common division of history not only between classical and Christian traditions, such as that seen in Mackay's *Progress of the Intellect*, but between classical and puritanical, or Protestant Christian, traditions, such as that epitomized in Matthew Arnold's *Culture and Anarchy*.

In addition, "continuous historical" exegetes developed the tendency toward periodization to an astonishing degree, representing history as more dense and complex than ever before perceived. They believed history, like the Apocalypse, accommodated many different schemes or structures at once: septenary, tertiary, binary, etc. Their mathematical computations of prophetic periods almost defy comprehension, as these expositors struggled to make all of ancient and modern history conform to the combined "sacred calendar" of Old and New Testament prophecies. E. B. Elliott's "Sketch of the History of Apocalyptic Interpretation," included in his fourth volume, illustrates this passion for structure perhaps better than any other single work. Summarizing apocalyptic structures posed by a large number of earlier exegetes, Elliott even tabulates many of them in charts, the better to make different conceptions of the historico-apocalyptic scheme clear. In his own exposition, he organizes material from the entire tradition into one grandly universal scheme. George Stanley Faber's move from the *Dissertation on . . . 1260 Years* to the *Sacred Calendar of Prophecy* also illustrates this tendency toward ever greater complexity and formal unity in the scheme of history. The earlier work deals only with the period of the 1260 years, or "three and a half times." The later work expands this scheme to the "SEVEN PROPHETIC TIMES" that takes in Daniel's as well as St. John's prophecies, and extends from far back in ancient history to the period *following* the millennium. In short, the "historical" expositors developed an ever more complex "poetry" of chronology. Not surprisingly, *Horae Apocalypticae* includes a graphic design of the scheme of history—a visualization of the "scroll written within and without" with the mystic figures of time (see p. 2).

While the "continuous historical" expositors were waxing more enthusiastic as the date of the millennium approached, criticism based on German hermeneutics was also appearing more frequently in English and gaining more supporters. In 1860 and 1861, no fewer than three writers personally known to George Eliot produced critical works on the Apocalypse. Each of these works sought not only to oppose the interpretation of the millenarians, but to reaffirm the prophetic significance of the Apocalypse in more humanistic terms.

Sara Hennell, one of George Eliot's oldest friends and her most faithful correspondent, published *End of the World* in 1860, an essay-length work that considered all New Testament prophecy but focused particularly on the Apocalypse. Hennell won the Baillie Prize with the essay, which was reviewed quite favorably in the *Westminster Review*.[66] George Eliot was given a copy of the essay and apparently read it, for she later commented on it in a letter to Hennell (*GEL*, 3:329). Hennell adopts the Romantic solution to the problem of disillusionment with both history and prophecy, affirming that the Divine order depicted in the Apocalypse will be accomplished, not by "*sudden violent interposition*" but by the "*gradual unfolding of the human mind.*"[67] Although Christ and the apostles were mistaken in their belief that the world would actually end in a violent apocalypse within their generation, the prophet nevertheless envisioned an eternal truth: the gradual apocalypse of the imagination. As for St. John's Apocalypse, it is a "glorious poem . . . an immortal picture fresh with the glowing colours that were burnt in his own imagination; and his work *is* for all ages, precisely because it was never *meant* for them. . . . Through all the wildness of its gorgeous imagery there burns a feeling of intense reality."[68] Hennell thus characterizes the Apocalypse as a work for the present despite the failure of its prophecy.

In 1861, F. D. Maurice published *Lectures on the Apocalypse*. George Eliot had once described Maurice's thought as "muddy rather than 'profound,'" but in 1861 she mentioned going to hear him preach, and she was deeply touched by his warm response to *Romola* after the novel was published.[69] Maurice explicitly distinguishes his interpretation from the prevailing rage for "continuous historical" exposition:

> But my plan precludes me from the attempt to detect any minute parallels between particular sentences in the book and particular events that have happened or that are hereafter to happen in one period or another. The principal historical allusions in these Lectures are to the state of the Roman world during the years preceding the fall of Jerusalem.[70]

Referring to the "latest and most advanced school of German Rationalists," Maurice, like Hennell, assumes the writer of the Apocalypse to have been an early Christian whose vision was limited to the historical events of his own time. But the seer's function was to interpret history, for in uttering "the mind of Him who is and was and is to come," he was to "explain the past and present," and in connection with these, to speak of the future.[71] Maurice accordingly interprets such apocalyptic images as the four horsemen, for example, as archetypes with a perpetually recurring significance in each historical era. The red horse thus stands for the civil war that rises up "in every time of the world history."[72] And while rejecting a divinely inspired numerology, he suggests a broad literary significance for certain numbers as used in the Bible: the number seven suggests perfect unity, for example, while the number six is a number that will never arrive at unity, and thus the number 666 is a triply emphatic symbol of incompleteness and disunity.

Most interesting, however, is Maurice's apparently Comtean interpretation of the "woman clothed with the sun" (Rev. 12).[73] Representing "the contrast between the old world which was passing away, and the new world which was commencing," the woman is a "striking symbol of humanity."[74] By the "old world," Maurice means any culture dominated by "male" values, whereas the mother and the child are universal symbols of "what the human is, and how it is related to the Divine." In Maurice's somewhat fuzzy distinction, the new age is not to be either effeminate or even feminine, but the feminine is "the highest and most universal symbol under which it can be represented." Maurice's interpretation strongly suggests the aspect of positivism emphasized in W. M. W. Call's 1858 review of Comte's *Catechism of Positive Religion*: that the "feminine element symbolizes the affective nature of men" and that the new age would exhibit an affinity with the nature of women, whose duty was "to repress the selfish and elicit the social instinct."[75] Maurice's exposition of the "woman clothed with the sun" thus suggests a link between the Comtean banner, with its image of a woman carrying a child, and the Apocalypse.

Both Hennell's and Maurice's works on the Apocalypse appear on the heading list of another essay written by Call, described as a "secular exposition" of the Apocalypse, and published in the *Westminster Review* in October 1861. Call was well known to George Eliot, for she had first recommended him as a contributor to the *Westminster*.[76] Since she noted in her journal that she had read the October issue of the *Westminster Review*, and since she was at the same time reading "Savonarola's Prophecy" and "Tiraboschi on Abate Giaochimo" (Joachim of Fiore), it seems most unlikely she failed to give Call's article particular attention.[77]

Call not only approaches the Apocalypse as a literary work, but identifies it as part of a distinctive literary genre. First describing the "cycle" or literary tradition of Judeo-Christian apocalyptic works from which the Apocalypse emerged—Daniel, the Jewish Sibyl, Enoch, and the fourth book of Esdras—he then analyzes the structure, style, and theme of the Apocalypse as characteristic of this tradition. The structure is divided into two "great series," the development of the second series beginning with the "woman clothed with the sun." Call explicates the prophet's use of numbers not as mystical symbols or as historical facts but as indication of "the artificial and imaginary character of the whole work." The prophet invokes the "septenary principle," or repeated use of the number seven, because "seven is a symbol of perfection or entireness," and the number four similarly because it is a symbol of unity:

> We thus see a reason for the septenary arrangement of the Apocalyptic vision, and are perfectly convinced that there could not be more than seven trumpets, seven vials, and seven seals, or fewer than three woes, or more than four cherubim. Does not Irenaeus assure us, on the authority of a somewhat different though equally cogent logic, that there could not be more than four Gospels, because there were not more than four winds, and was not Irenaeus right?[78]

Call even takes a playful sally at the symbolism of 666, the number of the beast, leaving his prophetic arithmetic to the consideration of Dr. Cumming and his fellow "mystagogues."

Call's secular exposition does not, like Samuel Davidson's essay that would appear in 1864, claim to remove the "dark drapery" of the prophecy and leave its meaning "patent to view," thus also denuding it of mystic potential.[79] Rather, the Apocalypse is a visionary landscape of the "imagined history" of the world, a "wondrous book of fate" in which symbolic pictures or images disclose "Divine purposes." Like Hennell, Call feels the Apocalypse is "a daring and wildly beautiful poem" and that it possesses a universal prophetic validity, newly significant in the nineteenth century:

> Our own times, since, at least, the French Revolution, have been stormy, turbulent, explosive, minatory as his. Old creeds are dying out; a new faith slowly and dimly growing up, social and national change advancing or impending. In the midst of the wreck of the past, the prophetic soul that is in man reawakens.... Our ideal is not a celestial but an earthly ideal.... We ask for no millennial resurrection, and for no impossible theocracy.... But not the less does "the hope that springs eternal" connect us with the future of the world: not the less do we look for some proximate realization of our dream of terrestrial justice, wisdom, and love; ... not the less do the bells from the ivy-clothed church-towers of our English towns and villages seem ... to "ring out the darkness of the land; to ring in the Christ that is to be."[80]

Call's essay, in short, both demonstrates a sophisticated awareness of apocalypse as literary genre and, like Hennell and Maurice, strives to relate its prophetic vision to his own time. But Call goes beyond Hennell and Maurice, and himself appropriates the voice of the prophet: in addition to explicating the structure and enduring significance of prophecy, he himself proclaims a "new faith" and envisions an "earthly ideal." His stance exemplifies what Joseph A. Wittreich, Jr., describes as the prophetic writer's characteristic movement beyond the epic poet's imposition of historical patterns: "Epic poets and prophets alike impose historical pattern upon historical pattern; but, whereas the epic poet translates pattern into model, the prophetic searches beyond pattern for a new model, his search causing him to turn closed patterns into open ones, which become not emblems of perfection but gateways leading toward it."[81]

Schooled in the "continuous historical" interpretation of the Apocalypse, George Eliot had available to her a complex model for imposing pattern on history; but for her, as for Call, Maurice, and Hennell, the apocalyptic landscape demanded a new interpretation. The "closed pattern" of history circumscribed by its theological premise could be reopened and made the vehicle of a new "earthly ideal" in which humankind could mirror its self-redemption. In this context of rekindling excitement about prophecy, George Eliot decided to write what she called a "historical romance" based on the life of the prophet Savonarola. Less than three months after the appearance of Call's article, she finally devised a "scheme" for the novel that satisfied her—a "scheme" that I shall argue was itself a radical revision of the landscape of history she had first discovered in the "school of the prophets." But before she undertook the difficult labor of composing *Romola* George Eliot seems already to have experimented with narrative schemes that interrogated conventional notions of history, as suggested by the subversive implications of chronology in *Adam Bede*.

CHAPTER 2

History and Hermeneutics in Adam Bede

Though *Romola* appears to be George Eliot's "apocalypse of history," her first attempt to fully appropriate and transform the hermeneutic scheme of history she had encountered in her youth, her earliest fictions bear evidence of her preoccupation with the problem of representing history. Each of the three long short stories or novellas in *Scenes of Clerical Life* dwells on aspects of "ecclesiastical history," from the changing appearance of Shepperton Church to the more widespread and less easily characterized changes wrought by the Evangelical movement. These tales demonstrate a surprisingly feminist energy in their depiction of "clerical life" as experienced, or endured, by women—a pervasive suggestion that clerical history as seen from a woman's perspective might differ substantially from the ecclesiastical histories written by men.[1] In "Janet's Repentance" also, the division of the narrative into two precise "halves" (between chapter 14 and chapter 15) that mirrors the break in Janet's marriage and the moment of decisive change in her life already predicts the more complex uses to which George Eliot will later put binary apocalyptic structurings, especially the very similar narrative division in *Romola*. But the three tales in *Clerical Life*, though they everywhere demonstrate their author's interest in questions of history, seem too short to permit the working-out of any detailed interpretive schemes.

In *Adam Bede*, however, George Eliot's ambivalence toward history forms a major thematic concern in the narrative, and her carefully plotted chronology provides the nexus for a scheme of hidden hermeneutics that repeatedly undermines and interrogates the assumptions of conventional history. Diane F. Sadoff has suggested that "the difficulty of reading rightly haunts every sign, every metaphor, every asserted meaning of *Adam Bede*."[2] Ironically, critics have often preferred to emphasize the narrator's discourse in chapter 17 on the "rare, precious quality of truthfulness" in Dutch painting and its supposed aesthetic of realism, while neglecting the narrator's more revealing comment in chapter 54 that "no story is the same to us after a lapse of time; or rather, we who read it are no longer the same interpreters."[3] But George Eliot's consciousness of the instability of narrative, the indeterminacy of language, the sheer difficulty of "reading" or interpreting narrative and history, permeates *Adam Bede*. Charles Palliser proposes that George Eliot exploits a "deliberate ambivalence" of presentation in the novel designed to force the reader to revise stock assumptions about the meaning of history.[4] I suggest that the chronology of *Adam Bede* further constructs that ambivalence, providing keys to a scheme of "hidden" hermeneutics that turns the narrative from a conventional historian's account of the silencing of Methodist women preachers to a ghostly interpretation of female prophecy as the "voice of one crying in the wilderness."

W. J. Harvey first pointed out that George Eliot's "treatment of time is less simple and straightforward than it appears" and that in the "astonishing chronological detail" exhibited in *Adam Bede* she concealed many cunningly structured parallels.[5] But Harvey wondered why George Eliot chose not to comment on "narrative ironies" that other writers—Thomas Hardy, for example—surely would have emphasized. Like the disturbing questions raised by Eve Kosofsky Sedgwick's reading of the novel, George Eliot's chronological coding suggests her dissatisfaction with the "easy" reading of her tale—her desire to interrupt the wedding guests happily speeding on their way to Dinah's wedding and make them strain to hear instead the "ghastly tale" of the deliberate silencing of women.[6] Jay Clayton points to a persistent "impulse to turn back within the context of an unceasing movement forward" in the narrative, and he suggests that this impulse eventually transforms the "hard" narrative of the "Law of Consequences" into a "vehicle for visionary sympathy."[7] But his reading assumes George Eliot's desire for coherence of both history and narrative, whereas the hidden hermeneutics in *Adam Bede* seem to work instead not only to "turn" the narrative from one reading to another but to school the reader in the duplicity of any story, including "history."

Accordingly, the dates specified in Adam Bede's history point to lectionary lessons that "interleave" the narrative, doubling or repeating narrative form and content and underlining certain parts of the narrative to produce new readings. Chronology both conceals and reveals readings that "turn" the narrative from a comedy ending with Dinah happily married to Adam into a frightening gothic tale in which Dinah's story cannot be separated from Hetty's tragedy. Turn-of-the-century history, conventionally read as that fortunate era when certain male poets possessed a "strange power of speech," becomes instead the haunting history of a brief moment when women also were empowered to speak.[8]

The hidden hermeneutics of *Adam Bede* thus produce a second reading of the story that consistently opposes the comforting conclusions the reader would draw from the first. Like the duck-rabbit illusion, the text appears to be readable in two irreconcilable directions—a narrative that is coherent and incoherent at the same time.[9] What one narrative, one way of reading history, ties together is perpetually undone by the suppressed stories coded into this history through their historical "connection"—the connection between historical dates in the novel and those same dates in the "universal" history of the church calendar.

Since the Anglican lectionary was a public discourse—as much a part of her readers' mental furniture as of her own—this subversive codification may represent a reading George Eliot wanted her readers to struggle for, as Bartle Massey's adult scholars had to struggle for something more than the "dry" meaning of letters. But whether public or private, the chronology produces a pattern of readings that undermines patriarchal ecclesiastical history—the Venerable Bede's history in which women do not speak. That it does so in a story ostensibly "written" by a male narrator who is a lifelong friend of our latter-day Adam suggests a level of narrative and historical sophistication already remarkable. But perhaps it is less remarkable for one created in the "school of the prophets" and then fortunately "fallen" in its exposure as the work of self-deluded historians.

I

As Felicia Bonaparte has noted of *Romola*, an undeclared reference to the Feast of John the Baptist (June 24) underlies the narrative structure of *Adam Bede*: the first twenty-one chapters take place from June 18 to June 24, 1799, or the week preceding and culminating in the Feast of John the Baptist.[10] This septenary structuring (note the *twenty-one* chapters and *seven* days) reaches a prophetic "fulfillment" in chapter 42 when Adam's baptism into suffering also writes him into the history of the apocalyptic witnesses. But chapters 19–21, all of which take place on June 24 or the day of the Feast, most plainly invoke a lectionary lesson associated with the Feast. In these chapters the narrator also pointedly alludes to the difficulty of reading and specifically to Adam's need to progress beyond the "alphabet."

On the morning of John the Baptist's Feast, the narrator discourses on the "lesson" of which Adam has so far learned only the "alphabet," and in the evening on the painful struggle of Bartle Massey's adult students to learn to read their lessons in their night school. The narrator thus suggests a progression from easy to difficult reading, from the simple recognition of letters plainly visible in broad daylight, to the complex act of interpretation involved in perceiving the "hidden" letters of texts only dimly visible in the poor light of night school. The narrative, I suggest, poses a similar spectrum from obvious to more difficult readings of the first lesson for the Feast of John the Baptist.

This first lesson, designated "For the Epistle," is not actually an epistle, but a prophecy from the Book of Isaiah that John the Baptist quoted: the "voice of one crying in the wilderness," he claimed, referred to him. I condense the Epistle here to the texts that seem most relevant to *Adam Bede*:

> Comfort ye, comfort ye my people, saith your God. Speak ye comfortably to Jerusalem, and cry unto her, that her warfare is accomplished; that her iniquity is pardoned: for she hath received of the Lord's hand double for all her sins. The voice of him that crieth in the wilderness, Prepare ye the way of the Lord, make straight in the desert a high-way for our God.... He shall feed his flock like a shepherd; he shall

> gather the lambs with his arm, and carry them in his bosom, and shall gently lead those that are with young. (Isa. 40:1–11)[11]

The prophet's image of the Good Shepherd seems to spell out quite plainly the lesson Adam needs to learn. As the narrator comments in chapter 19, the "secret" of Adam's "hardness" is that he has "too little fellow-feeling with the weakness that errs in spite of foreseen consequences." He needs to get his heartstrings bound "round the weak and erring"—as here in the Epistle, around the straying sheep and foolish lambs. Just as the pastoral imagery of the prophetic text appropriately parallels the pastoral world of the novel, so the narrator's comments suggest an appropriately simple and conventional reading of the biblical lesson: Adam should soften his hard heart and become a good shepherd to Hetty, lest she become a "lost lamb."

But if the Epistle provides the rather obvious lesson Adam must learn to read, it also provides the text Dinah "writes"—and this feminized hermeneutics proves far subtler and more difficult. As Bartle Massey exhorts his less diligent students, readers must also apply themselves to arithmetic, for dimly perceived numbers as well as letters haunt the text of *Adam Bede*. Only by laboriously adding and subtracting days, weeks, and months can the reader calculate George Eliot's devious hermeneutic designs in this novel.

The date when Dinah first appears in the text and when she preaches her outdoor sermon is June 18, or seven days prior to the Feast of John the Baptist. Yet this prophetic numerology at first seems to work against the text, for Wiry Ben describes Dinah as a sort of caricature of prophetic mission. Parodying Jesus' words concerning John the Baptist, he teases Seth: "'What come ye out for to see? A Prophetess? Yes, I say unto you, and more than a prophetess'—an uncommon pretty young woman" (52). Dinah's female form renders prophetic identity a wild improbability to her male observers: what they see, or the language of nature, "blinds" them to what cannot be seen but must be "read" in her words. As the elderly stranger comments, "'A sweet woman, but surely nature never meant her for a preacher'" (67).

Unlike John the Baptist, Dinah makes no explicit claim to prophetic authority herself. But she chooses for her sermon the text from Isaiah read by Jesus as testimony to *his* prophetic mission: "the spirit of the Lord is upon me, because he hath anointed me to preach the gospel to the poor" (Isa. 42:1). In the Gospel of Luke, which Anglicans began reading on the seventeenth of June, or the day just "outside" the *Adam Bede* chronology, Jesus' claim to fulfill Isaiah's words immediately follows John's. The biblical text tempts the reader to the "easy" reading that Dinah belongs in this train of prophets foretold by Isaiah, that the prophetic authorization claimed by John and Jesus should be extended to her—and specifically to her *preaching*, or speaking.

Yet the unspoken context of Dinah's theme tells quite a different story. In Luke's account, Jesus' listeners greet his interpretation of this text as referring to himself with skepticism: "Is not this Joseph's son?" they murmur (Luke 4:22). Their question, we should note, casts doubt not only on Jesus' claim to prophetic authorization, but on Luke's story of Jesus' birth from a virgin. Eventually Jesus' listeners drag him out of the temple and attempt to throw him down a hill. The full story of Dinah's text, then, not only underlines the skepticism with which her preaching is received, but foreshadows the parallel casting out of Methodist women preachers in the novel. But more than that, since Luke's story reminds us that both John and Jesus were "silenced," it also suggests we read the silencing of women preachers as prophetic martyrdom: it *affirms* the silencing of women by locating that "hard" fact in a different narrative—the history of prophecy. Finally, Jesus' words in self-defense, "No prophet is accepted in his own country," reverberate with particular irony in Dinah's case, for the voice of this woman prophet will be silenced in the very country that writes maternity, or female "nature," in large letters—the dairy country where production equals reproduction, and profits are weighed in pounds of milk.

We may read the first twenty-one chapters of *Adam Bede*, then, as a narrative exegesis of the first lesson for John the Baptist's day—a subversive midrash that exploits the difficulties of reading that lesson rather than simplifying it for the reader. But Bartle Massey's discourse presents the most difficult reading of all. Like those mysterious signs that his puzzled student discovers construct different "letters" depending on which way the "tail" is turned, the schoolmaster's discourse seems a prime example of the duplicity of language. Massey himself, both in his patient teaching of his slow adult scholars and in his tender care for his pregnant dog, plainly appears to fulfill the Good Shepherd prophecy. But the language he uses both appropriates maternal metaphors, or female "nature," to describe this prophetic labor, and in the same words patently degrades femininity.

A confirmed misogynist, in fact, Massey excoriates femininity in general and in particular vigorously dissents from the traditional biblical reading of woman's divinely appointed purpose as Adam's companion. He complains that his "woman" (which is what he calls his bitch Vixen) will do nothing with the food he gives her except nourish "those unnecessary babbies. That's the way with these women—they've got no head-pieces to nourish, and so their food all runs either to fat or to brats" (285). To Adam's scarcely less misogynistic defense of the usefulness of women—that they are needed to keep the workingman's house clean and comfortable—Massey compares his own superior housekeeping. He declares that "it's an impious, unscriptural opinion to say a woman's a blessing to a man now," and insists women have no use whatever except the unfortunate necessity of reproduction, and even that "had better ha' been left to the men" (286).

Yet ironically Massey cannot seem to describe the nature of his pedagogy without something of a "fall" into femininity himself: he compares teaching a grown man his ABC's to giving a calf "something to suck at" (292). Massey's misogynistic discourse subverts his own intentions: to the reader turning to the first lesson for the day, Massey's language "teaches" a reading of the Good Shepherd as one who *mothers*—one who provides milk for lost lambs and weanling calves, regardless of their merits. Though he scoffs at Vixen that "she's got no conscience—no conscience—it's all run to milk!" (292), any reader can see that he has a milky conscience himself. His behavior spells out male mothering, and his discourse constructs a more dissenting interpretation than he intends. Depending on which way the "tale" is turned, we may speculate that woman was *not* created to be man's companion, and that the Good Shepherd was really a mother.

II

Reading the first lesson for John the Baptist's day, then, turns both Adam's and Dinah's histories in unexpected directions. Rather than confirming the Law of Consequences, the interleaving of this lesson suggests the possibility of more than one interpretation, for each fact may be located in more than one narrative, and even the meaning of "letters" depends on the turn of the "tail." The first lessons for the next two dates specified in the narrative, like those for two later dates, both quote the prophetic theme of "turning" in contexts that mirror and interpret narrative form and content in *Adam Bede*. "Turning" becomes a model not only for the renewal of life but of history, for when we turn to history we always read a new story.

The whole of Book III takes place on July 30, the day when Arthur Donnithorne comes of age and announces Adam's new position as manager of the woods. It is also on this day that Hetty makes an assignation to meet Arthur in those woods. The first lesson for July 30, or Jeremiah 25, turns this celebration of pastoral life into an ominous prophecy of disaster among the "shepherds." The prophet Jeremiah exhorts the Israelites to "turn ye again now every one from his evil way," and warns: "Howl, ye shepherds, and cry; and wallow yourselves in the ashes, ye principal of the flock. . . . A voice of the cry of the shepherds, and an howling of the principal of the flock, shall be heard" (Jer. 25:34–36).

The lesson seems to underline or italicize the foreshadowing of ominous consequences when Hetty arranges to meet Arthur in the woods that have now become Adam's charge. But a fuller significance of this first lesson for July 30 becomes apparent only as the reader moves forward in narrative time to other dates and other lessons. The interleaved structure of lessons proves to repeat the prophetic theme of "turning" over and over again—four times in all—each time mirroring narrative form and each time converting Adam's history to a new story. In this case, we learn that Adam's misreading of the past—his failure to "turn" soon enough—will indeed culminate in a "cry" among the shepherds and especially of the "principal of the flock," or himself.

After the events of Arthur's birthday, the narrative moves to

August 18. Because of either a mistake or a deliberate change in chronology, George Eliot represents August 18 as an ordinary working day, whereas according to the calendar for 1799 it should have been a Sunday.[12] However, the first lesson for August 18 remains the same in the lectionary, regardless of the day of the week. In that lesson, Ezekiel 18, we find the prophet Ezekiel restating the crucial theme of "turning," again in a context highly relevant to Adam's misreading. To the Israelites' complaint that God's ways are not "equal," the prophet reiterates that God is not interested in equity—that is, in vengeance—for wrongdoing, but rather desires that the son should "turn" from the wicked ways of the father, and live. The lesson concludes, "turn yourselves, and live ye." On the date for this lesson, Adam sees Arthur kissing Hetty in the woods and suddenly "a terrible scorching light showed him the hidden letters that changed the meaning of the past" (342). The narrator's words suggest an obvious reading of the prophet's "hidden letters" into the text: Arthur Donnithorne is repeating his father's careless and self-indulgent stewardship and needs to turn from his ways. Adam, the figure of stern prophetic admonishment, now appears to warn Arthur of his error.

But narrative form suggests it is Adam who "turns" toward life at this point. Adam's first reaction to his discovery that Arthur's "history" is not what he had taken it to be is rage: feeling that Arthur has robbed him of what was rightfully his, he offers to fight, and the two engage in a nearly fatal combat. Only as he begins to fear what he has done to Arthur does Adam realize "the vanity of his own rage," that it has not rescued Hetty or "changed the past." As he kneels beside the unconscious Arthur like "an image of despair gazing at an image of death," Adam is forced to recognize the implacability of history as he has read it. If hard consequences follow deeds according to the law of equity, then history cannot be changed or the past redeemed.

At this crucial moment in Adam's education, narrative form also mirrors the prophetic theme that Adam should "turn" himself and live. In chapter 27, Adam nearly becomes a murderer; in chapter 28, as Arthur regains consciousness, Adam joyfully realizes his reprieve from what could have been a very "hard" consequence of his own rage. At this moment Adam turns from reading history as an unbending Law of Consequences, and begins moving toward that point where he will be able to "own up" to Hetty even as the acknowledged murderer of her own child. His reading of history begins to soften. This profoundly significant turning point in Adam's story takes place exactly in the center of the 55-chapter narrative sequence, or in chapters 27 and 28. But this precise binary division not only underlines the dramatic turn in Adam himself, it also suggests the reversibility of history: while Adam continues to journey forward toward the moment of Hetty's trial, it is possible also to read his story from this point on as a journey back to the significance of that "voice of one crying in the wilderness," to the identification of a prophetess to whom he did not even listen at the time.

III

On the next Sunday Adam takes the next important step in learning to interpret that significance. On that day, and apparently at about the same time in the evening, Adam reads Dinah's letter to Seth and Hetty reads Arthur's letter to herself. The two letters cross in several interesting ways, the first being that these two "lovers" each read a letter from another lover at the same time—obviously one of George Eliot's carefully constructed chronological parallels. The writer of Hetty's letter is her lover of the past, while the writer of the letter Adam reads will become his lover in the future, suggesting the crossing or intersection of narrative past and future in these two letters. Dinah's letter persuades Adam that the words of a "preaching woman" need not be "hateful," but Arthur's letter leads Hetty to conclude that the words she had formerly found so pleasant were indeed hateful.

But perhaps most important of all, Adam's reading of Dinah's written words seems to soften or enlarge his interpretation of the woman prophet, while Hetty's reading only retrenches her in the "narrow circle of her imagination," an ultimately self-destructive path. Hetty's reading accepts and confirms Arthur's statement that "the past cannot be altered," while Dinah's letter opens Adam's eyes to the notion that the meaning of words may be seen with "new clearness," thus permitting the reader to escape from the "narrow thought." Dinah's letter, in fact, provides a model for reading or interpreting history, while Arthur's models a misreading.

But this larger significance of Dinah's letter becomes especially visible in the context of a hidden letter—the Epistle for this August Sunday, presumably the fifteenth Sunday after Trinity. If the reader turns to this Epistle, taken from the sixth chapter of Paul's letter to the Galatians, Dinah's letter appears both to echo and interpret it. The Epistle begins, "Ye see how large a letter I have written unto you with mine own hand" (Gal. 6:11). Dinah's postscript underlines this opening statement of Paul's, but turns it to the self-deprecatingly feminine form, "I have not skill to write the words so small as you do" (375). But it is clear that Dinah, like Paul, writes "large." It is also clear that the word "large" can be read in more than one way. Dinah's letter, in fact, is a hidden hermeneutics, an interpretation that writes the Pauline doctrine of the cross as explained in the Epistle in the larger letters of sympathy for the "sin and sorrow of this world."

Dinah writes that she has heard the words "take up my cross," explained or "enlarged" as meaning "the troubles and persecutions we bring on ourselves by confessing Jesus." But, she comments, "surely that is a narrow thought." Her words read like a critical gloss on Paul's statement in the Epistle, "But God forbid that I should glory, save in the cross" (Gal. 6:14). Going Paul one better, Dinah's letter implies that glorying in one's own persecution is a "narrow thought" in comparison with sharing in the "sin and sorrow of the world." Her words "spell out" the thematic heart of the novel, defining the cross of Christianity as a narrow doctrine and "enlarging" it to the doctrine of sympathy, or George Eliot's "religion of humanity." Dinah's letter, then, crosses Pauline doctrine in more than one sense; it not only dramatically contradicts his self-glorification in persecution but in this act of reinterpretation "speaks out" against his dictum that women should not speak or hold authority over men (1 Tim. 2:12).

In addition, Adam's reading of Dinah's letter illustrates his progress in reading or interpreting: Adam now reads new meaning into a text he would once have interpreted in a "narrow," not to say "hard," sense. He would have thought a letter from a "preaching woman hateful," he remarks, had he not known her first. Instead, he seems to see and hear her speaking as he reads, and his interpretation enlarges. As in Dinah's hermeneutics, he crosses the dry words of the text with his own remembered feeling, and through such reading changes the meaning of the past. Preaching women are no longer hateful per se—although, as we shall see, Adam's reading has changed only to a degree on this matter. Ironically, Adam still sees Dinah as a perfect wife for Seth. With even greater irony, Hetty's reading of Arthur's letter turns her to the consideration of Adam as a possible husband.

The consequences of these misreadings are realized on the next specific date mentioned in the narrative: Sunday, November 2, or the twenty-fourth Sunday after Trinity in the Anglican calendar. On this day, walking home with Hetty after afternoon service, Adam asks her to marry him. The second lesson for evening prayer on this day not only underlines the irony of this supposedly happy moment but also provided the text for John Keble's *Christian Year* poem for the day: "The heart knoweth his own bitterness: and a stranger doth not intermeddle with his joy" (Prov. 14:10). Keble's interpretation of the text could be a narrator's comment on Hetty's situation:

> . . . all alone, so Heaven has will'd, we die,
> Nor even the tenderest heart, and next our own,
> Knows half the reasons why we smile and sigh.[13]

Adam, with the "tenderest heart," knows only half the reason for Hetty's tears: not only does she fear that Adam plans to marry Mary Burge, she also fears she is pregnant with Arthur's child. In its comparison of human isolation and pain with that of the Israelites wandering in the desert, the poem also suggests a subtler hermeneutics for Hetty's last name: "sorrel" is the name of a bitter herb such as the Israelites were to eat at Passover to remind them of the bitterness of their captivity and desert wandering—and Hetty is soon to begin a bitterly lonely "wandering."

Some weeks after her betrothal to Adam Hetty experiences the "first on-coming of her great dread"—presumably the first unmistakable stirrings of life within her (411). At this time the narrator comments on the "foolish lost lamb wandering farther and farther," and "tasting the bitterest of life's bitterness," reflecting that it is "no wonder that man's religion has much sorrow in it; no wonder he needs a Suffering God." Suddenly, as Jay Clayton comments, the story seems to "open itself" to an image of agony that transforms the narrative through its intensity of feeling.[14] Yet this intensity of feeling seems inadequately explained—why does the narrator suddenly rise to such transcendent sympathy for Hetty's suffering, discovering in the very landscape about him the image of a hidden agony, "the agony of the Cross"?

The narrator's discovery of the "Cross" hidden in the apparently benign landscape of Loamshire repeats, in effect, the kind of reading we have just seen in Dinah's reading of Paul's epistle, and in Adam's reading of Dinah's letter. The narrator, like these earlier readers, "crosses" the dry letters of the text with the hidden letters supplied by remembered feeling, now interpreting the "text" of the landscape in a new and enlarged reading.[15] If, for example, the reader now turns back in the text to those letters Bartle Massey's adult scholar struggled to read—"d,r,y"—and transforms them by supplying the hidden letters "a" and "i," the reader produces a word curiously saturated with feeling for the narrator. These "hidden letters" have already transformed the reading of the Loamshire landscape for the narrator, for what has previously moved him to outbursts of lyric passion have been the products of the dairy: cheese, butter, whey, and milk. As he describes Adam drinking whey in Mrs. Poyser's dairy, he reads his own remembered feeling into the text: "Ah! I think I taste that whey now—with a flavour so delicate that one can hardly distinguish it from an odour, and with that soft gliding warmth that fills one's imagination with a still, happy dreaminess. And the light music of the dropping whey is in my ears." (263).

For the narrator, the meaning of the Loamshire landscape centers in the dairy, that "damp temple of cleanliness" that, as he tells us in chapter 7, "was certainly worth looking at" (127). Milk, the product Mrs. Poyser discusses in terms of profit and loss, signifies remembered joy, the association of childhood history with "soft, gliding warmth" and "still, happy dreaminess," for the narrator. The crossing of that remembered significance with his present perception of motherhood as a "hidden dread" charges his reading of the landscape with powerful feeling. In this landscape, motherhood has become the sign of bitterness, and what he had formerly read as the landscape of the Good Shepherd he must now read as the "wilderness" in which a "cry of the shepherds" will be heard. Like Bartle Massey, the narrator here displays a "milky" conscience; his reading of the pastoral landscape becomes engorged, swollen with maternal feeling—he speaks as a male mother. But the cry he hears is not only that of the lost lamb but the voice of the prophetess, the voice that Hetty also hears.

IV

The journey Hetty now makes, as Clayton points out, is circular: she retraces in the "Journey in Despair" the same path she followed in the "Journey in Hope." Her journey, then, marks out a "turn."[16] After journeying toward Arthur for seven days, only to discover that he has already left Windsor, Hetty opens her red-leather case and the name Dinah Morris flashes upon her "like a newly-discovered message" (426). Hetty does not read the text written above the name, but she reads the letters of Dinah's name with new meaning, remembering for the first time Dinah's kindness. Because of this new reading, Hetty returns over the path she has already taken, now journeying toward Snowfield. After five days she reaches the black pool where she experiences profoundly contradictory yearnings for death and life. Almost against her will, it seems, Hetty turns at this moment toward life, leaving the black pool and taking refuge in a hovel near a sheepfold, where she kisses her own arms in sudden consciousness of a "passionate love of life" (433).

Only by mimicking Hetty's journey—by moving forward in the narrative and then turning back in it—can the reader discover the "hidden letters" that read new meaning into Hetty's turn from death to life. Although the narrative carefully marks out the stages of Hetty's journey by length of duration, seven days for the journey in hope and five for the journey in despair, we cannot deduce the dates of that journey until we read of Adam's attempt to find

Hetty. Adam leaves on Sunday, "the last morning in February" and therefore, February "28." Reaching Snowfield on this day, he learns that Dinah left Snowfield on the same day Hetty left the Hall Farm, or a fortnight before last Friday. Hetty, then, leaves on Friday, February "12" for Stoniton, where she spends the night. The next morning she sets off on her journey to Windsor, where she arrives in "the middle of the seventh day" or on Friday, February "19" (421). Because she faints when told of Arthur's previous departure, she spends the night and does not leave until the next day, Saturday, when Dinah's name "flashes upon" her. After traveling five days this time she reaches the pool as darkness is coming on. The day, then, would be Wednesday, February "24." Although George Eliot's calculation of the date differs from the calendar year by two days, this day would appear to be Ash Wednesday, the first day of Lent.[17] The second chapter of the prophet Joel provides the Epistle for this day, beginning "Turn ye even unto me" (Joel 2:12). The interleaved biblical lesson repeats for the third time the prophetic theme of "turning," even as it mirrors Hetty's "turn" from death to life. The "hidden letters" of the text underline this phase of Hetty's journey as a journey back to Dinah and toward life.

But if the reader turns still further back in the narrative and struggles to make out the text above Dinah's name, Hetty's "turn" takes on new significance. Dinah wrote the text in Hetty's red-leather case, we learn, one evening when she and Hetty were sitting together in the bedchamber, an evening when Dinah promised Hetty she would always be a friend in trouble. Most probably this refers to the evening described in chapter 15, "The Two Bed-Chambers," when an "inner voice" prompts Dinah to go to Hetty. Uncertain as to whether she interprets the voice correctly, Dinah allows her Bible to fall open and takes the first words she sees as direction. These words, "And they all wept sore, and fell on Paul's neck and kissed him," Dinah reads in the "light" of her memory of the rest of the associated text, for the evening light is too dim for "easy" reading (Acts 20:38). What she remembers, the narrator tells us, and reads into the visible letters of the text, is the "memorable parting at Ephesus, when Paul had felt bound to open his heart in a last exhortation and warning" (204). But the narrator does not quote Paul's warning to "take heed ... to all the flock" for "grievous wolves (shall) enter in among you, not sparing the flock." And Paul concludes, "I have shewed you all things, how that so labouring ye ought to support the weak" (Acts 20:17–38). Dinah's inner voice, we find, responded to a "hidden" reading: Hetty, this "weak" member of the flock, was vulnerable and needed support. Should we speculate that the text she wrote above her own name was "Turn ye even unto me" and should we read into this text the new meaning of a turn toward Dinah? For Hetty does indeed turn toward Dinah, the "voice" crying in her wilderness, and from that silent voice takes comfort, finds joy in her own life. Hetty's and Dinah's paths—which parallel each other in the narrative present—thus "cross" in the narrative past, merging or turning into each other with an uncanny sameness.

V

On the next day, the narrator leaves Hetty to continue her wanderings, doomed to taste her sorrow with "more intense bitterness" (435). "What will be the end?" he wonders, and exclaims, "God preserve you and me from being the beginners of such misery!" With this reference to beginnings and endings, another story interrupts Hetty's. For seven chapters the narrative turns to Adam's "journey" before returning to Hetty's—and Dinah's. In these seven chapters, Adam finally learns to read the "hidden letters" for the first "lesson," or Epistle, of John the Baptist's day. And it seems no accident that the schoolmaster should teach Adam how to interpret that lesson as a reading of both Hetty Sorrel and Dinah Morris. Most important, Bartle Massey teaches Adam to read himself into Hetty's narrative.

When Adam first hears of Hetty's arrest and imprisonment from Mr. Irwine, he finds he cannot read the letter that tells her story: "he could not put the words together and make out what they meant" (455). With passionate conviction he insists that these words are not Hetty's story, but Arthur's: "'It's *his* doing.... *He* taught her to deceive.... Let 'em put *him* on his trial—let him stand in court beside her'" (455). While resisting the story of guilt as properly belonging to Hetty, he still desires to position himself entirely outside that narrative. Like the Poysers, he cannot bring himself to affirm his association with Hetty. It is Arthur, he insists, who should "stand trial" with Hetty, for Hetty's troubles are Arthur's "doing" in the first place. Since he, Adam, had no part in the beginnings of Hetty's bitter sorrow, he has no place at the end: he does not belong in Hetty's story.

But on the eve of the trial, Mr. Irwine sternly admonishes Adam that he has no right to place the guilt for Hetty's crime solely on Arthur. In words that reiterate the "hidden letters" of the first lesson for August 18, the day Adam fought and nearly killed Arthur, Irwine tells Adam that "an act of vengeance on your part against Arthur would simply be another evil added to those we are suffering under" (469). He reminds Adam of his feelings after that nearly fatal fight in the woods, his words calling up for Adam a "vivid image of the past." But if Adam begins to change his interpretation of Arthur's part in Hetty's story at this point, he still places himself outside it. Not until his old schoolteacher gently interprets for him the fuller significance of Mr. Irwine's words does Adam see how to put the words of Hetty's story together—by reading himself into them.

On the day of Hetty's trial, Adam shares in her suffering so intensely as to experience a "baptism," or a regeneration into a new state. Yet he still shrinks from witnessing her trial, feeling himself powerless to contemplate such "irremediable evil and suffering" (470). Only when Bartle Massey returns from the trial—just to look in on Adam, as he puts it—does he hear any of the particulars of what has taken place. Massey tends Adam as solicitously as he did his "bitch," while describing for Adam the "foolish women" at the trial. Again, his discourse functions on two levels: though he has earlier declared that the sooner women such as Hetty are hanged the better, his description of her in the courtroom conveys Hetty's desperate need to Adam. Even more duplicitously, he chooses to emphasize not only Mr. Irwine's standing by Mr. Poyser, but that "it's a great thing in a man's life to be able to stand by a neighbour, and uphold him in such trouble as that" (474). Mr. Irwine will go so far, he tells Adam, as to witness for Hetty, despite her being one of these "poor, silly, women-things."

Hearing this interpretation of Hetty's story, Adam makes his decision to "stand by" her, to "own" her. Nerved by his active resolution to "witness" for Hetty, Adam now takes bread and wine with his old teacher.

Adam's baptism of suffering and his symbolic communion with Bartle Massey take place in chapter 42. The number of the chapter, like the dates in the narrative, signals the intersection of Adam's narrative with another, "larger" history outside the novel: the history of the "two witnesses" who prophesied for "forty and two months" (Rev. 11:3). In "continuous historical" apocalyptics, the two witnesses signified all those who testified or "witnessed" for "protestantism," meaning reformation and regeneration of the church throughout its history.[18] Three of George Eliot's later novels, including *Romola*, make this chapter number integral to the narrative design, signaling an intersection or crossing between narrative content in the chapter and one or another aspects of "continuous historical" apocalyptics. In these later novels, however, the number forty-two locates hermeneutic significance in a sevenfold "history" of humanity. In *Adam Bede* the number suggests instead Adam's place in a new history of prophecy—a history of prophecy constructed, not from man's, but from woman's perspective. The number "writes" Adam's decision to testify for Hetty into the history of apocalyptic witnesses: by owning up to Hetty, he testifies to the necessary reformation of the patriarchal church, "confessing" its exclusion and silencing of women.

Clearly, Adam's baptism into Hetty's suffering has taught him to "read" the Epistle for John the Baptist's day: new feeling now binds his heartstrings round the weak and erring and softens his hardness. His old teacher's double-ended discourse has taught him the lesson of the Good Shepherd as male motherhood—as the necessity not merely to care for "those with young," but to identify with them, to *name* oneself in maternal metaphors. Thus Adam now promises to "stand by" Hetty, to "own up" to her name as his own, to read her story as his.

Adam's new baptism also testifies to Dinah's hermeneutics: he does not merely bear the suffering he has "earned" himself, but shares in the "sin and sorrow of the world." In placing himself among Hetty's witnesses, Adam places himself among Dinah's.

Though he was not there on the green, Adam seems to hear Dinah's preaching now as the "voice of one crying in the wilderness." His baptism into suffering teaches him to read a "baptist" as one who fully shares in the suffering of "poor, silly, women-things." This new Adam testifies to *Eve*'s prophecy.

Still another number rich in hermeneutic significance underlines Adam's resolve to witness: the date on which Hetty's trial takes place. This day, the Friday following the Monday a week after Hetty buries her baby, is March "12," as the reader can discover by turning ahead in the narrative to the account of the trial (466, 479).[19] The Anglican lectionary designates Luke's account of Jesus' trial as the second lesson for March 12.[20] This narrative "crossing" takes on even greater significance when we realize that only in Luke's gospel does Jesus testify to the suffering of women, identifying it with his own:

> But Jesus turning unto them said, Daughters of Jerusalem, weep not for me, but weep for yourselves, and for your children.
> For, behold, the days are coming, in the which they shall say, Blessed are the barren, and the wombs that never bare, and the paps which never gave suck. (Luke 23:28–29)

The date of Hetty's trial appears carefully chosen to intersect with the reading of this particular narrative of Jesus' trial—the only gospel narrative in which Jesus, like George Eliot's latter-day Adam, "writes" the suffering of mothers as his own.

VI

Adam's education culminates in his baptism and resolve to testify for Hetty: he has learned to read the lesson for John the Baptist's day as a testimony both to the history of womankind and to the prophetess proclaiming that history. Only after this hermeneutically significant interruption of *seven* chapters "outside" Hetty's narrative—seven chapters that supply the necessary chronological information to determine the "beginning" and the "end" of this break in history—does the narrative return to Hetty's own account, the "inside" story of her history. In that story prophecy and history merge: the voice crying in the wood is both the voice of the prophetess and the silenced voice of womankind.

The circumstances of Hetty's confession to Dinah, like the break in her narrative, also contribute to the play on "outside" and "inside" perspectives. Dinah, who comes from outside Stoniton and outside Hetty's immediate family, immediately acknowledges kinship with Hetty (491). The elderly magistrate who had earlier listened to her preaching on the green as a "stranger" now admits her to the jail because he recognizes her as one with "a key to unlock hearts." And Dinah "unlocks" Hetty's heart only after the jailer turns "the harsh key in the lock" of the prison cell. In that unlocking, the silenced woman begins to speak, and history turns to prophecy.

With her first words, "I will speak . . . I will tell . . . I won't hide it anymore," Hetty finally speaks out, testifying to her suffering and producing in the darkness of the jail cell the sound of the voice crying in the wood. In that ghostly voice Hetty merges not only with her lost infant but with Dinah, "the voice of one crying in the wilderness," for Hetty's journey repeats her turn toward life at the black pool—doubles the interpretation of that earlier turn as a turn toward Dinah, and as Dinah's turn toward Hetty. She confesses to Dinah, "I turned back the way I'd come. I couldn't help it, Dinah; it was the baby's crying made me" (500). "Turning back" the way she had come, she continues to hear its "crying at every step," though we know from John Olding's testimony that he had removed the infant—whose life or death is strangely uncertain to him—by this time. The cry of Hetty's "lost lamb" merges with her own crying, the "voice" of her suffering as a mother, and with the voice of the prophetess crying in the wilderness.

From the beginning of her confession, Hetty compares her return to the baby's unceasing cry after her attempt to silence it with her earlier turn away from the black pool where she would have silenced herself, and toward Dinah: "I thought I could tell you," she now testifies to Dinah (498). Hetty's turn toward self-acceptance, toward "speaking" or testifying to herself, mirrors her earlier turn toward life, a turn underlined by the lectionary lesson for the day as a turn toward Dinah. The cry in the wood thus turns into Dinah's voice, and we read the "inside" meaning of Dinah's voice as that voice crying in the wilderness, "Comfort ye, comfort ye, my people."

It should be no surprise, then, that on the Sunday following the night in the jail, Dinah's first words to Adam are "Be comforted, Adam Bede: the Lord has not forsaken her," for Dinah's voice has reversed the history that forsakes or silences women (501). Nor should we be surprised that Bartle Massey, in his usual duplicitous fashion, further develops this interpretation of Dinah, telling Adam that "if there must be women to make trouble in the world, it's but fair there should be women to be comforters under it; and she's one—she's one" (503). Of course he adds that "it's a pity she's a Methodist, but there's no getting a woman without some foolishness or other."

VII

From the perspective of women's prophecy, the novel should have ended here with the production of the ghostly voice in the wood and its turn toward Dinah. But George Eliot not only continues with a final, septenary unit—the seven chapters of Book VI—but in these chapters appears to conspire in the silencing of her heroine. Adam recognizes Dinah as a "higher love" than Hetty, he proposes to her, and she accepts his proposal. In the epilogue we hear of the vote to silence Methodist women preachers—a vote Adam smugly affirms because, he says, most women are not like Dinah and do more harm than good with their preaching. For all he resembles the Good Shepherd and behaves like a male mother as he carries his young son on his shoulders, he remains a latter-day version of the Venerable Bede. On a Sunday he still chooses the Gospel of Matthew for pleasure reading—the gospel that most emphasizes the Law—and because he is a "good Churchman," disputes only apocryphal interpretations (542). Not only does Adam surely accept without dispute Paul's dictum that woman should not speak but find her salvation in childbearing, but George Eliot seems to have written her prophetess into Adam Bede's "history," merely substituting her name at the end where Hetty's appeared at the beginning.[21] The final seven chapters of the narrative, from the interpretive standpoint of women's prophecy, appear anything but visionary: by matter of factly permitting Dinah's reversion to the state of silenced motherhood, George Eliot seems to deliberately convert the soft or "milky" interpretation of Hetty's history back into the hard, dry prohibition of women's speaking.

But in this final narrative unit, chronology once again provides "keys" that turn the narrative from history to prophecy, once again undermines the supposed happiness of Dinah's fate with the bitterness of Hetty's. Perhaps the "hidden" number of this final narrative unit, produced by multiplying the number of chapters by the book number, is no more incidental than the narrative positioning of Dinah in the black invisibility of Hetty's jail cell, or seated in the cart with Hetty as she rides toward the gallows. In every respect, Dinah shares Hetty's fate, is written into her history.

Until the day of Adam and Dinah's betrothal, chronology appears somewhat hazy in Book VI; like the autumn sunshine, time floats somewhat indistinctly in the fall of 1801 "more than eighteen months" after the parting of Adam and Arthur. But as Adam rides toward Snowfield time crystallizes into the second Sunday in October. This day in 1801 was October 11, or in the Anglican calendar, the twentieth Sunday after Trinity. The landscape reminds Adam of his earlier journey to Snowfield, when he sought Hetty, not Dinah. At this juncture the narrator makes his comment that no story remains the same because we as readers do not remain the same. Indeed, Adam now recognizes that his journey in search of Hetty was all part of his journey toward Dinah; his "baptism" into Hetty's sorrow finds its fulfillment in his "better and more precious love" for Dinah (574).

But the narrative, as well as the narrator, also tells us that Adam's journeys toward two different women are, in another sense, a single journey—a journey marked by a crucial turning point. Adam not only retraces his own earlier journey to Stoniton but Hetty's, as she blindly sought both Dinah and the black pool. That blind quest began, as we know, when the letters of Dinah's name "flashed upon" her in the little red-leather case, and "ended" with her decision not to kill herself on the day that a later narrative clue suggests is Ash Wednesday. We now find that the hidden letters, or first lesson for the twentieth Sunday after Trinity, which is the second chapter of Joel, repeats that for Ash Wednesday. But the part of the chapter that was "hidden" or unread on Ash Wednesday now enlarges the meaning of the opening line, "Turn ye even unto me," for included in the Trinity lesson is the text, "I will pour out my spirit upon all flesh; and your sons *and your daughters* shall prophesy" (Joel 2:28, my emphasis). Adam's journey not only repeats Hetty's but doubly underlines the irony of "Turn ye even unto me," even as Dinah turns away from the scene of her preaching. The interleaved lesson turns us from Dinah back to Hetty, and we discover that women's prophecy is a black, silent pool, a moving emptiness, a lasting bitterness.

There are indeed numerous indications of Dinah's and Hetty's parallel paths through life in the narrative, as well as their ghostly merging of identity. Dinah sets out for Leeds on the same day Hetty sets out for Stoniton, for example, and Mrs. Poyser breaks a precious jug when she thinks she sees Dinah's ghost in Hetty's face. Hetty's and Dinah's names are written in the same little red-leather book, and until Dinah "unlocks" Hetty's heart and voice, Hetty does not testify to the difference between the two names. Hetty's real first name Hesther—which is never spelled out in the narrative—is a variant of Esther, whom the prophetic figure Mordecai warns not to think she can escape the fate of her people.[22] The narrative, as I have earlier pointed out, pictures Dinah as sharing Hetty's fate, not only her "locking-up" in the jail cell but her ride in the executioner's cart. The name Dinah, in fact, means "judged." And as I have already suggested, the cry from Hetty's own inner wilderness merges with Dinah's "inner voice" in that crying in the wood that will not stop even after it has been silenced.

If we now turn to the day of Adam and Dinah's wedding, we discover that it is more than merely "close" to the day of Adam and Hetty's betrothal two years earlier, as W. J. Harvey has noted, for it immediately follows the twenty-fourth Sunday after Trinity. This is the day underlined by the lectionary text, "The heart knoweth his own bitterness."[23] We may now read that text more complexly: it spells not only the biblical associations of Hetty's last name, Sorrel, but of Dinah's first name. If we turn to the only place in the Bible where the name Dinah appears, we find her to be the daughter of Jacob who was "defiled" or seduced. For the faithful Victorian Anglican reader, the biblical Dinah's story parallels Hetty's imprisonment, for it was the second lesson for the second Sunday in Lent, which in 1800 was March "7," or the Sunday before Hetty's trials. "Dinah" too, then, spells the bitterness of seduction, but the biblical Dinah was seduced because her lover not only "clave unto her," but "spake kindly" to her (Gen. 34:3).

The hidden hermeneutic structure of *Adam Bede* deconstructs its conventional narrative. The first "easy" reading of the plainly visible story with its traditional happy ending in a wedding grows darker and more difficult as stories from "outside" the text interleave those "inside" it. No more than Adam, we cannot read the same story twice. Dinah's submission, that seems so easy on the face of things, reads differently after a lapse of time. A brief "lapse" in the course of ecclesiastical history turns into a lapse of interpretation: the historian's perspective is brought into question, his narrative decentered, and a different story looms in the margins of *Adam Bede*. In her first novel George Eliot does not teach the reader how to read history but instead writes an account of the ambivalence of history, the duplicity of narrative, and the continuing difficulty of reading.

CHAPTER 3

The Scheme of the Apocalypse

I

Although *The Mill on the Floss* preceded *Romola* by only two and a half years, these two fictions of women's lives at first glance appear very different.[1] The earlier novel is set in nineteenth-century England, the later in fifteenth-century Italy. The earlier novel ends abruptly with the death of the heroine, the later with the heroine's establishment in a women's community. Autobiographical material and profoundly personal feeling permeate the earlier novel, while alien historical material and a sense of authorial distance characterize the later work, suggesting a level of abstraction akin to allegory.[2] These differences, however, do not preclude very striking similarities of apocalyptic structuring in the two novels: the later novel appears, in fact, to radically revise the septenary structure employed in the earlier.

As George Eliot's "apocalypse of history," the plot or "scheme" of *Romola* conceals a septenary structure, a sevenfold apocalyptic history of the world. *The Mill on the Floss*, however, is visibly divided into seven "books" with nonsequential chapter numbering between the books—a chapter arrangement that underlines the narrative's seven-part division. Narrative content in the relevant sections of the two novels suggests many parallels that are also reversals or mirror images, as in the double drownings at the conclusion of both narratives. A comparison of this parallel apocalyptic structuring suggests that in Maggie Tulliver's story George Eliot writes the "history of a witch" in seven books, a representation of feminine conflict that takes the form of a bitter parody of apocalyptic history, while in *Romola* she re-writes history as a sevenfold prophetic vision of "the woman clothed with the sun."

Apocalyptic structuring in *The Mill on the Floss* appears relatively simple and direct: fueled by powerful, apparently unimpeded emotion and uncluttered by researched material, its septenary division seems to encode only a readily accessible level of literary symbolism like the "stream of rhythmic memories" that George Eliot locates in Maggie Tulliver's consciousness.³ In contrast with both *Adam Bede* and *Romola*, chronology is blurred in this novel—dates are frequently only approximate—and I find little suggestion of elaborate or cleverly constructed narrative schematics.⁴ Nancy Miller has suggested that a suppressed female plot, an erotics of power, controls narrative structure in this novel, refusing the conventional happy ending in romance.⁵ A comparison of its narrative structure with that of *Romola* further suggests *The Mill on the Floss* may be read as a "black" apocalypse—a narrative in which George Eliot simultaneously liberates and "kills" off the witch in her own private history. She then proceeds in her next full-length novel to work out her own "continuous historical" apocalypse in which a female protagonist symbolizes the prophetic history of humanity. Yet both novels constitute sevenfold histories of Woman.

As a prelude to my discussion of the elaborate "scheme of the Apocalypse" in *Romola*, I shall first briefly describe the satiric, apocalyptic outline with which George Eliot constructs Maggie Tulliver's life as a "devil's history," or history of a witch. Outlines of a sevenfold prophetic history culminating in an undated "apocalypse," or Second Advent, were printed in many large Victorian editions of the Bible, such as the "family" Bible in which Tom writes his father's curse on Wakem. The lineage of these "indexes" to prophetic history may be traced as far back as Augustine's *City of God*.⁶ Representing a kind of historical Law of the Fathers—the authorized version of history written by the Fathers of the Church—this sevenfold biblical history seems to have been so familiar to Victorians as to be almost unconscious, functioning as a "landscape of time" that organized the individual's history as well as the world's. In *The Mill on the Floss*, each of the seven "books" into which Maggie Tulliver's history is divided parodies an age of prophetic history.

It is not hard to see Book I, "Boy and Girl," as an ironic version of the Creation, a Garden of Eden full of rats to be chased, toads

"A Chronological Index," inserted in an 1839 King James Bible.

to be pelted, and chickens that *want* killing. Tom Tulliver, that "pink-and-white bit of masculinity" so typical of English boyhood, nevertheless represents some of Nature's "most rigid, inflexible purposes," of which delight in the pursuit and destruction of other creatures is among the most prominent (30). But Maggie Tulliver herself is the thing most "out of nature" in this creation: instead of being sweet, doll-like and docile like the golden-haired Lucy Deane, she is black-haired, passionate, and "'cute," as her father laments—far too acute for the subordinate status for which Nature has clearly intended her. She learns early that she is a "naughty girl," and consoles herself for this frustration by driving nails into the head of her "Fetish" in the fashion of Jael destroying Sisera—an obviously effective biblical model of femininity (26). Even more telling is her early fascination with Defoe's *History of the Devil*, from which she takes her explanation of what it means to be a witch. If a woman swims, she's a witch and must be killed; if she drowns, then she's innocent, but as Maggie guilelessly wonders, "what good would it do her then, you know?" (17).

Maggie thus accurately though unknowingly prophesies her own predicament as a woman. If she "swims" with her own female nature, passionately reveling in her sexual energy as the opening narrative voice revels in the love of "moistness," she will be destroyed by the "Law of the Father": the internalized as well as external order of moral authority that governs her culture and her self.[7] But if she remains "innocent" and smothers that part of her that might "swim" as a woman, she will also perish, for this is the fate that the "Law" preordains for the witch: guilt and destruction.[8]

In Book II, "School Time," we find an ironic version of the Fall, or second age, interpreted as the fortunate education of mankind, for education is unfortunate for both Maggie and Tom. Designed to suit the traditional conception of their differing genders, education "wounds" Tom's pride of masculinity but confers little illumination, while Maggie's curiosity about grammar and syntax is considered mere proof of her feminine superficiality (127, 132, 134). From this maleficent schooling they are expelled by their father's misfortune, an expulsion couched in explicit allusion to *Paradise Lost*: "They had entered the thorny wilderness, and the golden gates of their childhood had for ever closed behind them" (171).

The third age of apocalyptic history is the Age of Abraham, the period marked by the first covenant and the prophecy of a Promised Land. Book III, "The Downfall," chronicles instead the period when the Tullivers are expelled from their "promised land," the mill that Mr. Tulliver considers rightfully his through generations of patriarchal possession but that a lawsuit he cannot even comprehend now removes. Instead of concluding with a covenant of forgiveness, this book concludes with Mr. Tulliver's instruction to Tom to write his undying curse on Wakem in the family Bible. That such rascals should prosper can only be "the devil's doing," in Mr. Tulliver's opinion (236). Thus does family history overwrite the book of prophetic history with a demonic text, and as in the exemplary illustration of the witch in Defoe's *History of the Devil*, Maggie's innocence and tearful protests against this hate-filled construction cannot save her from entrapment in it.

In Book IV, "The Valley of Humiliation," George Eliot writes a deeply insightful, ironic, yet almost grieving version of the fourth age of apocalyptic history—the Age of David, whom exegetes interpreted as a type of Christ, reading his psalms as celebrations of Yahweh's love for his bride Israel. For George Eliot this "age" reflects the inherent conflict for women produced by the Judeo-Christian hermeneutic of femininity as metaphor for sinful, dependent humanity. In *Romola* a complicated system of typological and apocalyptic reference makes the comparable section of Romola's history the thematic heart of the novel, the center of its prophetic vision. But in *The Mill on the Floss*, Maggie Tulliver's discovery of Thomas à Kempis and her consequent renunciation of the world are the crux of the predicament that will lead inevitably to her death by drowning. In striving to achieve sainthood through her particular "variation of Protestantism," Maggie opens her life to larger currents that keep her alive in what would otherwise have been a "thirsty, trackless uncertain journey," but she does not understand, as the narrator does, that "renunciation remains sorrow" even if that sorrow is voluntarily accepted (251, 255).

Constructing this stereotypically feminine story as the history of a witch, George Eliot writes Maggie's self-election to sacred brideship as the beginning of her self-immolation, even though it temporarily preserves her from the deadly "machinery" of her family's tempestuous history. As in both *Adam Bede* and *Romola*, numerical "signs" mark this apocalyptic turning point in Maggie's history: the beginning of Book IV marks the exact midway division in chapter sequence, with twenty-nine chapters preceding and twenty-nine chapters following it. But this "second half" of Maggie's life does not permit her—as it does Romola—to "reform" and regenerate her life in such a way as to escape the destructive elements inherent in her early history. Perhaps for this reason we may discover here a suppressed prophetic number comparable to that I noted in the last book of *Adam Bede*; by "crossing" or adding book number (four) and number of chapters (three) we obtain the "hidden" number seven, the numerical sign for completion or fulfillment, here ironically "buried" in the book where monastic teaching begins to bury Maggie alive.

The fifth age in prophetic history is the Age of the Babylonian Exile or Captivity. In *Romola* this is an age of painful human judgment, as in Frederick Temple's explication of it as a time of painful but necessary education.[9] The title of the fifth book in *The Mill on the Floss*, "Wheat and Tares," also plainly identifies this as a book of "judgment," of differentiating between wheat and tares. In both novels this is an era when the heroine begins to experience some disillusionment with the "prophecy" she had formerly adopted wholeheartedly, some awareness of its blindspots and prejudices, but for Maggie this new stage of pilgrimage only mires her deeper in the conflict in which she will eventually sink.

Ellen Moers has identified the "Red Deeps" where Maggie clandestinely meets Philip as a "female landscape"—a landscape that metaphorically figures Maggie's abortive sexual awakening.[10] Signifying pleasure, a "female self-indulgence," it fills her with guilt not only because she disobeys Tom's prohibition against associating with Philip but because she reads novels and poetry with him, a disobedience of the even more deeply instilled self-denial she has assumed in her devotion to Thomas à Kempis, that "voice from the past." Thus the "wheat and tares" of Maggie's fifth stage refer not only to her dawning doubts about certain aspects of her "Protestantism" but to the judgment already prepared for her: her eventual destruction by the network of conflicting desires and prohibitions that circumscribes the life or self permitted to a woman in St. Ogg's.

Book VI, "The Great Temptation," writes this parallel to the modern age or Age of Christianity solely in terms of Maggie's temptation—a temptation that is simultaneously a "crucifixion" because she cannot refuse the "cup" held out to her. As in the corresponding stage of *Romola*, the "tide" bears the heroine away. But in *The Mill on the Floss* this episode clearly represents a test by water, for if Maggie "swims" with Stephen she is a witch who deserves punishment by the outraged community and by her own self-condemnation, but when she refuses to swim with the tide she implicitly binds herself to a self-eroding acceptance of family and community demands. As Jane McDonnell comments, *The Mill on the Floss* represents a paradox at the "very heart of female identity": the conflict between "an ethical concern for others and the demands of the growing consciousness" (206).[11] Maggie is crucified by these conflicting desires, both of which seem to be her own "nature": the "nature" that craved the "fullness of existence" to be found in a life with Stephen, and the "nature" controlled by the "faith and sympathy that were the best organs of her soul" (402). In her decision to "kill" off the witch in herself by refusing to accept Stephen's love, Maggie embraces an equally fatal "innocence" that predicts her final death by water.

In Book VII, cynically titled "The Final Rescue," Maggie perishes in the flood locked in the arms of her brother. Her death proclaims her innocence, returns her to that moment in her history when brother and sister had "clasped their little hands in love, and roamed the daisied fields together." But the ending troubles readers exactly as it did young Maggie when she wondered what good it would do the witch to be innocent if she drowned anyway. In *Romola*, as we shall see, George Eliot writes this "double drowning" over again, but here the narrative kills off father and brother-husband. In her earlier "devil's history" of woman as a witch, George Eliot seems to have both produced and cast out the story of her life as feminine conflict. In her next novel, she set about a task evidently much more difficult for her: the radical transformation of a patriarchal scheme into a feminist apocalypse of history.

II

George Eliot's struggles with the "scheme" for her Italian novel suggest that she intended some dramatically new form. Comments in her journal indicate that her difficulties stemmed from the narrative structure of the work. In August 1861, she repeatedly referred to attempts to work out the "plot" or "construction" of her story. At one point she mentioned an idea for a "backbone" with which Lewes was "strongly satisfied," but this seems not to have been productive. By November she was so discouraged she almost resolved to give up the whole work. Not until December 11, when she noted that she had finally written "a scheme of my plot," did she begin to work out a structure that seemed acceptable to her. Even then she felt it necessary to write several drafts of the scheme.[12] Her labors indicate that her conception of form was both complicated and unconventional—a radical departure, apparently, even from her own earlier experiments with narrative form.

Yet only recently have critics begun to consider the work as something other than a conventional historical novel—a form in which many have judged it a failure.[13] Most illuminating among alternate critical approaches is Felicia Bonaparte's seminal thesis that we should read *Romola* as an "epic in prose" symbolizing the history of Western civilization. Bonaparte does not suggest any source for George Eliot's conception of a work that was to be half realistic narrative and half a "rich and encompassing poetic vision," but her description conforms precisely to the Apocalypse as it was read in the school of "continuous historical" exegesis.[14] The Revelation of St. John was seen as both a philosophy of history and an epic poem, both a mirror of chronology and a divine plan— in short, as both a realistic historical narrative and a poetic and prophetic vision of history. In *Romola*, I suggest, George Eliot wrote her own "continuous historical" apocalypse, appropriating the "scheme of the Apocalypse" in all its fascinating complexity of structure but revising it into a post-Christian and postpatriarchal vision of humanity. Romola progresses toward a new age governed by a Comtean conception of "feminine" values, values that emphasize devotion to the community but that also encompass a degree of female independence and autonomy unparalleled in any of George Eliot's other novels. With the composition of this novel, she strove to effect a complete revolution from a demonic to a visionary history of Woman.

The resulting complex narrative commands multiple levels of interpretation. The story of Romola di Bardi, daughter of a fifteenth-century Florentine family, represents a particular historical locality; dense with chronological and other factual detail, the narrative is a historical fiction that seeks to embed "real" historical data in an imaginary "story." Despite its "fantastic" elements, the novel thus makes a claim to be read as the realistic story of a woman living in a particular time and place. To some degree, then, the narrative functions on a level of psychological realism and may be read, as Mary Gosselink De Jong has proposed, as a female bildungsroman—a bildungsroman that writes the female self very differently from *The Mill on the Floss*.[15]

But Romola di Bardi is also "Romola," or the symbolic daughter of "Rome," the apocalyptic city of God.[16] As such the narrative invests her with still other levels of particular historical significance, for the city of Florence possessed a tradition of interpreting its own history in apocalyptic terms. This tradition of national historical interpretation, in turn, George Eliot plays off against her own political context. As in Florence, English exegetes had interpreted their country as the "sealed nation" of the Apocalypse, and like Girolamo Savonarola, these Victorian "prophets" had begun to identify the divine scheme with their own party politics.[17] According to them, England was specially commissioned to carry Protestantism to the rest of the world, for England was the isle in the sea on which one foot of the great Reformation angel rested (Rev. 10:2), and English Protestant hymns were the songs sung by the harpers beside the glassy sea of fire, in anticipation of the overthrow of the papal "beast" on the continent (Rev. 15:2).[18] George Eliot's attack on John Cumming in 1855 had criticized him for his greater interest in politics than the "kingdom within," and for giving a "charter to hatred." In her detailed study of Savonarola's "revolutionary" politics, she held up a historical mirror to the reactionary apocalyptics of the nineteenth-century Church of England.

But more important among George Eliot's artistic motives, I believe, is Romola di Bardi's signification as the "daughter" of an exegetical tradition that read the Apocalypse as a visionary history of the "church" or "mankind." On this level *Romola* represents a radical innovation, for not only does George Eliot invade a hitherto almost exclusively masculine domain of history but she writes the "education of humanity" as a development of "feminine" attitudes toward the community. She also writes the history of an idealized female figure in whose actions "protestantism" becomes a protofeminism. Romola protests against patriarchal authority and eventually frees herself from it. Her "history" thus radically rewrites Maggie Tulliver's inevitable destruction by the overwhelming tides of her feminine conflict.

Appropriately for such complex narrative ends, George Eliot employed even more elaborate and cunningly devised narrative schematics in *Romola* than in *Adam Bede*—schematics whose models can be found in "continuous historical" apocalyptics. Several critics have already described three- and four-part "allegorical" structures in the novel, such as J. B. Bullen's demonstration of one corresponding to the three Comtean stages of moral consciousness.[19] Tito and Bardi's paganism correspond to the first stage of polytheism, Savonarola's Christianity to the second stage of monotheism, and Romola's independent humanism to the third stage, or positivism.[20] But the Comtean structure of history was itself based upon a well-known prophetic scheme: the Joachimite Trinitarian division of history into the Age of the Father, the Age of the Son, and the Age of the Holy Spirit. The three stages of Romola's life in fact correspond about as well to Joachim's Trinitarian interpretation of history as to Comte's reinterpretation of it.[21] Romola first lives in an "age of the father" guided by her father, then in an "age of the son" guided first by the false son Tito and then by Savonarola's teaching of the true Son, and finally in an "age of the spirit," in which the institution of Christianity has withered away and Romola lives in a women's community guided only by a spirit of charity.

Interestingly, the tertiary scheme of the narrative also closely resembles the "continuous historical" interpretation of the three apocalyptic septenaries (seals, trumpets, and vials). In this interpretation, the seven seals were seen as the history of Rome pagan, the seven trumpets as Rome Christian, and the seven vials as the French Revolution. In Book I of the novel (chapters 1–20), in which Romola lives in the house of her father, the Renaissance revival of classicism dominates the city of Florence. In Book II (chapters 21–41), in which Romola lives with her husband Tito, Savonarola's preaching becomes prominent in the city. In Book III (chapters 42–72), in which Romola transforms Savonarola's teaching into a spiritual "religion" of charity, a revolution in Florentine politics takes place and Savonarola is eventually overthrown. Thus, Florentine history also takes on the tertiary apocalyptic configuration: the apocalyptic city in pagan, Christian, and "revolutionary" post-Christian eras.

But the tertiary apocalyptic scheme is only one of several that can be demonstrated in the novel. First and most significantly, the novel is divided into two halves that exemplify the Reformation—a Reformation both historical and visionary. Second, as several critics have already shown, Piero di Cosimo's "sketch" symbolizes the four-part division of Romola's spiritual progress.[22] Piero's sketch, I will argue, derives from interpretation of the Four Empires prophecy in the Book of Daniel. And lastly, the narrative falls into seven parts, four of which are very clearly delineated and three less so, a septenary structure that elaborates the universalized apocalyptic scheme of history already outlined in *The Mill on the Floss*. With this multileveled narrative web, George Eliot prophesies the spiritual destiny of humanity as an affirmation of both feminine and feminist values. The history of the apocalyptic nation will culminate, not in a "visible advent" in either fifteenth-century Florence or nineteenth-century England but in an apocalyptic "city" or community of women and children that demonstrates feminine nurturance but from which patriarchal authority has been purged. The conclusion of the narrative questions the "truth" of Savonarola's inspiration but leaves this question unresolved.

The difficulty of the extraordinary narrative project I have outlined here was undoubtedly further increased by the requirement for "secrecy." An essay written by George Henry Lewes in March 1860 (the year George Eliot began work on *Romola*) discusses the importance of the "construction" of a novel, whether simple or complex, but emphasizes above all the necessity of "art which conceals its art": "[T]here must be an easy play and fluctuation of various elements, all *secretly* and inevitably tending towards one point, but never ostentatiously tending towards it. The artist . . . must not permit us to see the strings and pulleys of his puppets; he must not betray his intention. Directly the machine creaks, our illusion vanishes."[23]

George Eliot had more than aesthetic motivation for desiring to conceal her "scheme" in *Romola*. The repossession and extensive manipulation of a scheme that embodied a "Law of the Fathers" must obviously have been fraught with psychological trauma as well as narratological difficulty.[24] The comparison of apocalyptic structures in *The Mill on the Floss* and *Romola* suggests that while it was "easy" for George Eliot to write the history of a witch, it was only with extreme effort that she could produce a visionary history of the human race as womankind. That this was her intention seems corroborated by her statements that the novel had been written with her "best blood" and that it had marked a well-defined transition in her own life, for she had begun it as a young woman and finished it an old one. To the very end of her life, she considered *Romola* her best work, and it is well to remember that when she donated money for the feminist purpose of founding a women's college (Girton), she signed herself "the Author of *Romola*."[25]

III

Precisely in the center of the novel, in the thirty-sixth chapter out of seventy-two, Romola is struck by a "vague but arresting sense that she was somehow violently rending her life in two."[26] An array of symbolic imagery reinforces this explicit binary division of the narrative. Romola prepares to seal forever the chest containing her wedding clothes, taking out instead a monastic garment whose plain dark veil contrasts strikingly with the bridal crown of pearls. On the crown rests a little sugarplum remaining from the wedding celebration, the sweetness of its bridal promise now turned to the bitterness of Tito's deceit and betrayal. Finally, Romola opens the little tabernacle or triptych, given her by her husband and painted with a fanciful Bacchic scene of love, and takes from it the austere cross given her by Savonarola. These acts and objects ostentatiously symbolize a major division in Romola's life between erotic and altruistic love, between the deceptive sweetness of romantic love and the inevitable sorrow of a broad sympathy with suffering humanity. Romola is about to enter a stage of existence in which the bridal prophecy of love will be reinterpreted, and given the new and larger meaning of charity.[27]

George Eliot's narratives exhibit binary division as early as "Janet's Repentance," and I shall attempt to demonstrate her continued development and complication of this narrative strategy to the very end of her writing career. In *Romola*, her construction of this midpoint division appears set off and deliberately italicized by her allusion to apocalyptic imagery and its interpretation, as if narrative here serves as a nearly explicit commentary on apocalyptic form and interpretation. The sugarplum sweetness now turned to bitterness, for example, suggests the apocalyptic prophecy that would be "sweet as honey" in the mouth, but "bitter in the belly" (Rev. 10:10), while the sealing of the wedding chest and opening of the triptych suggests the traditional hermeneutic division between the "sealed book" of the first principle prophecy, or pre-Reformation Christianity, and the "little open book" of the second prophecy, or Protestantism (Rev. 5:1, 10:2).

In this construction of binary division with imagery suggestive of the Apocalypse "midpoint," George Eliot appropriates "continuous historical" interpretation of both the Apocalypse and history as divided by the Protestant Reformation. But exegetes also interpreted the Reformation not only as a revolutionary change or division from the past but as a "reformation" of the old. "Reformation" thus reunited past and present by rehabilitating the past. George Eliot's italicization of binary division in *Romola*, as opposed to the less emphatic representation of division in Maggie's life, suggests her resolution of conflict and division through resorting to "continuous historical" interpretation of "Protestantism" as a prophetic call to active reform of the past. Following the midpoint division in *Romola*, a group of seven chapters elaborates the significance of Romola's "reformation" through apocalyptic symbol, type, and number.

Since the Reformation, Protestant interpreters had divided the Apocalypse into two parts. Joseph Mede, for example, states that "the whole Revelation, from the fourth chapter, is distributed into two principal prophecies. The first is of the seal and the trumpets. The second, or the little book opened, repeats the time of the former prophecies."[28] The precise point at which the Apocalypse was to be divided was not a matter of universal consent, but most felt the division came near the midpoint of the work—either between the first and last eleven chapters, when the seventh trumpet is sounded (Rev. 11:15) and the woman clothed with the sun appears (Rev. 12:1), or at the end of the tenth chapter, when the rainbow-crowned angel commands the prophet to "prophesy again" (Rev. 10:11). The apocalyptic work of the Old Testament, the Book of Daniel, was also divided at its numerical midpoint, between the first and last six chapters. This division into two parts eventually became the basis for a hermeneutical principle. The second part, or prophecy, explained the first, for as Bishop Newton commented, it was "the usual method of the Holy Spirit to make the latter prophecies explanatory of the former."[29]

Victorian exegetes interpreted the command of the rainbow-crowned angel that the prophet should take the little open book and "prophesy again" as the opening of the Bible—hitherto the "sealed book"—to the laity at the time of the Reformation. The "little book opened" thus symbolized the bringing forth of reformed Christianity from the "sealed book" of pre-Reformation Christianity—a Christianity usually identified with Roman and Greek thought. Romola's act of bringing forth the cross from the triptych repeats this interpretation of the "little book opened," suggesting that the Christianity symbolized by Savonarola's cross will proceed from and develop further the philosophy that guided the first part of Romola's life. Her meditation on her brother Dino's prophecy, though it seems at first only to confirm the truth of Dino's prediction of marital disaster, proves instead to illuminate both the first stage of Romola's life and the function of prophecy itself.

Dino had prophesied that her husband would have the "face of the Great Tempter" and that Romola would find herself wandering in a bare and stony plain where there was no water. Dino's prophecy appears correct, yet Romola feels she was right not to heed its warning:

> True as the voice of foreboding had proved ... to have renounced Tito in obedience to a warning like that, would have been meagre-hearted folly. Her trust had been delusive, but she would have chosen over again to have acted on it rather than be a creature led by phantoms and disjointed whispers in a world where there was the large music of reasonable speech and the warm grasp of living hands. (395)

But if Dino's prophecy, despite its accuracy, is not worth heeding, why is it given such importance in the narrative? Or to put it another way, if the prophecy is only part of a world of "phantoms and disjointed whispers," why should Dino nevertheless appear to have been correct in his prediction of events? The answer seems to lie in the episode's construction of an exemplum on the function of prophecy: its significance does not consist in any putative relationship to events but in its interpretation of "history" as philosophical or spiritual progress. Romola's meditation on Dino's prophecy repeats the message of "The Lifted Veil": mere prediction of the future, even if accurate, is a misguided and futile exercise. The real purpose of prophecy is to provoke interpretation of human "history," which is not the same as events that take place in history.

In this light, Dino's prophecy encompasses an interpretation of the inadequacy of the first two great philosophical visions of Romola's existence. The greater part of the prophecy, in fact, concerns the "wasteland" in which Romola now finds herself, a wasteland of dry parchment populated only by bronze and marble figures. In the dream, Romola seeks to revive her father's body with water held out by these figures, but even the water turns to parchment, and the parchments themselves shrivel up (215–16). After recounting his vision, Dino had told Romola it was a revelation intended "to warn thee against marriage." But this interpretation was limited and superficial, for Romola's greatest danger was not the possibility of a failed marriage, but the philosophical position in which a failed marriage would leave her. The destruction of her illusions concerning marriage leaves her no philosophic truth by which she can knit her life together again. Her father's Stoicism, which in Dino's vision she tries to revive through the parchments and figures symbolizing his library, allows her to conceive only "a solitary loveless life" and a "proud stoical heroism" (394). The sweetness of Tito's Hellenic vision of life, in turn, has become as bitter as her father's Stoicism is dry—neither is capable of providing the spiritual bread and water of life.

The parallel between this point in Romola's life and the "thirsty, trackless journey" of Maggie's existence before her discovery of Thomas à Kempis is clear. Like Maggie, also, Romola receives her revelation from a human, not an angelic, figure. In "silent" ironic response to apocalyptic hermeneutics, George Eliot emphasizes that for Romola, as for most people, revelation is not usually supernatural: "No radiant angel came across the gloom with a clear message for her. In those times, as now, there were human beings who never saw angels or heard perfectly clear messages (396)." The comment, however, covertly signals a conjunction between "continuous historical" interpretation and the narrative, for exegetes characteristically identified Savonarola as one of the apocalyptic angels or as one of the "two witnesses" who formed part of the great tradition of pre-Reformation "protestants." Bishop Newton, for example, describes Savonarola as one of the "good men, who called aloud for a reformation in faith as well as in morals, in doctrine as well as in discipline" while yet "in the bosom of the church of Rome" and thus suffered martyrdom for his witnessing.[30]

Moreover Romola hears this "arresting voice" in chapter 37, the precise beginning of the second half of the chapter sequence in the later novel, just as Maggie discovers her "voice from the past" in Book IV, the beginning of the second half of the chapter sequence in *The Mill on the Floss*. For both women, the encounter with a Catholic theologian marks the second "principal prophecy" of their lives. But Romola's encounter with Savonarola differs significantly from Maggie's with Kempis because George Eliot interprets Savonarola as a "Protestant" and in this interpretation comprehends Romola's ability to externalize and protest against a patriarchal authority that remains an internalized and inchoate conflict for Maggie Tulliver.

Bonaparte finds it surprising that George Eliot should give so little space to the "Protestant era" in the novel and suggests that she chose Savonarola as a prophetic figure partly because of a characteristically Victorian fascination with Roman Catholicism.[31] But in George Eliot's major sources, Savonarola was not seen as a Catholic but as an "early Protestant," a voice of the Reformation. In the *History of Girolamo Savonarola and of His Times* (1863), which George Eliot studied carefully, Pasquale Villari summarizes the work of earlier biographers and emphasizes the German tradition of considering Savonarola a "martyr of Protestantism."[32] Villari specifically cites Karl Meier's biography, which George Eliot owned, as one that considered Savonarola a martyr of the Reformation.[33] Villari himself saw Savonarola as an "evangelical prophet" and one who clearly stood "at the head of the new era."[34]

The change from a Catholic theologian advocating renunciation to one identified with "Protestantism" dramatically revises the significance of Romola's second "principal prophecy." Where Maggie's "variation of Protestantism" binds her to a self-abnegating rule of renunciation and obedience rooted in a medieval monastic ethic, Romola's "arresting voice" witnesses to the need for reform and regeneration and ultimately to active protest against a corrupt patriarchy.

George Eliot's review of Robert Mackay's *The Progress of the Intellect*, published in the *Westminster* in 1851, may clarify her construction of the Protestant Reformation in *Romola* as symbolizing the character of prophetic religion:

> The judicious reader of the Hebrew Scriptures, however orthodox his faith, cannot fail to perceive that they exhibit a progress from degrading to enlightened views of Divine nature and government. The writings of the prophets are full of protests against the conceptions of popular ignorance, and by continually expanding and purifying the Jewish Ideas of Deity, prepared the way for the reception of the teachings of Christ.[35]

In the review she commends Mackay's explanation of Christianity as "an expansion of the prophetic spiritualism," or a reinterpretation and renovation of the Jewish religion.[36] *The Progress of the Intellect* is, in fact, an English *Universalgeschichte* that traces religious development to its roots of "Greek Philosophy and Christianized Hebrewism," a scheme obviously similar to that of *Romola*. And Mackay's fundamental principle is that Christianity results from "prophetic spiritualism," or the prophets' spiritual interpretation of Hebrew ritual and form. He restated this principle in his later work, *The Rise and Progress of Christianity*, published in 1854, and expanded it to the conception of reform as the basic principle of all religious development:

> If it be allowed that the principle best suited to human imperfection is that of reform, it seems a necessary inference that a principle so important ought not be overlooked by religion; and undoubtedly the Christian religion was originally a reform of that narrow Judaical formalism....
> Protestantism is a good general name for religious reformation. It is the protest of reason and conscience against those superstitious abuses which have ever tended to substitute human precepts for the laws of God.... To define Protestantism, then, is to define Christianity; it is to verify the possibility of effecting reform by restoration.[37]

Savonarola's call to Romola embodies this sense of the Reformation as symbolizing all religious reform. He reinterprets for her the meaning of her marital bond, emphasizing her "sisterhood with the neighbour who kneels beside her," her duty to her community (432). Speaking to her as a "messenger" of "simple human fellowship," he urges her commitment to a "higher law" of a new "fellowship with suffering" (428, 435). Though he insists she return to her husband and submit herself again to the marriage bond, it is because that bond represents "the bond of a higher love." Savonarola's call "reforms" the meaning of marriage for Romola at this time, changing her understanding of it from a bond of romantic love only to one of participation in human suffering.

In *The Mill on the Floss*, the section in which Maggie discovers Thomas à Kempis and accepts his "call" appears marked or signed by an ironic reference to the prophetic number seven, obtained by adding book and chapter numbers. In *Romola*, a group of seven chapters that begins with the apocalyptically significant number forty-two and takes place on October 30 and 31, 1496 constructs Savonarola's call to Romola as her "Protestant Reformation" through an elaborate system of allusion to apocalyptic symbol, type, and number. In this narrative core of George Eliot's prophecy, Romola becomes, like Adam Bede, a "witness," but her witness is not to the suffering or exclusion of women but to the need for reform of a politicized Christianity into an ecumenical religion that makes charity its only institution.

Chapter 42 opens with the abrupt announcement of a different time: "It was the thirtieth of October, 1496" (443). The "new Charlemagne," as the French king is described in terms of apocalyptic legend, has deserted the city of Florence, leaving it not only in a politically perilous position but suffering from plague and famine. In this context, Romola now appears in her new role of ministering madonna. Carrying out Savonarola's instructions, she has reaccepted her marital bond as a part of her bond to her city and now devotes her life to this larger community.

Just as in *Adam Bede*, Chapter 42 of *Romola* represents a symbolic eucharist: Romola revives a dying man with wine and bread. The dying man proves to be Baldassare, Tito's deserted foster father, and in rescuing him Romola not only enacts a precise opposite to her husband's self-centered behavior but symbolically revives the past. Moreover, Romola's eucharist provides a solution to the problem envisioned by Dino's prophecy: in the "higher law" taught by Savonarola, she has found both the "water of life," or the personal inspiration she so desperately needed, and the means to escape the human isolation that was the inevitable end of the Stoical philosophy. The dry parchments and lifeless figures of her father's library have been transformed into "the large music of reasonable speech and the warm grasp of living hands." Yet Romola's succor of the suffering Florentine citizens clearly emanates from a personal stoicism: her father's philosophy of self-denial and heroic commitment to a moral existence is essential to her charitable activities. Thus, Romola's revival of Baldassare suggests a second "principal prophecy" that grows directly out of the first but also reforms it.

In Chapters 43 and 44, entitled "The Unseen Madonna" and "The Visible Madonna," Romola becomes the visible embodiment of charitable love signified by the hidden madonna carried in a "painted tabernacle." The sequence of tabernacle to visible embodiment of Christianity obviously recalls the sequence of the little triptych, also called a "painted tabernacle," and the cross. Both sequences symbolize progression from myth or fanciful belief about love to human enactment of self-sacrificing love or charity.

Less obviously, both sequences also suggest a typological interpretation of Revelation 7, known as the "harvest of the Church," and interpreted as the fulfillment or antitype of the Old Testament Feast of Tabernacles. According to Edward Bickersteth, the Hebrew festival of the harvest was a type of the "harvest of the Church" depicted in the 144,000 sealed "in the forehead" and standing before the throne.[38] From the ancient feast of tabernacles, then, emerged the apocalyptic antitype of the "invisible," or unmarked servants of God. In the novel, George Eliot in effect "seals" or marks her apocalyptic servant, symbolically bringing her forth from the tabernacles of ancient myths about love. The dates of the seven chapters in which Romola enacts her role of "visible madonna" further suggest Revelation 7, for October 30 and 31 are the two days before All Saints' Day, on which Revelation 7 is read as a lesson. Keble's poem for All Saints' Day in *The Christian Year* describes the "unseen armies of God" and takes its text from Revelation 7. Nor does it seem a coincidence that on October 31, the Eve of All Saints' Day, Tito sarcastically calls Romola "my angry saint."

Romola's anger is also an important aspect of her "reformation," for it is in becoming a "Protestant" that her spiritual progress differs most radically from Maggie's. Suspecting Tito of a plan to betray Savonarola, Romola publicly compromises him in such a way that he dares not carry out the plan. She then challenges Tito, in private, to "begin a new life" (493). The fact that these acts of protest take place on October 31 suggests a prophetic type of the nailing of Luther's 95 theses to the door on October 31, 1517—a prominent part of "continuous historical" exposition of the second principal prophecy. The day when the witnesses "stood upon their feet" was interpreted as the day when Luther nailed his theses to the door and the Reformation began (Rev. 11:11). Reference to "continuous historical" apocalyptics, then, identifies Romola both as an apocalyptic witness and as an "early Protestant" who testifies to the need for reform *before* the Reformation.

It seems more than probable that George Eliot here also deliberately invokes the apocalyptic image that Mede calls "truly a most beautiful image and representation of the Primitive Childebearing Church," the "woman clothed with the sun, and the moon under her feet, and upon her head a crown of twelve stars" (Rev. 12:1).[39] Roman Catholic exposition interpreted the woman as the Virgin Mary, but most Protestant exegetes agreed that she was an emblem of the church and that the dragon menacing her represented the devil. Like the woman in the Apocalypse, Romola is "clothed" with the sun of righteousness in this section of the novel, and she brings forth a spiritual "child" in response to the prophesying of the witness Savonarola, even as she is also menaced by Tito's deceptions and betrayals. As "visible madonna" of Florence, Romola clearly portrays F. D. Maurice's Comtean interpretation of the woman clothed with the sun as a "striking symbol of humanity," an emblem of the new age that was to be characterized by the nature of women, whose duty was "to repress the selfish and elicit the social instinct." The old, "masculine" age of individual heroism was to be replaced by the new, "feminine" age of social concern.

But if Romola typifies a feminine concern with the community, she also enacts a feminist protest against masculine egotism and error. From beginning to end, this septenary unit emphasizes her courage and independence as much as her devotion to community. In chapter 42, for example, she confronts and defies the hungry crowd who would snatch away the bread she carries for the neediest. Her introduction in this chapter as the ministering madonna who brings a saving "eucharist" to a dying man further suggests her identification with the "woman clothed with the sun," whom exegetes saw as symbol of the church triumphant in its reformation, regenerated with new life and vision. Where Adam Bede testified to the unjustified suffering and exclusion of women in the patriarchal church, Romola testifies to a church revived by feminine vision and feminist action.

IV

Several critics have pointed to the prophetic significance of Piero di Cosimo's sketch on the wall of Nello's barbershop.[40] Building on W. J. Sullivan's explication, Felicia Bonaparte develops a lengthy analysis of the sketch as a prophetic mural that not only portrays the four stages of Romola's life but also functions as "a pictorial synopsis of the history of Western civilization" (*Triptych*, 37). The relation of the sketch to the carnival structure of the novel, however, has not been pointed out, nor has its probable source in nineteenth-century interpretation of the Four Empires prophecy in the Book of Daniel. By examining three of George Eliot's sources for exegesis of the Four Empires, we shall see that the sketch does indeed function as prophecy but primarily in the form of a prophetic critique, imaging those "masks" of religious error that distort truth and write history as "carnivals" of superstitious rituals, myths, and mistaken interpretations.

Nello the barber clearly identifies Piero's sketch as visionary rather than realistic, claiming that Piero is "a strange, freakish painter, who says he saw it by long looking at a mouldy wall" (79). The picture consists of

> three masks—one a drunken, laughing Satyr, another a sorrowing Magdalen, and the third, which lay between them, the rigid, cold face of a Stoic: the masks rested obliquely on the lap of a little child, whose cherub features rose above them with something of the supernal promise in the gaze which painters had by that time learned to give to the Divine infant.

Tito comments that the picture is clearly "symbolic" and suggests that the child represents the Golden Age, or perhaps "the wise philosophy of Epicurus," to which Nello responds that Piero says his pictures are an "appendix" to the universe.

Warning against too simple an identification of the sketch with Tito the "Greek," Bardo the Stoic, and Savonarola the martyr, Sullivan suggests that each mask represents a different vision of life: the "grossness" typified by Tito and Dolfo Spini, the Stoicism of not only Bardo but Bernardo del Nero, and the mask of the Magdalen as a kind of Christian Stoicism to be found not only in Savonarola but in the Piagnoni and Fra Luca. Stoicism is thus central to Romola's development, as it appears to be in the sketch. Romola's final stage of development, according to Sullivan, is a kind of higher stoicism based on her godfather's, rather than her father's, life and philosophy. The child in the sketch, like the campanile in Florence, the frescoes in St. Mark's, and the village with the plague, is a representation of this "possible higher development."[41]

Bonaparte interprets the identity of the masks in much the same manner, but suggests that the central position of the Stoic mask reflects not the centrality of Stoicism in both pagan and Christian manifestations but the importance of feeling and passion represented by both the "mystery gods," Bacchus and Christ. The Satyr and the Magdalen, in her interpretation, represent the Bacchic symbolism associated with Tito and the symbolism of both the saint and the "pure prostitute" associated with Savonarola. Both Dino and Romola are rebels against the absence of feeling portrayed by the "rigid, cold fact" of the Stoic mask, and Romola's spiritual journey takes her first to the Bacchic sensuality of her husband Tito and then into the fellowship of suffering and sorrow offered by Savonarola. Stoicism is thus "central" only in a negative sense. Bonaparte also interprets the child as an image of the final stage of Romola's journey, but for her the child represents a transformation of the Christian vision and a "birth" of modern man, rather than a higher form of Stoicism.[42]

The painter himself, Piero di Cosimo, remarks only that "if any man is in doubt what they [his pictures] mean, he had better inquire of Holy Church" (79). Piero's cryptic comment suggests a double interpretation, not only that Christianity can provide the means for explication of the sketch but also that the church itself may be the subject of it. This comment in turn suggests the Four Empires of Daniel, for "continuous historical" exegetes read the Apocalypse as simply an enlargement or further explication of Daniel's fourth empire, or "Rome," and the history of Rome is seen also as a history of the church. Daniel's Four Empires and the Apocalypse therefore demonstrate the prophetic "method" of beginning with a sketch or outline of events and afterward elaborating upon it—a method that the early appearance of the prophetic sketch in *Romola* seems to imitate precisely.[43]

Interpretations of the Four Empires prophecy were very current in nineteenth-century British exegesis, and George Eliot seems to have exploited them in her last novel, *Daniel Deronda*.[44] But I shall explore here three sources that appear particularly relevant to the writing of *Romola*: Savonarola's sermons, Mackay's *Progress of the Intellect*, and Frederick Temple's "The Education of the World," printed in *Essays and Reviews* (1860). Each of these works provides an example of interpretation of the scheme, and each was read by George Eliot during or before the writing of *Romola*.[45]

Savonarola's interpretation of the four seals of the Apocalypse as a four-stage history of the church obviously resembles and is probably modeled on explication of Daniel's prophecy of the Four Empires of world history. Most significantly for *Romola*, however, he emphasizes these stages as stages of spiritual "sickness" in the church's progress toward eventual "health." Donald Weinstein describes his interpretation of the four seals as: (1) the age of the apostles (white horse); (2) the age of the martyrs (red horse); (3) the age of the heretics (black horse); and (4) the age of the "tiepidi," or lukewarm (pale horse). The Florentines, according to Savonarola, were then in the fourth stage, since a lack of feeling especially characterized their "spiritual sickness." The remaining three seals of the Apocalypse were to include some form of scourge and renovation, but Weinstein states that Savonarola was never as clear about these later three stages as about the first four.[46] In another version of the fourfold scheme, Savonarola explicated the four days from Lazarus's sickness to his resurrection as an allegory of Florentine church history. The first day represented the Medici rule, the second the need for repentance, the third the beginning of tribulations, and the fourth a "war of all" and a "resurrection" of the city.[47]

Nineteenth-century sources did not characterize the four stages as a progress from sickness to health but from ignorance to knowledge, the stages thus representing partial knowledge or steps in educating the human race. Mackay's *Progress of the Intellect* also further interprets the Four Empires as an "archetypal" or universal mythical structure discernible in *all* histories. He compares the Four Empires, for example, to Hesiod's Four Ages, as also to the "hindoo mythical series of four ages."[48] This explanation provides a clue to the contrasting interpretations of the sketch offered by Tito and Piero, for they suggest the same link Mackay does—Hesiod's Four Ages and Daniel's Four Empires. Tito's reference to the child as the "Golden Age" is both appropriate to his identity as "the Greek" and significantly incorrect. In Hesiod's cycle of Four Ages, the Golden Age is the first, paradisal age, from which the state of mankind progressively declines further and further until, finally, the cycle begins again. Tito, however, appears to believe the ascendant figure of the child represents some "Golden Age" or "wise philosophy" dominating the course of time or history. His interpretation of the sketch is in a sense an interpretation of himself, for it is *he* who is the "child" in the story. As Mackay explains, the Greeks represented a kind of "mental childhood" in the history of religious development, for they accepted even ecstasy and frenzy as divine and believed "doctrine" which even the barbarous Scythian repudiated.[49] The mask of the drunken, laughing Satyr appears to symbolize this conception of Greek religion as one so primitive that intoxication is confused with the divine, while Tito himself is the "child" of a Golden Age, living in a paradise created by his capacity for self-delusion.

Like Mackay's work, Frederick Temple's "The Education of the World" is a version of *Universalgeschichte*.[50] The first essay in the epoch-making *Essays and Reviews*, Temple's article proposes a childhood, youth, and manhood of the world.[51] In his scheme, however, the Four Empires are reduced to "tutors" or "Educators" of the world during its childhood: from Rome, mankind received the spirit of order and organization, or discipline; from Greece, science and art, reason and taste; from "Asia" (Babylon and Assyria), spiritual imagination and otherworldliness; from the Hebrews, human conscience. George Eliot had read Frederick Harrison's *Westminster Review* article on *Essays and Reviews*, which protests that the four nations chosen for this scheme by Temple are only a "meagre classification" of the significant races, omitting the Egyptians, Confucians, Buddhists, and Mohammedans.[52] Both the ancestry and the rationale for Temple's selection seem evident, however, when we consider the traditional interpretation of the Four Empires as Babylon, Persia, Greece, and Rome.[53] Temple converted the Four Empires to an educational scheme and daringly considered the Hebrews as merely one of those educators (for which he was castigated by Harrison). He continued to interpret all human development, however, as the development of the "church," considering all non-Christian forms of religious or spiritual development as comparatively insignificant.

Temple's scheme is not far removed from Savonarola's fourfold spiritual progress of the church, except that each "Educator" has become an aspect, rather than a progressive stage, of spiritual development. Moreover, each culture provides only a single aspect that can in itself represent an extreme and must be balanced by the others. For example, Grecian art and science require the balance of Roman discipline, Hebrew spiritual morality that of Asian spiritual imagination. Each of the spiritual aspects, as in Savonarola's scheme, represents a kind of spiritual sickness or error. This variation for the Four Empires scheme suggests large implications for Piero's sketch, for we can also interpret it as representing not only four stages of a spiritual journey but three "faces" of spiritual error. This interpretation, in turn, points to another major prophetic structure in the novel—the cycle of the three carnivals.

The first mask represents not only hedonism and pleasure-giving love but drunkenness and sensuality—an aspect of the Bacchic myth manifested at the first carnival, when Tito and Romola are betrothed in the midst of revelry and "grossness" of all kinds. The second mask, in turn, may be interpreted as representing not only Stoic coldness but also—as Bonaparte suggests—the rigidity of a narrow, Christian puritanism. The second carnival manifests this destructive puritanism when Savonarola's "pyramid of vanities" destroys great works of secular art along with cosmetics and fripperies. In this construction of "puritanism" or "stoicism," George Eliot seems to spell out for Romola a religious error that for Maggie Tulliver remains obscure but intrinsic to her problem.

Lastly, the third mask, representing the penitence and sorrow at the heart of Christian reformation, may also represent a love of martyrdom, thus pointing to the third carnival and Savonarola's bid for martyrdom or a miracle. Each mask in effect prophesies a carnival "theme," and each theme in turn symbolizes a religious or philosophical extreme, or distortion—a "costume" that at once reveals and obscures religious truth.

Piero's sketch may thus include a much more comprehensive prophetic significance than has yet been suggested. It is indeed a prophecy, modeled on the Four Empires, both of Romola's spiritual progress and of the history of Western civilization. Just as Western civilization may be construed as moving through periods dominated by Greek civilization, the Roman Empire, Christianity, and a visionary post-Christian period, so the major spiritual influences of Romola's life are Tito's love, the Stoic philosophy of her father and godfather, and Savonarola's Christian "reformation," after which she passes into an independent but community-oriented stage of post-Christian and postpatriarchal values.

But the sketch is not only visionary but "freakish" or satiric, representing the three types of spiritual sickness or errors present in each of Romola's "Educators" and dramatized by one of the three carnivals. Through carnival masks, we see each of the "reforms" needed in Romola's life: the concept of love as entirely "sweet" and pleasure-giving; religious discipline that becomes narrow and blind, rejecting secular arts as it rejects human feeling; and penitence that grows into an egotistical desire for martyrdom. The order of the masks, which does not conform to the order of Romola's spiritual stages, conforms precisely to the order of the carnivals.

Piero's sketch, then, represents in miniature the "continuous historical" apocalyptic scheme centered on the Protestant Reformation as both historical and symbolic. It envisions history both as humanity's spiritual pilgrimage and as a carnival cycle of errors that masks truth, and must be seen *as* masks in order to reform and rehabilitate the past. Perhaps nothing in *Romola* so clearly exhibits George Eliot's prophetic method and intention as Piero's sketch drawn on "a mouldy wall."

V

I have described two of the multiple structures of time from the "scheme of the Apocalypse" that George Eliot implicates in her "historical romance": the division into two great prophecies, or history divided by the Reformation, and the four-stage prophetic "sketch" based on the Four Empires, and here treated both as a spiritual history of mankind and a prophetic critique of religious error. But the narrative also manifests an even more complex and universalizing apocalyptic structure in its sevenfold division of Romola's journey, framed by apocalyptic proem and epilogue. Through this septenary construction Romola's journey takes on the symbolic significance of the apocalyptic "city" journeying through time. Tito's history, meanwhile, exhibits a contrasting cyclical form similar to the Hesiodic cycle he perceives in Piero di Cosimo's mural—a form symbolizing self-limitation, and lack of direction and progress.

"Continuous historical" exegetes saw the Apocalypse as the keystone that completed the biblical arc of time, its sevenfold vision of the End balancing and completing the seven days of creation, and the seven ages of time. The narrative of *Romola* similarly appears to be divided into seven sections or "visions" that correspond to the days and eras of creation, and to the apocalyptic imagery of the End. Even the proem and epilogue of the novel also resemble apocalyptic structure, for the Apocalypse is most often seen as a poetic structure of prologue and epilogue enclosing "septenaries" of visions.[54]

The proem, with its angelic machinery, its spirit or "shape" surveying the city of the future, and its reference to the Joachimite myth of Pope Angelico, who was to "come by-and-by and bring in a new order of things," almost obviously sets the stage for a prophetic vision. Its chronological setting in 1492, the year when Columbus set out to discover the New World, is not only near in time to the Reformation but was symbolically identified in "continuous historical" exegesis with apocalyptic times. On Edward Bickersteth's chart, the year 1492 marks the dividing point between the evening and the morning of the sixth "day," or last age before the millennium.[55] But the epilogue also suggests an echo of the Apocalypse, though instead of looking ahead to the fulfillment of the plea to "Come quickly!" Romola looks back to one who gave help when it was greatly needed.

Within this framework of apocalyptic proem and epilogue, Romola's journey proceeds from an age of innocence to an apocalyptic city, as will be shown. But this progress through time toward a historical goal pierces through Tito's path, which ends where it began. The contrast between symbolic shapes of the two journeys suggests a conscious dialectic between the Christian conception of history as linear and progressive and the Greek conception of time as cyclical.[56] In the novel, however, the Greek conception is identified also with Judeo-Christian symbolism of evil, while Romola's sevenfold journey culminates in a community of women and children, not a "city of God."

Bonaparte has pointed out that Tito's ring, which first attracts Bratti's attention on April 9, 1492, is one of the images that links Tito with Bacchus, "the epiphanic god of the sea who numbers among his special creatures the serpent" (*Triptych*, 93). This interpretation represents only a part of George Eliot's complex symbolic allusion, however, for Mackay describes the serpent, fish, lion, dragon, and Leviathan all as biblical imagery symbolizing "a ghostly adversary or principle of evil." Tito's rings, whether the "fish with the crested serpent" or the "Cupid riding on a lion," all identify him as the principle of evil cloaked by romantic or erotic love.[57] His own interpretation of his serpent-ring as a symbol of good fortune "especially at sea" is another example of his significant misinterpretation, for he will meet his death by water (88).

The serpent-ring not only suggests Tito's primary identification with the "adversary" but particularly symbolizes the circularity of evil—its endless recurrence throughout time and failure to progress. This conception of evil is by no means new with Mackay but part of a familiar typological interpretation of Genesis.[58] In an article published in the *Christian Observer* in 1840, for example—the same year in which Mary Ann Evans published her first poem in the journal—the prophecy pronounced against the serpent in the garden is said to be fulfilled in the twelfth chapter of the Apocalypse, where "the great dragon" is to be cast out.[59] The *circle* of evil—the deceptive serpent in the garden mirrored by the "dragon" who threatens the woman in Apocalypse and drives her into the wilderness—is thus implicit in nineteenth-century typological interpretation of the Old Testament.

In *Romola*, the symbolic chronology of Tito's story doubles the circularity of evil symbolized by his ring. Bonaparte has pointed out, for example, that Tito is discovered in Florence and is killed there on the same day, April 9. His cycle of existence lasts exactly six years, a number not only associated with the "beast" in Apocalypse, but with the failure to reach the completion or perfection of seven. In addition, the first six chapters of the novel all take place on April 9, 1492, the day of Tito's discovery in Florence, and his death on the same day six years later takes place in the sixth chapter from the end of the novel (chapter 67). A "circle" of sixes at the beginning and end of the narrative figures the endless cyclical recurrence of evil and its failure to achieve any kind of linear progress. We may note the similarity between the circular "flood" that encloses Maggie's story, finally engulfing Maggie herself, and the extensive circular symbolism in *Romola* that eventually culminates in Tito's death in a "flood."

In the later novel, not only is the septenary and linear structure of Romola's narrative sharply differentiated from Tito's cyclical rise and fall, but George Eliot enormously complicates the significance of Romola's sevenfold history, loading it with multiple levels of symbolic and allegorical meaning. This narrative scheme accommodates the seven days of creation, the seven ages of time, the structure of the Apocalypse, and the liturgical year.[60] To George Eliot this poetic structure was not only a familiar part of her own education but a prominent aspect of her source materials for *Romola*.[61] I have already mentioned Savonarola's reference to a sevenfold periodization of world history, but I should emphasize the awe felt by his nineteenth-century biographers for his imaginative exegesis of the Bible, in which meanings were heaped up in "prodigal confusion":

> ... he is said to have learnt the Bible by heart. But it was that book, read by an imagination which opened out the biblical language with a boldness and luxuriance, certainly as yet untried, and perhaps hardly surpassed in later days: every image, every allegory, every parable, every figure has not one but a thousand meanings,—meanings, each of the same authority with its plainest and most literal significance,— meanings heaped one upon another with prodigal profusion; and that not in wanton ingenuity, but with a vehemence and fervour which enforce the belief that the preacher had the fullest confidence in every one of his wildest interpretations.... At the same time he ... has full

faith in the poetic mythology of the middle ages, in the Virgin, and in the Saints.[62]

Villari quotes this comment in his chapter and note on Savonarola's biblical interpretation.[63] To further illustrate the extraordinary "luxuriance" of Savonarola's exegesis, Villari devises a chart demonstrating his multiple levels of interpretation of the Creation. Such a sevenfold structure of all time and history was probably long since familiar to George Eliot, however, as is suggested by Bickersteth's chart, in which historical events are set into a framework of the six days of creation, with the seventh millennial age expected during the 1860s. I have already suggested that Mary Ann Evans's own chart, which was to have included the apocalyptic prophecies, would probably have taken a similar form.

The septenary structure in *Romola* begins, appropriately, with chapter 7, following the first six chapters that take place on the day of Tito's awakening in Florence. Possibly of ironic relation to the structure of the Apocalypse is the fact that chapter 7 is an "epistolary" chapter, dealing with a Platonist squabble carried on by letter, for the Apocalypse also begins with an "epistolary portion." In any event, the "epistolary" chapter marks the beginning of four clearly demarcated chronological periods, each of which takes place in either seven or fourteen chapters and begins with a chapter whose number is a multiple of seven. These sections correspond to the first four days of creation and the first four ages of time, as well as incorporating a New Testament order that begins with the nativities of John the Baptist and the Virgin Mary, and proceeds through an Advent, Christmas Eve, and spiritual "birth" or All Saints period. After the first four stages a strict septenary division of chronological periods is no longer evident, but the narrative continues to echo apocalyptic imagery and to be divisible into three final stages of Romola's journey. This division between four clearly demarcated periods and three less definite stages also resembles Savonarola's explication of the stages of the church.[64]

The epistolary chapter, which takes place on an undesignated "May afternoon," is followed by five chapters that take place on the Eve and Feast of St. John the Baptist, or approximately June 24 and 25.[65] These are followed in turn by several chapters that take place on the Eve and Feast of the Nativity of the Virgin Mary, or September 7 and 8. Following these focal periods, time flows by unmarked until the carnival or pre-Lenten season of 1493, when Tito and Romola are betrothed. This group of fourteen chapters (7–20) make up the first symbolic unit in the prophetic structure of time: an "Age of Creation" and paradisal beginnings, but also of illusion and unreality.

Bonaparte has suggested that the double significance of the Feast of St. John as both Christian feast day and pagan celebration of Midsummer dramatizes Romola's (and Florence's) choice between two gods—Bacchus and Christ (*Triptych*, 134–35). But John Keble's interpretation of the feast may have an even more pertinent relation here to George Eliot's new apocalypse, for Keble's poem emphasizes the relation of the past to the present as symbolized by the filial relationship. Taking as his text Malachi 4:5–6 (from the lessons for the day), "he [Elijah] shall turn the heart of the fathers to the children, and the heart of the children to their fathers," Keble develops the theme that filial duty as a symbolic turning to the past is necessary to preparation for the "great and dreadful day," for the world must learn "first filial duty, then divine."[66] Tito's deliberate decision in this section to turn his back on his foster father not only sharply contrasts with this theme associated with John the Baptist, but underlines the larger symbolic significance of his betrayal as a denial of the past.

George Eliot frames Tito's denial of the past, in turn, with a "Golden Age" that is also a Comtean "age of fiction." As Mackay explains, "the real age of innocence was one with that of fiction; men seemed to know more when they believed more, as to be good when they knew not evil."[67] Although it is an "Age of Creation"—a time when "prophets" (Dino and Tito) and "virgins" (Tessa and Romola) appear, and a time when young love blossoms, it is also an age of superstition and magic, of innocent but childish belief. Ironically, Tessa half believes that Tito is St. Michael, the apocalyptic opponent of the dragon. The extended light of Midsummer suggests the creation of light on the first day, but in Florence Midsummer was originally the feast of Mars, and the darkness of pagan rites shadows the Christian feast. With even greater appropriateness this section ends with Tito's and Romola's carnival

LITERAL INTERPRETATION.	SPIRITUAL INTERPRETATION.	ALLEGORICAL INTERPRETATION with reference to the Old Testament.
First Day: Heaven, Earth, Light.	Soul, Body, Action, Intellect.	Adam, Eve, the light of Grace.
Second Day: The Firmament.	The Will, between the oppositions of Soul and Body.	Noah's Ark.
Third Day: Separation of the Waters from the Earth. — Dry Places. — Grass and Plants.	The movement of the Passions, and the errors which take possession of the intellect. The Intellect craving for knowledge.	Gentiles separated from the elected people. . . . . Multitude of the Elect.
Fourth Day: Sun, Moon, Stars.	Metaphysics and Ethics, Natural and Political Sciences.	High Priest, King, other priests.
Fifth Day: Birds, Fishes.	Contemplation of higher and lower objects.	Maccabees (who always fluctuated).
Sixth Day: Animals, Land animals, Beasts of burden. Man in the image of God.	Ferocious instincts. . . . . Sense. Man, who controls the Passions.	. . . . Hebrew people (given to avarice in the time of Christ). The Good. Christ (who was the expected of the Old Testament).

N.B.—It is to be observed, that although in the two interpretations, moral and different senses; in one case, e.g., reason means that force which rules the passions, in which we have given, must of necessity be imperfect, because it has been made out

"Tabular View of the Different Interpretations of the Bible, by Savonarola." From Pasquale Villari, History of Girolamo Savonarola *(1863).*

ALLEGORICAL INTERPRETATION with reference to the New Testament.	MORAL INTERPRETATION.	ANAGOGICAL INTERPRETATION.
Hebrew people, Gentiles, Jesus Christ.	Soul, Body (in the sense of reason and instinct) Light of Grace.	Angels, Men, visions of God.
The Apostles, and other Saints.	Moral strength.	Eternity of bliss and Condemnation.
Tribulations which separate many from the Church. . . . . The sound doctrines of the Church.	Struggle of the passions with duty. Reason.	Joy of the blest who were free from tribulations. . . . . Their praises and perfect works.
Pope, Emperor, Doctors.	Laws of Charity ancient and new, minor precepts.	Christ, the Virgin, the other Blessed.
Contemplative Life, Active Life.	Contemplations of things Divine and human.	Angels, and Men who enter the choir of the Angels.
Anti-Christ, with his followers. Christians given up to earthly things. The Elect of God. The perfect who will abound in the time of anti-Christ.	The bad. Persecutors. . . . . He who improves by tribulations.	Those who were persecutors. . . . . The Preachers. . . . .

spiritual, the same significations are given, they must always be understood in two the other case, it means that faculty by which truth is apprehended. This division from interpretations that are incomplete, sometimes scarcely indicated.

[370] SACRED CHRONOLOGY,

ARRANGED BY THE

MILLENNIA FROM CREATION.

FIRST EVENING.

A M
    Darkness, Fall. Gen. i. 2, 5, iii. Jer. iv. 23.
1 Creation and Fall, B C 4006 Abel's death; Cain's exile.
131 Seth b.
236 Enos b.
326 Cainan b.
396 Mahalaleel b.
461 Jared b. Apostacy. Gen. vi.

MORNING.

    Light, Gen. i. 3, v. 25. Prophecy, Jude 14
623 Enoch b. [cycle]
688 Methuselah b. [perfect cycle]
875 Lamech b.
931 Adam d. Gen. ii. 17
988 Enoch translated, Gen. v. 24
    Seventh from Adam,—prophet, Jude 14

SECOND EVENING.

    Waters under firmament, Gen. i. 6, 8, vi. 1—7, 11—13; Psalm xciii. 4; Isaiah xvii. 12, lvii. 20
1042 Seth d.
1057 Noah b.
    Violence, Gen. vi. 11. Curse, Gen. v. 29
1141 Enos d.
1236 Cainan d.
1291 Mahalaleel d.
1423 Jared d.

MORNING.

    Firmament, Gen. i. 6, ix. 8—17; Ezra i. 22—28
    Waters above firmament, Gen. i, 7; ix, 18; xi, 9
1537 Ark preparing
    Forbearance, Gen. vi, 3; 1 Peter iii, 20
1557 Noah's sons b. [cycle], Gen. v, 32
    Founders of New World. Gen. ix, 19

VOL. II.—71

A M
1652 Lamech d.
1656 Methuselah d. Flood begins. Eight saved by water, Gen. vii, viii,
1657 Flood ends B C 2350
1659 Arphaxad b. B C 2348
1694 Salah b.
1724 Eber b.
1758 Peleg b. [cycle]
1774 Chaldean era, B C 2233
1778 Reu b.
1820 Serug b.
1850 Nahor b.
    Dispersion, Gen. x, 25, 32
    Seventy families, Gen. x, Deut. xxxiii, 8.
1879 Terah b.
1949 Haran b. Gen. xi, 26
1997 Peleg d.—8 Nahor d. B C 2010
    Dispersion complete

THIRD EVENING.

    Land in the midst of the waters, Gen. i, 9, 10; xii, 1—7; xv, 7—21; xvii, Exod. vi, 1—8
2007 Noah d.
2009 Abraham b.
2019 Sarai b.
2027 Reu d.
2050 Serug d.
2084 Call of Abraham, xii, 1, B C 1923
    Sojourning, 430 years, current, [cycle]
2095 Ishmael b. æt. 86
2097 Arphaxad d.
2109 Isaac b. [100] B C 1898
2127 Salah d.
2159 Shem d.
2169 Esau and Jacob b. [60]
2184 Abraham d. [æt. 175]
2188 Eber dies
    Last Patriarch, Gen. x, 21; xiv, 13
2246 Jacob's exile, Gen. xxviii, [æt. 77]
2260 Joseph b. [91]
2290 Joseph's rule, Gen. xli, [30]
2299 Descent to Egypt

"*Sacred Chronology.*" *From Edward Bickersteth,* A Practical Guide to the Prophecies *(1841).*

The Scheme of the Apocalypse   89

A M
2370 Joseph d. [110] B C 1637
     End of Genesis.
2430 Aaron b.
2433 Moses b.
2473 Moses in Midian

MORNING.

Earth yielding fruit? Lev. xxvi;
  Deut. xi.
2513 *Exodus*, B C 1494
2553 Entrance to land
2559 First year of tillage, Lev. xix,
  23. Josh. xiii, xiv, B C 1448
  Division, date of jubilees
2593? Othniel d.
2672? Ehud. Second rest ends. Judges
  iii, 30
2712? Barak and Deborah. Third rest,
  Judges v, 31
2751? Gideon. Fourth rest ends, Judges viii, 28, 32
  Abimelech rules
2754? Abimelech slain. Jub. IV
2777? Tola d.
2799 Jair d.
2806 Jephthah d. Interv. 252 yrs.
  Judges xi, 26
2812 Ibzan d.
2822 Elon d.
2830 Abdon d.
  Philistines rule
2850? Samson d.
2889 Eli d. Ark at Kirjath, 1 Sam.
  iv, v
2909 Ark returns, B C 1098
  Close of period, Acts xiii, 20
  Samuel and Saul, xiii, 21
2949 David at Hebron, B C 1058
2956 David at Jerusalem, B C 1051
2989 Solomon r. B C 1018
2992 Temple founded, B C 1015
3000 Dedication, Jubilee ix, B C 1007
  Height of Jewish state

FOURTH EVENING.

Light to rule the night, Gen. i, 14
  —18; 2 Peter i, 19; Daniel xii,
  13

A M		B C
3029	Rehoboam, Jeroboam	978
3046	Abijah 3 years	961
3049	Asa 41 years Jubilee x	958
3050	Nadab 2 years	957
3052	Baasha 24 years	'955
3074	Elah 2 years	933
3075	Zimri, Omri 12 years	932
	— 79, Samaria built	
3086	Ahab 22 years	921

A M		B C
	Jericho rebuilt, 1 Kings xvi	
	Elijah pr. 1 Kgs. xvii	
3090	Jehoshaphat 25 years	917
3108	Ahaziah 2 years	899
3110	Joram 12 years	897
3114	Jehoram 8 years	893
3120?	Elijah rapt? cycle	887?
3121	Ahaziah 1 year	886
3122	Athaliah—Jehu 28 years	885
3128	Joash 40 years	879
	Zechariah slain, 2 Ch. xxiv, 20	
3143	Jonah pr.	864
3150	Jehoahaz 17 years	857
3168	Amaziah 29 years	839
	Elisha d.	
3182	Jeroboam II, 41 years	825
3197	Uzziah 52 years	810
3205	Joel pr.?	802
3218	Amos pr.?	789
3231	Era of Olympiads	776
3235	Shallum Menahem	772
3246	Pekakiah	762
3248	Pekah	759
3249	Jotham 16 years	758
3254	Era of Rome	753
	Micah pr.	
3260	Era of Nabonassar	747
3265	Ahaz 16 years	742
	Hosea pr.	
3276	Hosea 9 years	731
3278	Captivity of Israel	729
3281	Hezekiah	726
3286	Samaria taken	721
3294	Sennacherib's invasion	713
	Overthrow, Jubilee xv.	
	Nahum, Isaiah	
3310	Manasseh	697
3331	Second captivity, Is. vii, 8	676
3365	Amon r.	642
3367	Josiah	640
	Zephan. and Habakkuk	
3379	Jeremiah begins to prophecy	628
3398	Jehoahaz—May B C	609
	Jehoiakim—August B C	
3401	Nebuchadnezzar	606
	First Empire, Dan. ii, 38; vii, 4	
	Captivity, first date, 2 Kings xxiv, 2. Isaiah xxiii, 15	
	Times of the Gentiles begin? Luke xxi	
3404	Daniel's first vision	603
3409	Jehoiachin 3 months, March	598
	Zedekiah 11 years, June	
3418	Siege of Jerusalem, Jan.	589
3419	Sabbath in siege, Jer. xxxiv	588
3420	Jerusalem taken, June	587
	Temple burnt, 2nd date of captivity	

A M		B C	A M		B C
	420 years, 70 Sabbaths, 2 Chron. xxxvi, 21		3574	Sanctuary cleansed, Neh. xii - - - -	433
3421	Ezekiel prophes. xxxiii, 21, January - - -	586		Evening and morning, sec. date, Dan. viii, 14	
3446	Evil Merodach, Jan.	561		Close of sacred history	
	Close of 2 Kings and Jer.		3576	Peloponnesian war -	431
3448	Neriglissar		3582	Xerxes II. Sogdianus	425
3451	Laborosoarchod		3583	Darius Nothus	424
3452	Belshazzar, Daniel vii	555	3602	Artaxerxes Mnemon -	405
3454	Daniel's second vision	553	3603	Athens taken. Lacedemonian headship -	404
3469	Babylon taken, Dan. v	538		Leopard, second head? Daniel vii, 6	
	Darius the Mede, Dan. v, 31, ix			Close of seven weeks, Dan. ix, 25	
3471	Cyrus the Persian, Dan. x; Ezra i, 1	536	3636	Leuctra, Theban headship	371
	Second, or Persian Empire, Daniel ii, 32, 39; vii, 5; viii, 3, 4			Leopard, third head? Daniel vii, 6	
	Captivity, first close		3648	Ochus	
3478	Cambyses, first king, Dan. xi, 2 - - - -	529	3669	Arses—Philip's headship, Chaeronea - -	338
3485	Smerdis, second king, Daniel xi, 2 - - -	522		Leopard, fourth head, Dan. vii, 6	
3486	Darius Hystaspes, third king	521	3671	Darius,—Alex. the Great	336
3489	Haggai and Zechariah	518		First horn of goat, Dan. viii, 5; xi, 3	
3490	Jubilee xix, begins? September - - - -	517	3676	Arbela, fall of Darius -	331
3491	Second temple dedicated Ezra vi, 15, Feb. -	516		Third, or Grecian Empire, Dan. ii, 32, 39; vii, 6; viii, 5—7; xi, 3	
	Zerubbabel and Josh. Zec. iv, 1—9		3684	Philip Aridaeus - -	323
3497	Athens freed - -	510	3695	Era of Seleucidæ -	312
3499	Consuls at Rome - -	508		Ptolemy Soter, Seleucus Nicator xi, 15	
	Sec. Head of 4th Beast, Rev. xvii, 10		3701	Fourfold Division, Dan. viii, 8; xi, 4 - - -	306
			3722	Philadelphus, v, 6 - -	285
	MORNING.		3727	Antiochus Soter -	280
	Light to rule the day; dawn of the gospel, Gen. i, 16; Mal. iv, 2; Luke i, 78; 1 John ii, 8.			Kingdoms of Pergamus, Pontus, Cappadocia, and Bythinia; Pyrrhus in Italy; Achaean league; Gauls in Greece.	
3522	Xerxes, fourth king, Dan. xi. 2 - - - -	485	3746	Antiochus Theus, v, 6	261
3527	Thermopylæ and Salamis	480	3760	Euergetes, v, 7, 9 -	247
	Athenian empire. Leopard first head?			Bernice and Son slain, v, 6	
3542	Artabanus - - -	465	3761	Seleucus Callinicus, v, 7, 8	246
3543	Artaxerxes Long: Ezra vii, Neh. i, and June -	464		First Punic War ends	
3550	Ezra's commission, Ez. vii	457	3781	Seleucus Ceraunus, v, 10	226
	Seventy weeks, first date, Daniel ix, 24		3784	Antiochus Magnus, v, 10, 13, 15 - - - -	223
	Evening and morning, first date, Daniel viii, 14		3785	Philopator, v, 11	222
	Fresh date of jubilees?		3790	Battle of Raphia, v, 11, 12	217
3563	Nehemiah's commission. ch. ii,—March - -	444	3802	Epiphanes, v, 14 -	205
			3805	Battle of Zama, Second Punic war ends - -	202
	Sabbath of sec. week, Neh. viii—x		3809	Battle of Panium, v, 15, 16	198
			3811	Greece declared free -	196
				Græco-Roman Horn, viii, 9, 10, 25; Rev. xii, 3	
			3815	Antiochus in Greece, v, 18	192

The Scheme of the Apocalypse   91

A M		B C
3817	Romans in Asia, v, 18	190
3820	Selencus Philopator, v, 19	187
3826	Philometor	181
3832	Antiochus Epiphanes, v, 21	175
3839	Pydna, Fall of Macedon	168

Roman Legation, Livy xlv, 11, 12; Dan. xi, 30.
Fourth, or *Roman Empire*. Dan. ii, 33, 40; vii, 7; ix, 26; xi, 31. Numb. xxiv, 25.

3845	Antiochus Eupator	162
3847	Demetrius Soter	160
3857	Alexander Bala	150
3861	Demetrius Nicator, Euerg. II.	146

Carthage and Corinth fall. Dan. xi, 31.

3925	Sulla Dictator	82

Fifth Head? Rev. xvii, 10.

3944 Temple profaned by Pompey - 63
Abomination, Dan. viii, 11.

3963	Cæsar's death	44

Sixth Head, Rev. xvii, 10.

3982	Temple of Janus closed	25
4001	BIRTH OF CHRIST? B C	6

FIFTH EVENING.

Living creatures in the seas. Gen. i, 20. Ez. xlvii, 9—11. Matt. iv, 18; xiii, 47.
Kingdom of the Stone, Dan. ii, 34.

Depression of *Visible Church*.

A D
27? Baptism of John, Luke iii, 1
Sixty-two weeks close, Dan. ix, 24, 26
30 CRUCIFIXION, ASCENSION?
Pentecostal Church, Rev. xii. 1
41 Call of Gentiles, Dan. xi, 32
53 Council of Jerusalem, Is. ii, 3
St. Paul in Greece, Zech. ix. 13
62 St. Paul at Rome, Dan. xi, 33; Gen. viii, 27
70 Fall of Jerusalem
First Seal. Rev. vi, 2; Dan. ix, 26
Literal abomination, Daniel xi, 31
Triumphs of Gospel, Gibb. xv.
Persecutions, Dan. xi, 32, 33; viii, 12; Rev. xii, 4; Gibb. xvi.
81 Domitian—St. John in Patmos
96 Close of Sacred Canon
98 Trajan—Pliny, Bithynian persecution

A D
117 Hadrian
138 Antoninus Pius
161 Marcus Aurelius
Persecutions, Polycarp m.
180 Commodus, Troubles in Empire
Fire cast on earth, Rev. viii, 5; Gibb. vii.
Preparation, viii, 6; Gibb. viii, ix.
250 Decius, persecution
Persian and Gothic Invasions
First Trumpet. Rev. viii, 7, 250—303
253 Valerian, persecution
Goths in Asia, Franks, Alemans
303 Diocletian's persecution
Travail of church, Rev. xii, 2
Ten days' tribulation, Rev. ii, 10; Dan. xi, 33
313 End of Persecutions
Monasticism, Rev. xii, 6; Gibb. xxxvii.
305——323 Paganism overthrown, Gibb. xiv.
Victory in heaven, Rev. xii, 7—12
324 *Empire Christian.* Constantinople founded, Gibb. xvii, xx.
Second Seal. Rev. vi, 3, 4; Gibb. xviii.
Help of the church, Dan. xi, 34
Seventh Head, Rev. xvii, 10
325 Council of Nice
336 Death of Constantine, threefold division, Goths and Persians
Exile of Athanasius
361 Julian Emperor
364 Valens and Valentinian
Alemans, Burgundians, Scots, and Persians
Second Trumpet, 365—476
378 Hadrianople, Valens' death, Gibb. xxvi.
379 Theodosius the Great, Gibb. xxvii.
381 First Council of Constantinople
Close of First Trumpet
395 Arcadius and Honorius, Gibb. xxix.
Separation of Latin Empire
Eagle wings given? Rev. xii, 14
404 Ravenna seat of Empire, Gibb. xxx.
Mountain cast into sea? Rev. viii, 8
410 Sack of Rome by Alaric, Gibb. xxxi.
Third part, blood, viii, 9
Britain revolts; Goths, Sueves,

A.D.		A.D.	
	Almans, Vandals, Burgundians, &c.	666	Papal authority in Britain Latin service in the churches pressed by Vitalian
412	Religious war of the East, Gibb. xlvii.	680	Third Council of Constantinople
	Third Trumpet, Rev. viii, 10	698	Carthage falls
431	Council of Ephesus	710	Saracens in Spain
451	Council of Chalcedon	728	Greg. II, Revolt of Rome, Gibb. xlix
476	Fall of Western Empire, Gibb. xxxvi.		Little horn risen, Dan. vii, 8
	Second trumpet ending	762	Bagdad founded, City of Peace
	Seventh head falls, Rev. xvii, 10; xiii, 3	774	Lombards overthrown Third King uprooted, Dan. vii, 8
	Odoacer, King of Italy, Dan. vii, 8, 20, 24. *First King*		Rise of second beast, Rev. xiii, 11
	Beast rising from the sea, Rev. xiii, 1	786	Harun Al Rashed, 2 Saracen Empire at height
493	Ostrogoths in Italy		*Five months end*, Rev. ix, 5
	Second King. Dan. vii, 8	787	Second Council of Nice
		800	Charlemagne crowned, Gibb. xlix
	MORNING.		*Seventh Head revives*, Rev. xiii, 3
	Exaltation of visible church	869	Fourth Council of Constantinople, and last Eastern General Council
533	Justinian's Code; Empire orthodox, Gibb. xliv.	936	Fall of Caliphate
	Third Seal. Rev. vi, 5, 6		*End of Locust woe*, Rev. ix, 12
	Wars of Belisarius, Rev. xii, 16; Gibb. xli.	988	Conversion of Russia, Gibb. lv Christendom complete, A M, 4994
	Time, times and half? Dan vii, 25; Rev. xi, 3; xii, 14		Height of visible church
	Mystical Abomination, Dan. xi, 31; xii, 11		SIXTH EVENING.
553	Ostrogoths overthrown, Gibb. xliii.		Living Creatures of the earth— Christian Polities established
	Second Council of Constantinople		Depression of true Church
	Second King uprooted, Dan. vii, 8	997	The Turks, Mahmud the Gaznevide first Sultan, A M 5003, Gibb. lvii
565	Death of Justinian		Angel of the East? Rev. ix, 14
	Fourth Trumpet, Rev. viii, 12, 565—622	1009	Jerusalem raised, Fatimite Caliphs
568	Lombards conquer Italy, Gibb. xlviii.		Angel of the South? Rev. ix, 14
	Third King, Dan. vii, 8	1016	Normans in Italy, Gibb. lvi
602	Phocas, Persian War, Gibb. xlvi.	1060	Normans conquer Sicily
	Darkening of East, Gibb. xlviii.	1066	Normans conquer England Angel of the North?
608	Pantheon dedicated; Mahomet's preaching	1063	Alp Arslan crosses Euphrates Armenia and Georgia lost
	Fifth Trumpet. Rev. ix, 1, 2; Gibb. xxviii.		*Sixth Trumpet*, Rev. ix, 13 Month and year, or 390 days?
	Ten Kingdoms; Beast from the sea rises, Rev. xiii, 1; xvii, 12	1073	Hildebrand Power of second Beast, Rev. xiii, 11
	Forty-two months? Rev. xi, 2; xiii. 5		*Fourth Seal*, Rev. 6, 7
612	Islamism begins, Gibb. 1.	1081	Normans invade East
622	Hegira, or flight of Mahomet	1095	Council of Clermont
637	Jerusalem taken, Rev. ix, 11?		First Crusade, Franks and Normans against the Saracens and Turks
	Locust, or *Saracen* woe, Rev. ix, 3		
647	Saracens invade Africa	1098	Jerusalem won from Saracens
660	Paulicians, Gibb. xlix; Rev. viii, 13?		Days of Chivalry, Rev. ix, 14, 16
		1123	First Lateran Council

The Scheme of the Apocalypse

A D
- 1139 Second Lateran Council
- 1147 Second Crusade
- 1179 Third Lateran Council
- 1189 Third Crusade. Richard I, Lion-hearted
- 1198 Innocent III. John in England Fourth Crusade. Height of second Beast
- 1203 Latins take Constantinople
- 1206 Mogul Empire begins
- 1207 Crusades against Albigenses, Rev. xiii, 12?
- 1209 Interdict on England, xiii, 13
- 1215 Fourth Lateran Council
- 1243 Close of Albigensian Crusades
- 1245 Council of Lyons
- 1261 Greek Empire restored
- 1274 Second Council of Lyons
- 1299 Othman invades the East
- 1311 Council of Vienna
- 1326 Prusa taken
- 1353 Ottomans in Europe
- 1370 Timour reigns
- 1378 Great Schism of the West
- 1396 Last Crusade
- 1409 Council of Pisa
- 1414 Council of Constance Jerome and Huss burnt, Rev. xiii, 15
- 1431 Council of Basil
- 1433 Council of Florence Re-union of Eastern Church, ix, 20, 21. Empire Papal *Fifth Seal*. Rev. vi, 3
- 1453 Fall of Eastern Empire, May 29 Month and year end? Rev. ix, 15 Papal despotism at height, xiii, 14—18; ix, 20, 21 Witnessess lie slain, Rev. xi, 7, 8
- 1492 Discovery of America by Columbus

MORNING.

Exaltation of true Church, Gen. i, 26; ii, 21—24; Rev. xix, 7—9; Eph. v
Revival of learning, 1453—1517; Rev. x, 1?
- 1514 Fifth Lateran Council, 9th Session
Exposure of witnesses, Rev. xi, 9
Embassies, Indulgences, &c. xi, 10

A D
- 1517 REFORMATION, Theses of Luther Witnesses revive, Rev. xi, 11
- 1521 Diet of Worms Re-prophesying, Rev. x, 11
- 1529 Protestation at Spires, xi, 1?
- 1556 Edward VI; Council of Trent; Luther dies; Altar measured? Court cast out? Rev. xi, 1, 2
- 1552 Treaty of Passau Time of the end? Dan. xii, 4, 9; Rev. x, 8
- 1553 Mary, Persecution in England Cry of the Martyrs? Rev. vi, 10
- 1558 Elizabeth; English Establishment
- 1588 Spanish Armada
- 1648 Peace of Westphalia Charles I, beheaded; Commonwealth
- 1688 English Revolution
- 1789 French Revolution Tenth part falls, Rev. xi, 13 *First Vial*, Rev. xvi, 2 *Sixth Seal*, Rev. vi, 12
- 1792 Jacobinism throughout Europe *Empire Infidel;* French Republic Era of liberty; Infidel Calendar Era of missions, xi, 12; xiv, 15? Close of 1260 days? xi, 3; xii, 14
- 1793 French Atheism; Reign of Terror *Second Vial*, Rev. xvi, 3
- 1795 Directory; Conscription Italian Campaigns; French Victories *Third Vial*, Rev. xvi, 4
- 1802 Napoleon Supreme; Popery restored *Fourth Vial*, Rev. xvi, 8
- 1815 Empire headless; Fall of Napoleon *Seventh Seal*, Rev. viii, 1; vii, 1 Occupation of France 3 years *Fifth Vial*, Rev. xvi, 10; Ex. x, 22 Congress of Four Powers at Vienna *Pause in Heaven*, vii, 1; viii, 1
- 1822 Greek Independence; wasting of Turkish empire *Sixth Vial*, Rev. xvi, 12 Close of 1290 days; time of end? Dan. xii, 11; xi, 40 Preaching of Second Advent, Rev. xvi, 15. A M 5828

betrothal: the union of this "Adam and Eve" begins at a time of masking and pretense, suggesting the first mask in Piero's prophetic sketch. Time and the Hours appear as frightening specters whose true nature cannot be ascertained, any more than Dino's prophecy can be correctly interpreted.

Following this "Creation," we expect a Fall, or Age of the Flood. The next fourteen chapters, 21–34, take place on November 17 and November 21–28, 1494, and are identified both with the Age of the Flood and with the season of Advent through Savonarola's preaching. In his Advent sermons, Savonarola has prophesied that the invasion of the French king will be the "deluge" or "flood of waters" by which Florence would be both scourged and renovated: "He believed it was by supreme guidance that he had reached just so far in his exposition of Genesis the previous Lent; and he believed the 'flood of waters'—emblem at once of avenging wrath and purifying mercy—to be the divinely indicated symbol of the French army" (269).[68] The French king's arrival coincides with that of Baldassare, who is, as Bonaparte comments, Tito's personal scourge. Tito does not "fall" during this section, however, for Tito has already fallen, committing himself to deceit and betrayal from the very first—the serpent is always in the garden. It is Romola who "falls" here—a fortunate fall from innocence into the first knowledge of her husband's deception, when she discovers his sale of her father's library. Baldassare also falls from grace in this section. By adopting vengeance as his motive, Baldassare identifies himself with Tito's evil. From here on, the serpent and beast imagery associated with Tito are also associated with Baldassare, and he becomes more and more "entwined" in Tito's fate.

Savonarola's interpretation of the French king as God's purifying scourge not only invokes the symbolism of the second day (creation of the waters) and of the second age of time (the Flood), but suggests a subtle critique of apocalyptic exposition in George Eliot's time. During the reign of Louis Napoleon (1848–70), debate raged in England as to whether he was the "Antichrist" prophesied in the Apocalypse.[69] The parallel between this political aspect of mid-Victorian apocalyptics and Savonarola's predictions concerning the son of the "subtle Louis" in the fifteenth century is too clear to ignore, as is the reminder that the Second Advent imminently expected by Savonarola was still imminent for Victorian "prophets."

Just as the lectionary theme of filial love heightens the irony of Tito's failure to ransom his foster father, so now an Advent lectionary theme subtly underlines his continued betrayals. In response to Baldassare's appearance in Florence, Tito purchases a coat of armor, the wearing of which Niccolo describes as "like carrying fear about with one" (306). Romola even more specifically calls the armor "this fear" (316). Both comments bring to mind the opposing "armor of light" in the Advent Collect, an "armor" that protects against the "works of darkness." As Tito moves further and further into the works of darkness, he dons the appropriate symbolic garment—an armor that not only symbolizes the cold weight of fear upon him but that will eventually be the means of his exposure, rather than of his protection.

The narrative moves to a new period of time in chapter 35 as the French king leaves Florence, and chapters 36–41 take place on December 23 and 24. On December 23 Romola feels she is tearing her life in half as she removes her wedding ring and seals her wedding chest. On the morning of the 24th, or Christmas Eve, she sets out on her historic journey and encounters Savonarola and Fra Luca. At this point the narrative interrupts Romola's story and returns to Tito's "last supper" in the Rucellai garden, in which he not only becomes involved in a political game of "triple deceit" but once more publicly denies and betrays Baldassare (312). The supper in the Rucellai garden, which seems to take place on December 22, is thus enclosed as a "flashback" or retrospect within the significant period in which Romola's reformation takes place.[70]

George Eliot's extensive use of a "flashback" technique in this narrative deserves comment. Although we have seen a similar interruption and turning back in *Adam Bede* when Hetty confesses to Dinah in the jail cell, in *Romola* George Eliot resorts to this narrative strategy more frequently and even more designedly. By enclosing events that actually took place at an earlier time within a symbolically significant chronological period, the strategy appropriates other levels of interpretation for the enclosed or framed events. This technique had been the subject of discussion in apocalyptic exegesis since the seventeenth century. Mede's interpretation of the Apocalypse rested on his principle of "Synchronisme," or the concept that prophecies described at different points in the narrative actually occur at the same time.[71] Faber discusses Mede's principle of "abstract synchronisation" at great length, considering it the fundamental means by which the Apocalypse may be ordered and interpreted.[72] E. B. Elliott, in his history of apocalyptic exposition, also speaks of how Mede "advanced the science" of interpreting the Apocalypse, "inferring the structure of the prophecy from its own internal evidence ... its synchronisms and the mutual relationship of its several parts."[73] By the principle of "synchronism," separate parts of the Apocalypse may actually be considered as "flashbacks," or events prophesied to take place at the same time even though described separately. Narrative interpretation thus "synchronizes" the symbolic, especially numerological, significance of apparently separate narrative units.

George Eliot's use of "flashback" in the narrative appears highly similar to apocalyptic synchronism. Events linked in this way symbolically or "prophetically" parallel each other. In this third or Christmas Eve section of the narrative, for example, Tito's Judas-like betrayal of Baldassare at the Rucellai supper precisely contrasts with Romola's move toward reformation and inner renewal. He exemplifies the "works of darkness," she the light beginning to shine in the midst of darkness. Tito poisons his "communion" with Baldassare, ending his possibilities for reform and regeneration; Romola, meanwhile, takes the first step toward that inner reformation that will enable her to offer bread and wine to Baldassare in the next section. Tito's action points toward the death of the "Christ child," or spirit of love within himself, Romola's toward the "birth."

As in the two preceding sections, the events of this section also invoke the corresponding periods in the prophetic structure of time—the third day of creation, and the third age of time. In the third age, Abraham leaves the land of his forefathers and sets out for a promised land: he receives a new covenant. On the third day of creation land appears, and exegetes interpreted this as corresponding to Abraham's departure. The correlation between Romola's leaving her father's house and setting out toward a distant city, and her receipt of Savonarola's "new covenant," is obvious.

Less obvious but equally significant is the "covenant" that Tito also accepts at this time—a political commission that entails complicated deceptions and intrigues. (We should be reminded here of the "devil's covenant" at the end of Book III in *The Mill on the Floss*, when Tom writes his father's curse in the family Bible.) And Tito also, after undertaking this commission, sets off for another city. Finally, the Christmas Collect, recited on the Eve as well as the day of Christmas, petitions for regeneration and renewal, the process that Savonarola is about to inaugurate for Romola.

The fourth section into which the narrative divides, chapters 42–48, takes place on October 30 and 31, 1496, and describes Romola as both an "unseen" and a "visible" madonna. Just as the preceding section symbolizes the eve of a spiritual rebirth in Romola, this section symbolizes the birth itself. I have already described its relation to the second principal prophecy and to the apocalyptic "woman clothed with the sun." The section also corresponds to the fourth day of creation, for on that day the sun, moon, and stars are created. Mackay's discussion of the six days of creation suggests a delicate poetic balance between Romola as the "bride of Christ" here, and the bride of Bacchus, or Tito, in the first section. According to Mackay, the sixfold creation exhibits a symmetrical poetic balance: the creations of each of the second three days balances those in the first three:

> The first day brings forth universal light, which on the fourth is embodied and personified in sun, moon, and stars; on the second day are made the firmament and sublunary waters, which on the fifth are inhabited by birds and fish; on the third day the land with its vegetable covering emerges from the deep, and on the sixth it receives its appropriate living occupants.[74]

In the first prophetic section, the time of midsummer and greatest light, Romola falls in love with Tito; here, in the fourth section, where she herself shines with the "sun" of righteousness, she becomes the spiritual bride of Christ.[75] As in *The Mill on the Floss*, this fourth section of the narrative clearly corresponds to the fourth age or the Age of David, whose psalms celebrate the love of Yahweh for his bride Israel. Even more significant, however, than the striking parallel between the two novels is the subtle but crucial difference that George Eliot works in her second heroine's brideship. Maggie adopts a veil of "humiliation," of self-destructive renunciation, but Romola learns the principle of "reformation," of the revision and regeneration of past spiritual error into a new life.

Tito appears in this section as a false prophet, one who takes the place of the rightful messenger with the news of the ships' arrival. Moreover, the respite from famine that he announces is only temporary. In this section as in the preceding one, the light that illuminates the portrait of the Virgin renders Tito's "darkness" more visible.

We can easily discern the fourfold "history of the church" in these first four sections of the narrative: Romola progresses through a paradise of innocence, a fall from that innocence, a darkest moment that is also an epiphany, and finally a reformation. The remainder of the narrative, though it continues to fall into sections that correspond to a sevenfold prophetic structure, does not seem to utilize septenary symbolism, with one significant exception. Apocalyptic imagery, however, becomes more and more striking as the events of the narrative approximate those of the "little open book," or second principal prophecy.

From chapter 49, "A Pyramid of Vanities," to chapter 54, "The Evening and the Morning," Romola experiences a painful insight into the true nature of Savonarola as well as Tito. The flaming pyramid both demonstrates Savonarola's puritanical extremes that lead him to reject secular works of art and symbolizes the beginning of a new epoch in Romola's life, when she will first perceive not only his but her own blindness. In the ensuing five chapters the fanatical prophetess Camilla Rucellai forces Romola to recognize Savonarola's limitations, and Baldassare reveals to her not only that Tito is his foster son but that Tito has another "wife" and children by her. The title of chapter 54, "The Evening and the Morning," suggests the end of another prophetic "day," or epoch, in Romola's life. In the following chapter, Savonarola is excommunicated, plague spreads, and Baldassare disappears.

As the image of the flaming pyramid suggests, this section represents a kind of Pentecost for Romola—a fiery baptism, or "illuminating fire," that makes all life "look ghastly" to her (527). As such, the structure of the narrative continues to correspond to the days of creation and the ages of time. Bickersteth associated the fifth day, on which birds and fishes are created, with the image of the final judgment as a letting-down of a fishing-net, a gathering of the "good" into the vessel and casting away of the bad (Matt. 13:47–50).[76] As in Mackay's exposition, this is a poetic balance of the second day's creation of the waters and association with the Flood, which is also a type of both judgment and baptism. The fifth age of time, in turn, is the Age of Exile or Captivity, an age that Frederick Temple explicates as a time of painful but necessary education.[77] In *Romola*, as in *The Mill on the Floss*, George Eliot has transformed the image of divine judgment into an epoch of human judgment—a period in which one human being painfully evaluates others and achieves a greater illumination both into what they stand for and what she herself believes.

Beginning in chapter 56, "The Other Wife," Romola enters a sixth stage that is, in many ways, a final or culminating stage of her existence, for with the last and seventh stage she begins a new life. In an action that both manifests her identity as "visible madonna" once more and foreshadows her role in the future, Romola returns Lillo to his mother. There, through the prophetic "link" of Tito's chain-mail armor, she discovers that Tessa is Tito's other "wife." Her attempt to intervene for her godfather Bernardo del Nero with Savonarola now completes her disillusionment with the prophet, for prophecy has clearly become synonymous with party politics. When Bernardo is executed, on August 21, 1497, Romola feels that "all clinging was at an end for her" (585). She no longer has any ties: each of the "Educators" of her earlier stages—Greek, Christian, and Stoic—has been decisively put behind her. At this point in Romola's story, George Eliot seems to italicize and sharply demarcate the particular "spiritual errors" that Maggie Tulliver is unable to separate from her own "best organs." For the later heroine, a radical division separates the "Educators" of her old life from the new life she is about to begin. As in the Evangelical Christianity of George Eliot's youth, Romola's sixth age is apocalyptic—poised on the eve of a new dispensation.

In chapter 61, "Drifting Away," Romola sets out to sea in a small boat, an action that critics from Sara Hennell on have judged as inappropriately unrealistic, but that George Eliot defended as part of the "romantic and symbolical elements" planned from her earliest version of the story (*GEL*, 4:104). Those elements clearly echo the apocalyptic imagery of the flood of waters that carry "the woman clothed with the sun" away into the wilderness. But George Eliot's manipulation of this apocalyptic flood imagery in *Romola* becomes more interesting still when we compare it with that in *The Mill on the Floss*. In the earlier novel, "drifting away on the tide" identifies the heroine as a "witch" or perhaps as the specifically apocalyptic "Whore of Babylon" because it implies her capitulation to erotic and romantic desires she will be unable to integrate with other parts of her feminine nature. In *Romola*, however, the heroine drifts away alone, leaving behind all menacing "dragons." Maggie's tidal drift, as I have pointed out, predicts her death by water, the appropriate apocalyptic conclusion for the "devil's history." Romola's, in revolutionary contrast, marks her separation from all patriarchal authority and the beginning of her elevation as the foundress of a new "church" that adopts children of all nations.

Like the woman in the Apocalypse, Romola now takes refuge in the "wilderness," although the narrative does not reveal her destination until chapter 68. Virgil Peterson has commented on the "structural" hiatus between Romola's departure and the narrative's return to her story, suggesting that "the inadequacy of the philosophies of Tito and Savonarola" is dramatized by their contrast with the "reassertion of moral values" that Romola experiences at the same time.[78] Narrative order does indeed appear deliberately "structural" here: another instance of "synchronization," this one clearly suggests the synchronous periods when the serpent casts out a flood of waters to carry away the woman, while the "beast" and the "false prophet" attempt a final victory. Savonarola's "miracle" as the sunlight strikes the uplifted chalice during the third carnival suggests both the Whore of Babylon's poisoned cup and the "false miracles" worked before the "beast" (Rev. 17:4 and 19:20). The mob captures and imprisons Savonarola on Palm Sunday—in chapter 66, suggesting the association of the mob with "the number of the beast"—and the same mob throws Tito into the river on the next day, April 9. At this point in her writing of the novel, George Eliot noted in her journal that she had "killed Tito in great excitement!"[79] Tito dies locked in the arms of his foster father, a mirror image of the double drowning with which *The Mill on the Floss* concludes. The contrast illuminates George Eliot's "excitement": while the unresolved feminine conflict of the earlier novel led inevitably to the drowning of the "witch" and her fraternal consort, the later narrative appears to dissect out and distance this conflict from the heroine, locating the "devil" and his "image" in male characters who can now be cast out with even greater unconscious satisfaction.

These events take place in six chapters, while the narrative returns to Romola in the seventh, thus once again creating a symbolically meaningful septenary unit. In her green valley Romola has experienced a "new baptism," a new perspective on life, during the same period when Savonarola, Tito, and Baldassare are judged and either imprisoned or drowned. The events of Romola's life "synchronize" with those of Tito's and Savonarola's, portraying the progress of the "church" simultaneously with the downfall of "Satan," the principle of evil.

As Bonaparte points out, Romola reenters Florence on Easter Eve (*Triptych*, 242). Her rediscovery of Tessa completes a prophetic "chain," for not only does her recognition of Tessa's chain or necklace bring it about but the connection is made by honest Bratti, the peddler who first discovered Tito at the narrative beginning. The narrative thus comes full circle in the seventieth chapter, suggesting an appropriation of Daniel's prophecy of the "seventy weeks," at the end of which the Messiah would appear. A Comtean "New Jerusalem," founded in a feminist "Protestantism" opposed to patriarchal politics as well as a feminine devotion to community needs, has been established.

Yet the conclusion of the narrative lacks finality. The final two chapters raise the question of Savonarola's significance as a prophet but leave it unresolved. Romola "only knew that Savonarola's voice had passed into eternal silence" (671). The epilogue suggests an "eleventh hour"—a continuation eleven years later, on the eve of the anniversary of Savonarola's death—at which time there are no surer answers than there were at the time of the execution. In this last refusal to write the "truth" of history, George Eliot again reminds her reader of the difficulty of interpretation. Even in her "laborious" apocalypse of history, constructed with a care and effort that she felt had turned her into an old woman, she can conclude only with an example of the ambiguity of prophecy and the unreliability of prophets.

I have sought to demonstrate that both *Romola* and *The Mill on the Floss* are built on subversive appropriations of an apocalyptic structure, but that the earlier novel writes Maggie Tulliver's story as the history of a witch while in the later George Eliot struggled to produce a visionary history of Woman clothed with the sun of righteousness. In this perspective, the later work appears obviously the more radical conception: indeed, I have emphasized the clearly feminist elements of the heroine's "Protestant" stance toward patriarchal politics. Yet to even the most sympathetic readers, the narrative machinery of this novel creaks audibly while *The Mill on the Floss* flows with an energy and feeling that only the sudden violence of its conclusion interrupts. How can we account for the seeming passivity of narrative in *Romola* if the novel does in fact represent George Eliot's revolution against that most formidable authority, the "Law" of history and narrative written by the Fathers of the church?

Mary Jacobus has argued that what is at stake in "all such acts of appropriation, naming, or legitimation" is the "literariness" or the "fiction" of genre itself. Genre allows us to "find our own faces in the text rather than experience that anxious dissolution of identity which is akin to not knowing our kind, or should I say, gender?"[80] Perhaps the difficulty of *Romola* stems not from George Eliot's radical conception but from her attempt to "legitimize" what should have been an illegitimate offspring, to authorize with the literary conventions of the historical novel and with accepted Comtean doctrine what should have been the product of an "unwed" mother—an even more radical narrative form. Although the attempt to re-write the culminating prophetic text of Christianity as female prophecy was surely the most illegitimate, the most "impure" of all George Eliot's narrative projects, her attempt to fence out illegitimate desires from that text may have constituted a disabling struggle for purity. Though her heroine drifts away from patriarchal control and even protests against it, her journey culminates in a community bound by "feminine" values that seem to offer little potential for the future. Romola's final situation appears lacking in energy and direction, even if free from marital and Christian constraints.

By contrast, George Eliot seems to revel in the deliciously illegitimate construction of the "history of a witch," killing off the "naughty girl" engendered by the Law of the Father. The very violence of the conclusion seems appropriate when we read it as the artist's willingness to permit the dissolution of a feminine identity only unconsciously recognized as feminine guilt. But in *Romola*, George Eliot seems anxiously to try to find in her text the face of a female self not yet born—the face of a *legitimate* prophetess. The resulting "apocalypse of history," as W. M. W. Call said of the Revelation of St. John, exhibits an "artificial and imaginary" character—a densely allusive and symbolic art that elicits more respect than enthusiasm from the modern reader. Yet when we read it as George Eliot's most deeply studied "landscape of time," *Romola* achieves a distinction unique among her works, at once the least and the most Victorian, and at once the least and the most her own.

CHAPTER 4

Transposing the Apocalypse in Middlemarch

The scheme of the Apocalypse serves as epic design in *Romola*—a metaphoric structure for George Eliot's "historical romance" or prophetic vision of history in which she seeks to rewrite the "Law of the Fathers" of the church as a sevenfold history of the Woman clothed with the sun of righteousness. In *Middlemarch*, begun some eight years later, George Eliot returns to the apocalyptic landscape of time but now manipulates this fiction to expose it as a source of mystifying patterns that lock her characters into visionary castles of their own construction.[1] The "keys" necessary for escape from these prison-houses are both epistemological and musical: one must recognize ancient error in order to perceive new truths, one must eschew ancient harmonies to hear the new rhythms born of Romanticism. In particular, one must transpose the exalted melodies and universal harmonies of apocalyptic symphony into a "lower" key—the simpler rhythms of a "middle march," of a musical comedy rather than an oratorio, of an earthly rather than a heavenly music. Though *Middlemarch* is far from a simple work, many of the delightful complexities of its multiplot narrative depend on musical "plays" on the apocalyptic structurings George Eliot treated in more serious mode in *Romola*. What she labors to construct in the earlier work she seems to dance with in *Middlemarch*.[2]

J. Hillis Miller has brilliantly elucidated not only George Eliot's awareness of "the irreducibly figurative or metaphorical nature of all language" but of the existence in *Middlemarch* of a subtle theory of signs and interpretation.[3] Moreover, he demonstrates that *Middlemarch* deconstructs traditional assumptions about the nature of history. The narrator demystifies the various illusions of characters in the novel, all of which are based on the assumption that details are "governed by a single center, origin, or end."[4] Miller postulates that the "moving web" is the structuring metaphor both for the narrator's process of deconstruction, or "unravelling," and for the characters' mystifying beliefs.[5] But the image of the web may itself incorporate unsuspected levels of irony, for it appears to derive from an apocalyptic vision whose possibilities George Eliot now exploits in a witty formal design.

I suggest here that her rereading of one of her favorite authors, Sir Thomas Browne, was George Eliot's preeminent instigation for her comic revision of apocalyptic metaphor and structure. In Browne's "quincunxial web" we shall find the common origins of several apparently separate metaphorical clusters in *Middlemarch*— the subtle, "microscopic" links connecting things epistemological and scientific, musical and apocalyptic. Most interestingly, we find Browne drawn to the uses of apocalyptic numerology, particularly to its metaphorical or "Hieroglyphical" functions:

> Lastly, Though many things have been delivered by Authors concerning number, and they transferred unto the advantage of their nature, yet are they oft times otherwise to be understood, then as they are vulgarly received in active and causall considerations; they being many times delivered Hieroglyphically, Metaphorically, Illustratively, and not with reference unto action or causality.[6]

Following in the revolutionary train of Baconian empiricism, Browne strove to detect those ancient and "vulgar" errors that stood in the path of truth, one of the most persistent of which was the superstitious belief in number. Yet having deconstructed many numerological beliefs in his *Pseudodoxia Epidemica*, Browne later wrote *The Garden of Cyrus*, in which he perceives a mystical pattern of five—the quincunxial web—everywhere in the universe, linking all things in time and space. In a disconcertingly similar process, George Eliot's narrator both unravels the mystifying webs of more limited characters than he and constructs another whose connections are more difficult to see but that nevertheless seem to be affirmed by his creator.[7]

These connections revolve around the musical implications of Browne's web and their relation to other visionary schemes, some far more ancient. As Browne explains, the quincunxial web of *The*

Garden of Cyrus is both a moving and a musical web, for its basic "X" figure derives from Plato's figure for the musical motion of the universe. In Pythagorean-Platonic theory, the intersection of the eight circles or "spheres" produces the eight tones of the octave: the music of the spheres and the harmony of the universe. Thus, Browne's quincunxial webs must be imagined as perpetually resounding with music at their moving intersections.[8] But in the exquisite metaphoric wit of George Eliot's "elegant historian," the musical web often figures the discords that resound between characters and their various "schemes of the universe" as they intersect.

Miller suggests George Eliot's narrator is himself entangled in his own web of metaphors and that history, in the novel, has "no ordering principle or aim" for "the concepts of origin, end, and continuity are replaced by the categories of repetition, of difference, of discontinuity, or openness, and of the free and contradictory struggle of individual human energies."[9] Yet George Eliot seems to affirm a kind of order and progress in the world of *Middlemarch*, even as she deconstructs its inhabitants' various apocalyptic schemes. Though subtly undermining her characters' belief in a universal harmony—the music of the spheres—she transposes their apocalypse into an entirely human but progressive music. Neither motion nor music ceases in the artist's "visionary" web, but prophecy takes a new "key" and musical wit rather than a subversive chronology underlines the narrative.

In *Middlemarch*, then, George Eliot seems to act on the insight Roger B. Henkle postulates as central to comic writers: "Somehow the attitude that we can define as 'noncomic,' the tendency to see things in their most serious and consequential terms, contains the potential of freezing and stultifying human response and leads, comic writers tell us, to a vision that will prove painfully inflexible."[10] Seeming to adopt in this novel what Henkle describes as the comic writer's objective, George Eliot seeks to make her readers understand that their habitual behavior is made up of "fictions." If in the process she resorts to "elaborate plans and exotic constructs," even to apparently private jokes, perhaps we should not conclude that these go against the grain of her "realism." As George Eliot herself commented:

O Aristotle! if you had had the advantage of being "the freshest modern" instead of the greatest ancient, would you not have mingled your praise of metaphorical speech, as a sign of high intelligence, with a lamentation that intelligence so rarely shows itself in speech without metaphor—that we can so seldom declare what a thing is, except by saying it is something else?[11]

In *Middlemarch*, she seeks to define human progress by demonstrating first of all what it is not, and in so doing she could have no more excellent example than that seventeenth-century seer of a "capacious credulity," Sir Thomas Browne.

I

Before attempting to elucidate George Eliot's witty transposition of Browne's apocalyptic "fictions," it may be helpful to point out a number of overt, as well as covert, clues to the seminal influence of his works on *Middlemarch*. These include quotations from Browne within the novel, such as the thematically significant epigraph for chapter 45.[12] As John Clark Pratt and Victor A. Neufeldt point out,

> No matter what their particular subject, George Eliot's authorities all seemed to remind her of what she had read in Sir Thomas Browne, that "the mortallest enemy unto knowledge, and that which hath done the greatest execution upon truth, hath been a pre-emptory adhesion unto authority; and more especially, the establishing of our belief upon the dictates of antiquity."[13]

Although Browne was by no means George Eliot's only source for her theme of the rejection of ancient error, the *Pseudodoxia Epidemica* seems to have been the most important. This is not surprising, since her references to Browne go back to 1851 and document an extensive acquaintance with his works over a period of at least two decades.

For *Middlemarch*, however, George Eliot seems to have methodically reread and taken notes on most of Browne's major writings. At this time, she presumably used the 1852 edition of Browne's *Works*, edited by Simon Wilkin, which remains in the George Eliot–George Henry Lewes Library.[14] Her notes, which take up the largest part of some seven pages in *Middlemarch Miscellany*, follow the order of Browne's works as printed in the 1852 edition—with one significant exception. There are no notes from *The Garden of Cyrus*.[15] If George Eliot's headings—"Sir Thomas Brownisms" and "Brownisms"—indicate, as seems likely, that her initial motive for rereading Browne at this time was her typically Victorian admiration for his prose style, the omission of *The Garden of Cyrus* might represent an also typical estimate of this paradoxical essay as the least impressive (or most absurd) of Browne's works.[16] But if this was her reason for omitting any notes on *The Garden of Cyrus*, then it is a remarkable coincidence indeed that a leading character in *Middlemarch* should be a physician intent on discovering the "primary web."

Once the connection is suggested, Tertius Lydgate recalls Sir Thomas Browne in a number of ways.[17] In the same chapter in which the narrator's "particular web" is first introduced, the "belated historian" describes Lydgate's ambition not only to contribute toward enlarging the "scientific, rational basis of his profession" but to uncover certain "primary webs of tissues" that would reveal the "fundamental knowledge of structure" (102). When Lydgate later remarks to Farebrother that he is "more and more convinced that it will be possible to demonstrate the homogeneous origin of all the tissues," Farebrother insightfully replies, "I have no power of prophecy there" (314). The web Lydgate seeks is in truth, as the narrator later comments, a "scheme of the universe," and a power of prophecy will be more required to find it than microscopic researches.

As a physician engaged in endless experimentation to discover empirical truths, and yet also the author of the Neoplatonic, prophetic conception of a "primary web" in *The Garden of Cyrus*, Browne certainly appears to be Lydgate's medical and visionary ancestor. Lydgate combines within himself the same "magnificent incongruity" that George Eliot remarked on in Browne, whose works she described as "the most remarkable combination existing, of witty sarcasm against ancient nonsense and modern obsequiousness, with indications of a capacious credulity."[18] Anxious to reform "ancient nonsense" in medical care, Lydgate is nevertheless guilty of "modern obsequiousness" to Bulstrode. And he is easily persuaded by a "capacious credulity" both for a universal harmony of organic structure and for the feminine mystique. In particular, he recalls the seemingly incompatible perspectives not only of Browne's empiricism and visionary propensities but of Browne's essay on the futility of human life and passion, *Urn Burial*, and his formally similar *The Garden of Cyrus*.

Simon Wilkin evidently did not perceive the relationship between *The Garden of Cyrus* and Browne's more popular essay *Urn Burial* that a twentieth-century biographer and critic, Frank Huntley, has proposed.[19] Pointing out the identical five-chapter structure of the two essays, their precise thematic contrasts of death and life, and their interlocking imagery, Huntley suggests that Browne intended the two essays as a literary unity. The prophetic web-pattern of the universe in *The Garden of Cyrus*, everywhere associated with light, fertility, and rebirth, was meant to complete and resolve the themes of shadowy uncertainty, darkness, and death in *Urn Burial*—a pairing similar to Milton's "L'Allegro" and "Il Penseroso." Wilkin, however, not only reversed the order of the two essays in his editions, placing *Urn Burial* after *The Garden of Cyrus*, but in the 1852 edition even placed them in separate volumes.[20]

George Eliot clearly appreciated Browne's profoundly poetic meditation, *Urn Burial*, for she quotes extensively from it in her notebook.[21] Despite Wilkin's separation of the two essays, the highly similar pairing in *Middlemarch* of Casaubon's preoccupation with the shadowy uncertainties of the past and Dorothea's pervasive association with images of light, fire and rebirth also suggests that George Eliot did not fail to appreciate the paradoxically balanced conceptions of the two essays. A far more subtle clue that she did compare them derives from a chain of evidence suggesting that the name she chose for her visionary physician encodes the poetic significance of Browne's other essay, *Urn Burial*.

U. C. Knoepflmacher, who has illuminated the generally extensive poetic allusiveness of *Middlemarch*, has also pointed out the probable origin of Lydgate's name in the late medieval poet, John Lydgate.[22] George Eliot's source for Lydgate was Thomas Warton's *The History of English Poetry*, which she read in conjunction with Edwin Guest's *A History of English Rhythms* in August 1868.[23] Although Knoepflmacher has suggested that John Lydgate's work "The Fall of Princes" may have attracted George Eliot because of its relation to her theme of forgotten men, the first work of Lydgate's discussed by Warton—and the one mentioned by name in George Eliot's notebook—is "Dance of Death."[24] What more suitable name could be chosen for a character inspired by the author of the well-known *Urn Burial* than that of the author of the little-known "Dance of Death"?

Moreover, the "Dance of Death" suggests a most appropriate musical metaphor for the nature of Tertius Lydgate's relationship with Rosamond, a marital rhythm that indeed proves fatal to his cosmic ambition. Several meanings associated with Lydgate's first name suggest an ironic appreciation of "hidden" connections between John Lydgate, Sir Thomas Browne, and Tertius Lydgate. In addition to being the *third* man (Tertius) associated with a "dance of death," the word *tertiary* can refer to the medical term for tertiary ague, according to the *OED*, in which death is caused by a paroxysm occurring every third day. Tertiary also denotes a perfect third in musical terminology. The name George Eliot chose for Lydgate, then, may have carried insidious links to other medical and poetic visions of a "dance of death" ensuing from blind human passion.

But Tertius Lydgate is not the only *Middlemarch* character with subtle but significant links to the paired essays of Sir Thomas Browne. Much of George Eliot's conception of Edward Casaubon, including his name, may derive from *Urn Burial*, just as Casaubon's mythological "key" obviously resembles Browne's search for the "quincunxial web." Knoepflmacher, who has pointed out associations between the *Middlemarch* Casaubon and both Isaac and Meric Casaubon, leans toward Isaac Casaubon as the more suggestive source, primarily because George Eliot commented in her notebook that it was "curious to turn from Shakespeare to Isaac Casaubon, his contemporary."[25] But in a footnote to the third chapter of *Urn Burial*, Browne refers his reader to "the most learned and worthy Mr. M. Casaubon," and in the essay immediately following *Urn Burial* in the 1852 edition (*Brampton Urns*), comments on observations on various burial urns made by "Dr.

Casaubon."[26] Browne thus identifies Meric Casaubon as the author of treatises on burial urns comparable to his own—except that, even by George Eliot's time, Meric Casaubon's treatises were as long forgotten as the burial urns on which they were composed. Even more suggestively, Meric Casaubon wrote a dry-as-dust treatise on enthusiasm, as well as two vindications of his father. He was also a contemporary of Milton and Locke, with both of whom the near-sighted Dorothea confuses her prospective bridegroom.[27]

But it is *Urn Burial* itself that comments most potently on the character of Edward Casaubon. From this "dead" subject, Browne produced an immortal meditation on the perpetual hopes and strivings of human beings whose only certainty in life is death, while Edward Casaubon's similar speculations on extinct beliefs might have served as additional subject matter for Browne. Browne's succinct comment on the greatest human grief—the approach of death unrelieved by any sense of immortality—seems to underlie the tragic moment when Edward Casaubon realizes his approaching death also spells the doom of his long-planned visionary work: "It is the heaviest stone that melancholy can throw at a man, to tell him he is at the end of his nature; or that there is no further state to come, unto which this seems progressional, and otherwise made in vaine" (*Major Works*, 305). The very yew tree under which Casaubon's melancholy figure is seen when Lydgate informs him he is "at the end of his nature" takes on ironic poignance from *Urn Burial*, for Browne reminded his readers that yews are planted in churchyards as emblems of resurrection (299). Edward Casaubon, whose "Key to All Mythologies" would have been a mythological counterpart to Browne's metaphysical scheme of the universe, instead embodies Browne's moving meditation on ancient passions come to nothing but ashes and "incrassated" tears.[28]

Browne's deepest influence on *Middlemarch*, however, may inhere in his thought-provoking insights concerning the nature of vision itself, especially in his observation on "quincunxes." *The Garden of Cyrus* is full of examples of "quincunxial" patterns that remind us of *Middlemarch* metaphors of vision: the web of the retiary spider, the network of human blood vessels, the microscopic patterns of germinal seeds, the telescopic patterns of planetary movement. But for Browne, the mechanism of sight is itself a "quincunx," and this leads to an interesting connection between physiology and metaphor:

> Lastly, It is no wonder that this Quincunciall order was first and still affected as gratefull unto the Eye: For all things are seen Quincuncially; For at the eye the Pyramidal rayes from the object, receive a decussation.... Whether the intellectual and phantastical lines be not thus rightly disposed, but magnified diminished, distorted, and ill placed in the Mathematicks of some brains, whereby they have irregular apprehensions of things, perverted notions, conceptions, and incurable hallucinations, were no unpleasant speculation. (*Major Works*, 376–77)

The "webs" envisioned by many of the characters in *Middlemarch* result from just such distorted perceptions and are in fact "perverted notions" or even "hallucinations"—as Mrs. Cadwallader astutely observes of Dorothea's illusions.

Browne thus seems well aware that vision depends upon the "lens"—metaphorical as well as physiological—through which one sees the world. George Eliot's emphasis on the distortions of vision in *Middlemarch* may subtly appropriate the observations of this ancient medical seer. Yet Browne's sophisticated conception inevitably raises questions about *The Garden of Cyrus*. Was his perception of quincunxial patterns in all things "artificial" and "natural" the result of his own "phantastical lines"—a mystifying belief in Neoplatonic harmonies? Or was the quincunxial web a "Hieroglyph," a metaphor only, for a divine order that could never be demonstrated by empirical methods alone?

For Browne, the distinction may well have been meaningless. He was both a Platonist and an Aristotelian, and *The Garden of Cyrus* is inspired both by the visionary harmony of the spheres and the direct observation of quincunxial patterns.[29] The quincunxial web is in fact similar to a typological interpretation, in which a person, event, or object is considered to have both a literal reality and a figurative or prophetic value.[30] But Browne proceeds in reverse order, from Platonic figure to empirical proof. In the final chapter of his prophetic discourse, Browne explains his holistic methodology for penetrating the "Labyrinth of Truth":

A large field is yet left unto sharper discerners to enlarge upon this order, to search out the *quaternio's* and figured draughts of this nature, and moderating the study of names, and meer nomenclature of plants, to erect generalities, disclose unobserved proprieties, not only in the vegetable shop, but the whole volume of nature; affording delightful Truths, confirmable by sense and ocular Observation, which seems to me the surest path, to trace the Labyrinth of Truth. For though discursive enquiry and rationall conjecture, may leave handsome gashes and flesh-wounds; yet without conjunction of this expect no mortal or dispatching blows unto errour. (*Major Works*, 386)

Vision beyond "discursive enquiry and rationall conjecture" is necessary to deal a "mortal" blow to error: the "quaternios," or Pythagorean figures suggestive of the totality of things and their underlying design, must first be sought out, although these "delightful Truths" can then be confirmed by "sense and ocular Observation."[31]

Whether George Eliot still considered Browne's quincunxial web only as a Neoplatonic absurdity is a question I shall postpone for the moment. In *Middlemarch*, it is demonstrable that she utilized Browne's "mystical Mathematicks of the City of Heaven" as a *quaternio*—a Pythagorean figure here suggestive of the *artist's* totality of design. But this numerologic web has been turned back upon itself, transformed into a "Hieroglyph" for apocalyptic vision now seen as a "fiction" for the dead hand of the past. In a kind of silent laughter at errors already ancient in Browne's time, yet still lively in the "modern" England of the Reform Bill, this "web" figures a labyrinth of error, not of truth.

II

Dorothea's pilgrimage not only passes through four early stages of spiritual growth that closely parallel Romola's (and Maggie Tulliver's) but also exhibits a similar chapter sequence appropriating septenary symbolism. Even more provocatively, chapter numbers become satirical hieroglyphs in *Middlemarch*—a witty design whose decoding reveals the insignificance, rather than the significance, of the apocalyptic schemes in which both Dorothea and Casaubon are enmeshed at the opening of the narrative. The solemn music of visionary progress here becomes a sprightly comic dance, but it is a music Dorothea does not hear.

As in *Romola*, the seventh chapter carries particular significance for apocalyptic, or anti-apocalyptic, structure. But rather than signifying the chronological beginning of Dorothea's age of innocence, the seventh chapter in *Middlemarch* is a subtle structure in which musical and prophetic "keys" to Dorothea and Casaubon's mystifying webs are cunningly woven into the narrator's more explicit satire. The chapter is, in effect, an ironic sign, a "key" to Edenic mythology.

Opening with Casaubon's expectations that Dorothea will provide "the solace of female tendance for his declining years," and Dorothea's conviction that she can outdo Milton's "naughty and stupid" daughters, these indications of future discords are sounded again in their discussion of music with Mr. Brooke. Casaubon's conception of music as the "measured noises" of a minuet, his dislike for that new instrument, the piano, and his possession of a harpsichord all associate him with baroque music—a well-chosen musical metaphor for his search for ancient harmonies. But the harpsichord at Lowick has been silenced under piles of books, for Casaubon has no ear even for the music he seeks. Dorothea, who admits her ignorance of the language of music, nevertheless intuitively responds to its "grander forms," such as that heard on the great organ at Freiberg. Romantic theorists considered the organ the greatest of all instruments, since it was believed capable of "Totality," or universal music.[32] Dorothea's preference thus indicates her search for a prophetic harmony as well but in the different key of Romanticism. Mr. Brooke's remark that music is "not like ideas, you know" encapsulates his usual confusion, for music reflects the ideas—or lack of them—of all the participants in this discussion.

Not incidentally, the name of Casaubon's great work is revealed for the first time in this chapter, which itself supplies a key to at least some of the *Middlemarch* "mythologies." The number of the chapter similarly provides another "key" to its "musical" mythology. Prophetic expositors unanimously agreed that the number seven signified totality or unity and therefore, as John Cumming explained in his *Lectures on the Book of Revelation*, seven was fundamental to the nature of music: "All know that seven colours are the component elements of pure light; and seven notes in the range of the musical scale; and thus the sacred symbol may be laid in the nature of things."[33] With exegetical wit, George Eliot incorporates the number seven as a most unsacred symbol of the mystifying nature of things, both musical and prophetic.

Following this prophetic beginning, Dorothea proceeds through three more stages of apocalyptic history that parallel Romola's, each of which the artist marks or "signs" in a septenary chapter. Like Romola, Dorothea also experiences a "fall" that is both marital and prophetic, but in Dorothea's case the "fall" involves a crumbling of her vision of the apocalyptic city as well. Having married in Eden, Dorothea proceeds directly to Rome, but far from serving as the "spiritual centre and interpreter" of her world, the apocalyptic city seems like "a disease of the retina," its "stupendous fragmentariness" ever after serving as an image for the wreck of her own "ambitious ideals" (134–35). As in Browne's remarkable observation, the perception of this particular quincunx resulted from Dorothea's own "phantastical lines."

Although this anti-apocalyptic period is first introduced in chapter 19, where Naumann acutely perceives the "consciousness of Christian centuries" in Dorothea, the narrator does not speak of Dorothea's marital disillusionment as an "epoch" in her experience until the septenary chapter 21:

> But Dorothea remembered it to the last with the vividness with which we all remember epochs in our experience when some dear expectation dies, or some new motive is born. To-day she had begun to see that she had been under a wild illusion in expecting a response to her feeling from Mr. Casaubon, and she had felt the waking of a presentiment that there might be a sad consciousness in his life which made as great a need on his side as on her own. (146)

Romola also begins her "fall" from faith in Tito in chapter 21, while Savonarola begins to prophesy the seemingly unrelated fall of Florence. In *Middlemarch*, the "fall" of the apocalyptic city is clearly integrated as a metaphor for the sudden collapse of Dorothea's Protestant mythology, in which she had seen herself as bride to an apocalyptic bridegroom. Apocalyptic and musical imagery also appear again in this twenty-first chapter, here appropriately suggesting an abrupt reversal of prophetic roles. Where Dorothea had earlier seen Casaubon as modeled on Milton's archangel, Will now thinks of him as a "dragon." Will himself now appears in angelic colors, his hair seeming "to shake out light," while Casaubon stands "rayless" (145). And it is Will who now hears prophetic music, thinking of Dorothea as an Aeolian harp and waiting for the "melodious fragments" that came forth so ingenuously from her.

Romola's third stage is the crisis, or turning point, in her life: reaching a point of utter despair with her marriage, she sets off alone and encounters Savonarola, who will become the force for reformation and regeneration in her life. A similar third stage, marked by both despair and the potential for renewal, begins in Dorothea's life on her return to Lowick, which is described in another septenary chapter, the twenty-eighth. Again, the change marked in the earlier novel by a new set of symbolic objects figures in *Middlemarch* as a metamorphosis of vision. The view from the window of Dorothea's boudoir at Lowick seems distant and shrunken, like her vision of a noble and sacrificial purpose in marriage. Her faith has become a "solitary cry, the struggle out of a nightmare in which every object was withering and shrinking away from her" (190). Yet Dorothea herself is like the fire burning on the hearth—an image of an "incongruous renewal of life and glow" (189). Like Romola, she seeks some solution to her isolation, some way to renew that "sense of connection with a manifold pregnant existence."

And again, as in not only *Romola* but *Adam Bede*, the first marked development of this renewal or "reformation" takes place in chapter 42. But Dorothea's reformation results not from a Protestant Reformation but from the disintegration of Casaubon's visionary project, his "Key to All Mythologies." It is in chapter 42 that Lydgate informs Casaubon he has not long to live, thus also sounding the death knell for Casaubon's illusory hopes of completion. The prophetic "key" introduced in chapter 7 reaches its ironic fulfillment in the chapter with the even more apocalyptically significant number, forty-two. Where Romola's first reformation renews or reinterprets the Protestant Reformation, Dorothea's reformation begins with her "fall" from the illusions created by that prophetic tradition. Yet a human "angel" still remains for Casaubon—Dorothea herself. "Then she went towards him, and might have represented a heaven-sent angel coming with a promise that the short hours remaining should yet be filled with that faithful love which clings the closer to a comprehended grief" (294). But at this point, Casaubon shrinks from her, and leaving the emblematic yew-tree arbor, shuts himself up alone in his library. Only after hours of self-imposed solitude does he finally permit Dorothea to make that movement of fellowship toward him and to walk down the "broad corridor" with him hand in hand.

Chapter 42 in *Middlemarch*, then, signifies the ironic reverse of that prophetic tradition whose spiritual significance George Eliot reaffirms in *Romola*. Here the apocalyptic heritage figures as the distorted "Mathematicks of some brains," culminating in "incurable hallucinations" and an equally incurable mortality. Dorothea, however, begins to be cured of some of her hallucinations at this point, and I would point out that her "reformation" begins at the midway point in the novel—the end of the fourth book. As in both *The Mill on the Floss* and *Romola*, there is a suggestion of dividing not only Dorothea's pre- and post-reformation periods, but a political and historical "reform" as well, into these two roughly equal halves. Until this point in the novel, references to the Reform Bill have echoed only faintly in the town of Middlemarch. But in the fifth book, the struggle for both political and medical reform becomes dominant in the town, a state of affairs made explicit: "While Lydgate, safely married and with the Hospital under his command, felt himself struggling for Medical Reform against Middlemarch, Middlemarch was becoming more and more conscious of the national struggle for another kind of Reform" (316). *Middlemarch* thus seems based on the same binary "continuous historical" structure demonstrated in *The Mill on the Floss* and in *Romola*, a structure in which history revolves around a reform both historical and metaphorical.

But the recapitulation of four apocalyptic stages in an ironic mode is not the only example of satirical numerology in *Middlemarch*. The motif of ancient error extends to a more direct example of disastrous consequences resulting from an inheritance from the past. In *Romola*, it will be remembered, the heroine makes her reentry into Florence on Easter Eve, and this prophetic fulfillment of her apocalyptic role is appropriately symbolized also by the chapter number 70. Seventy symbolizes the prophecy in Daniel commonly interpreted as the period of years to be fulfilled in the restoration to Jerusalem. In *Daniel Deronda*, George Eliot grounds her narrative structure in an extensive manipulation of the hermeneutics of this prophecy. But in *Middlemarch*, this chapter number marks a covert anti-apocalyptics linking two instances in which characters accept an inheritance that should have been rejected and that leads to a most undesirable "fulfillment." In chapter 14, old Featherstone unlocks his casket in order to grudgingly advance one hundred pounds to Fred, who promptly loses it in an expensive gamble on a "stone" of no value—the horse named "Diamond." In chapter 70, Lydgate accepts one thousand pounds from Bulstrode, thus irredeemably tying himself to the banker's crime. The second sum of money, precisely ten times greater than the first and received in the septenary chapter whose number symbolizes a restoration of inheritance, ironically reinforces the theme of the profound consequences of uncritically accepting a dubious inheritance.

A final, striking instance of George Eliot's incorporation of the "secondary and ironic" possibilities of Sir Thomas Browne's web of ancient error provides an ironic hieroglyphical frame for the dangers of Lydgate and Bulstrode's entanglement. Among the errors of superstition explored by Browne in *Pseudodoxia Epidemica* was the "climacterical year," or the common belief that the sixty-third year of a man's life was the most dangerous year of his existence. Perhaps the telling significance of the "climacteric" for George Eliot was that Browne identified it with all of the ancient numerological beliefs. Tracing "the extraordinary power and secret virtue conceived to attend these numbers" back to Pythagoras and Plato, as well as Philo, "the learned Jew," Browne points out that "all or most of the other digits have been as mystically applauded" as the numbers seven and nine, from which the climacteric sixty-three is produced, and suggests that the real power of these numbers is "many times delivered Hieroglyphically, Metaphorically, Illustratively" (*Major Works*, 232–34).

Certainly, George Eliot's numerology in Book VII of *Middle-*

march appears to have reference "hieroglyphically, metaphorically, illustratively," for there the numbers of Browne's "climacteric" are found framing the section of the narrative that relates the most dangerous period of Lydgate and Bulstrode's lives. Beginning with chapter *sixty-three*, the *nine* chapters of the *seventh* book tell the tale of Lydgate's increasing indebtedness and his consequent entanglement in the web of Bulstrode's attempts to escape the past. These chapters detail the "climacteric" period in both men's lives—a period of mortal danger created by Bulstrode's failure to reject an inheritance not rightfully his and by Lydgate's willingness to allow himself to become part of that shadowy morass. By steadily enmeshing himself in Evangelical hypocrisy, Bulstrode becomes a "false prophet," and Lydgate allows himself to become "the beast created in his image." As in *Romola*, this apocalyptic section of the narrative—the seventh book—takes place while the "woman clothed with the sun" is offstage, taking refuge in the wilderness. That is, while Lydgate and Bulstrode weave their mutual destruction, Dorothea is off visiting a neighboring county, intent on the discovery of a suitable site for her "Pythagorean" (!) community.

The numbers of chapter and book in which the narrative reveals Lydgate and Bulstrode's story become another "key" to error and illusion, as seen from *outside* their maze. Miller's comments illuminate the metaphor of the key as both intrinsic and extrinsic to the novel:

> A "key," as in the "Key to all Mythologies," is both an intrinsic pattern organizing from within a large body of apparently heterogeneous material and at the same time something introduced from the outside which "unlocks" an otherwise hidden pattern. A key is a formula which cracks a code, as when George Eliot in *Daniel Deronda* says, "all meanings, we know, depend on the key of interpretation" (chap. 6). The meaning of a text is both intrinsic to that text and yet present in it only when it is projected by a certain extrinsic set of assumptions about the code or "key." This shifting from intrinsic to extrinsic definitions of "key" is present in the various meanings of the word, which include mechanical, architectural, musical, and botanical senses.[34]

As we shall see, the "meaning" of *Daniel Deronda* depends even more on a certain key of interpretation than *Middlemarch*. But in

Middlemarch also, George Eliot integrates both intrinsic and extrinsic patterns around certain "keys" to their meaning. What *Middlemarch* characters persuade themselves is the key to a visionary scheme, the author treats as an ironic key that "cracks the code" in a different sense. But this artfully constructed labyrinth of error is itself part of a larger "Labyrinth of Truth," more complex because less fixed. If the web of ancient error figures as "fixed distorting patterns" in *Middlemarch*, the artist-historian's "particular web" is a moving, musical web of minute human progress, "audible" to the thoughtful reader in a silent modulation of keys.

III

In what one critic has termed his "Romantic irony," Beethoven incorporates numerous musical puns and witticisms in his music and also moves through unusual successions of keys. Key relationships that had become standard in his time are rejected in favor of innovative ones; "old" keys are modulated into revolutionary "new" harmonies.[35] That George Eliot—who loved and practiced Beethoven's music—understood it thus as a metaphorically witty art cannot be documented, but it can be demonstrated that *Middlemarch* involves a revolutionary progression of "keys" that are both real keys to cabinets and other locked domains, and "keys" to an elaborate musical discourse.[36] The ancient prophetic harmonies of Browne's musical web are transposed into an equally apocalyptic Romantic "key"—a "key" that is in turn a musical *quaternio* for the historian's "particular web."

The formal structure of the novel visibly parallels musical structure, with its eight books evoking the eight tones of a scale or octave placed between a Prelude and a Finale.[37] The narrative itself becomes a "march" in the middle, "up" or perhaps "down" the scale. Or perhaps we may image the division into eight books as a *quaternio* for the eight spheres of the universe, resounding with sweet harmonies or blaring discords, as the case may be. In any event, George Eliot's scale or octave resonates with musical witticisms: keys from the past are tried and weighed in a different kind of "scale," rejected as too costly, and then modulated through a series of unexpected relationships into a new harmony that turns out—surprisingly—to be "lower" than the old. Or again, the scale appropriates the Neoplatonic scale or monochord, such as figures in Keble's poem for Palm Sunday, proceeding from "silent stones" to "angel choirs"—but this scale moves downward, starting with the jewels of the apocalyptic city and ending with the homely tunes of Stone Court. Yet what is "lower" or more human in George Eliot's composition is paradoxically "higher."

Because of individual varieties of tone deafness, the characters in *Middlemarch* do not necessarily hear the artist's intended harmonies. Although the music of "Totality" moves Dorothea, for example, she admits she does not understand "the language of music," and we may infer her tone deafness to certain melodies. Will, who comes the closest to true musicality among all the characters, rejects the idea of any "universal significance" in the various languages of art, suggesting that he is impervious to the larger harmonies (132). What Rosamond plays is a very artificial and shallow music, and that is what Lydgate hears. The narrator can thus form a musical web that is—like the numerologic web of error—extrinsic to the characters, outside their capacity to perceive it as a total system. What the characters hear as isolated tones, and what they must trace through the single paths allotted to them, emerges as the artist's web or labyrinth of truth: a "fiction" visible to those whose more "microscopic" or "telescopic" lenses enable them to detect motions invisible to others. The first chapter, for example, sounds a number of musical tones that are heard faintly, if at all, by the individuals involved.

Among the facts George Eliot noted in Warton's *History of English Poetry* was his description of the "dumb show" in old plays. This was, Warton commented, "a piece of machinery ... shadowing by an allegorical exhibition the matter that was immediately to follow." He suggested further that such dumb shows were "commonly too mysterious and obscure, to forestal the future events with any degree of clearness and precision."[38] Such a preliminary "allegorical exhibition" suggests a certain similarity to the sketch of the Four Empires in *Romola* and to the hermeneutical concept of a prophetic sketch appearing early within a larger prophetic narrative. In any event, references to certain other *Middlemarch* notes and sources suggest that the first chapter episode of the jewels from the cabinet is just such a mysterious and obscure "dumb show," calculated to mirror exactly not only the mystery and obscurity of Dorothea's prophetic schemes but to sound the two major prophetic "keys" in the novel. Dorothea's call for "the keys, the keys!" is a "prelude" of silent music in which the motifs for each of her two bridegrooms, "baroque" and "Romantic," are sounded.

Dorothea's comments, on first selecting emeralds from her mother's jewel box, appear ingenuous enough:

> "How very beautiful these gems are!" said Dorothea, under a new current of feeling, as sudden as the gleam. "It is strange how deeply colours seem to penetrate one, like scent. I suppose that is the reason why gems are used as spiritual emblems in the Revelation of St. John. They look like fragments of heaven. I think that emerald is more beautiful than any of them." (6)

But her remark that the gems are used as "spiritual emblems" in the Apocalypse would have suggested more than one clue to any reader well versed in apocalyptic exposition, including the artist. John Cumming's lecture on the apocalyptic city—in the volume on Revelation reviewed by George Eliot in 1855—in fact illuminates a number of obscure connections between the jewels and the particular harmony they suggest to Dorothea:

> All that is beautiful in nature may have its counterpart in something beautified by grace; and these two strings—once dissonant—may be touched anew, and prove again harmonious chords in the great and eternal harmony.
> All the precious stones in the crowns of kings, and in the cabinets of museums, are the scattered fragments of that explosion which sin kindled in ancient Paradise.[39]

Although George Eliot asserted in her essay that she had found no passage in Cumming's writings that impressed her as worth extracting, his old-fashioned metaphors were apparently just the thing for Dorothea's "ancient" religious views.[40] Jewels perceived as "fragments of heaven" reveal Dorothea's allegiance to an Evangelical Neoplatonism that looks back to an ancient, mythical harmony and prophesies its return in an apocalyptic city. Dorothea's first response to the jewels, then, provides the "key" to her first bridegroom's harmony—a harmony to be sought in the dim recesses of the past.

But Cumming's sermon suggests further insights into the veiled significance of the *Middlemarch* jewels. His discussion clarifies a chain of associations by which jewels symbolize both the "living stone"—the particular jewel of inheritance that is the right "key" to harmony—and "spiritual emblems" for particular individuals:

> The people of God are represented in Scripture under various names. They are frequently compared to living stones, and occasionally to precious stones. Thus it is declared by God, "They shall be mine, saith the Lord of hosts, in that day when I make up my jewels." These jewels, or precious stones, sparkling in the light, have each its own peculiar characteristic ... the purple amethyst may be dedicated to the grave and dignified James; and the emerald, so agreeable to the eye, the cultivated and holy Luke.[41]

Thus we understand that Dorothea has chosen for herself a jewel signifying an evangelist, the "holy and cultivated Luke," often called the poet of the New Testament. To her sister she willingly consigns the amethysts suggesting dedication to the "grave and dignified James," but doubtless only the artist appreciates this joke.

If Cumming's "key" to the *Middlemarch* jewels seems almost too obscure, another clue from outside the text confirms the emerald's poetic—and especially "musical"—symbolic value for George Eliot. A note in the *Middlemarch Miscellany*, tersely headed "Music 32," refers to the thirty-second chapter of Ecclesiasticus, where we find this passage:[42]

> Speak, thou that art the elder, for it becometh thee, but with sound judgment; and hinder not musick.
> Pour not out words where there is a musician, and shew not forth wisdom out of time.
> A concert of musick in a banquet of wine is as a signet of carbuncle set in gold.
> As a signet of an emerald set in a work of gold, so is the melody of musick with pleasant wine.

Commenting delightfully on Dorothea's "wisdom out of time"—both ancient and out of step, we may speculate—the passage tends to confirm the musical significance of the emerald for the artist.

But Dorothea's association of the emeralds with a lost Neoplatonic harmony is only a part of her response to them. The jewels also clearly call forth a response in another prophetic "key"—the Romantic. Her "current of feeling," her sense that the colors penetrate her as a "scent," and later, that they are like "little fountains of pure colour," signify her Romantic poetic sensibility.[43] And when she exclaims, "Yet what miserable men find such things, and work at them, and sell them," or draws elaborate plans for model cottages for workingmen, we should hear the first notes of those "angelic choirs" that Caleb Garth declares he hears in her voice. Like John Cumming, Dorothea muddles her metaphors—she can hardly be expected to remember where these "keys" were originally "hidden." The jewel scene is thus an appropriately mystifying allegory of the prophetic harmonies Dorothea has yet to disentangle.

As already shown, the Neoplatonic "key" sounds in the seventh chapter, itself a hieroglyph for the seven tones of the scale. Neither Dorothea nor Casaubon hears the subtle discords between their conceptions of prophetic harmony at this point, although Dorothea's response to organ music signals her Romantic predilections. But in chapter 42, when Casaubon learns of his approaching death, Dorothea has begun to perceive the futility of his "key." Not until the second half of the novel, however, does she finally and definitively reject both Casaubon's "Key to All Mythologies" and the keys to her material inheritance from him, Lowick.

After Casaubon's death, Dorothea requests the keys to Lowick and goes to the house in search of some sign of feeling in the papers remaining from her husband (343). Keys within keys are manipulated by the artist as well as Dorothea here: unlocking desks, and drawers within desks, Dorothea discovers Casaubon's final "key" to his intended "Key" to all prophetic myths—his "Synoptical Tabulation for the Use of Mrs. Casaubon." But the "key" for which Dorothea searches, the sign of some bond of human feeling, is lacking. Not finding this, she locks away forever the distorted "Mathematicks" of Casaubon's brain and later rejects the actual keys to Lowick as well.

Just as the keys to ancient harmony in the novel are chiefly associated with Lowick, that "dying flame," so the keys to Romantic prophecy are to be found at Stone Court, that other metaphorical domain whose name we may now speculate suggests the "living stone" of a true prophetic restoration. Through unexpected modulations of the keys to Stone Court, Mary Garth receives the inheritance she originally rejected, while the "precious" stone Bulstrode sought to inherit becomes the stone of his affliction. And Stone Court itself, like the name of its original owner Featherstone, proves to be of paradoxical value—of none to those who value it for monetary reasons, but of precious value to those who perceive it as a "living stone," or key to the Romantic vision of laboring humanity.

The keys to old Featherstone's caskets are the first pair of keys in the Stone Court "scale," for the key that Mary Garth refuses to give the old man parallels the first key used by him, when he unlocks a little casket in order to give his nephew one hundred pounds. But Mary's key has an unexpected relationship to Fred's: where he looks forward to his inheritance from his uncle, she prevents that inheritance by refusing the key to Featherstone's last will. Mary's awareness of the dangers of inheritance from a possibly tainted source opposes Fred's eagerness to inherit a gentlemanly "harmony" of idleness. Yet by a strange succession of keys indeed, Mary and Fred eventually do "inherit" Stone Court.

The next pair of keys to appear in this scale are the keys to the fateful Stone Court brandy chest. From the beginning, these keys are linked to Bulstrode's incrimination. When Rigg Featherstone takes out his keys and goes to unlock the brandy, Raffles picks up and hides a piece of folded paper: this paper later allows him to threaten Bulstrode with the revelation of the past (287). The next appearance of the brandy-chest keys implicates Bulstrode in a much more deadly affair, for by handing them to Mrs. Abel, he knowingly sets the stage for Raffles' death.

The keys to the Stone Court brandy chest, then, suggest a theme sharply opposed to the keys to Featherstone's caskets, for where Mary refuses a doubtful inheritance, Bulstrode purchases the keys to Stone Court with an inheritance he knows to be dishonest. Stone Court thus becomes the banker's "rock of offence," a stumbling stone that can be traced to his failure to reject a "key" to the past. Yet through still further, unexpected developments, the keys to Stone Court return to Mary Garth and her husband Fred. They inherit, however, not the land and the buildings, but Caleb Garth's "sublime music"—the "business" of farming. Mary also, like Dorothea Brooke, has rejected the key to an ancient kind of harmony—the life of the wealthy, useless gentlewoman—and transformed it into the "sublime music" of labor.

But the keys to Stone Court pass through one other unexpected modulation. Mr. Rigg Featherstone, far from clinging to the inheritance of Stone Court, is only too happy to exchange its keys for those of a money-changer's shop (360). Rigg Featherstone's sale of Stone Court, and Bulstrode's purchase, suggest that in this musical scheme or "scale," Stone Court is of paradoxical value. Like the name that Rigg also inherits, Stone Court has no intrinsic "weight" or worth. It can only be "inherited" by those who know it for the "precious stone" it is—the "silent stone" at the foot of the universal monochord that culminates in the Romantic celebration of common humanity rather than in the otherworldly choirs of ancient music.

The keys to Stone Court thus also function as keys to an elaborate and witty musical discourse. Reversing the usual apocalyptic progress, *Middlemarch* begins with the jewels of the apocalyptic city and descends to the "living stones" of Stone Court. Dorothea and Mary Garth perform parallel musical movements, rejecting keys to the inheritance of an ancient but dying harmony. But beyond this initial motion, can it be said that Dorothea and Will have any further part in the Romantic harmony centered on Stone Court? We know that Will detects the sound of the Aeolian harp in Dorothea's voice in that first encounter when he appears, significantly, as the artist of the yew tree. But are those musical fragments ever reborn in new form? What hitherto "hidden facts of structure" link Will and Dorothea's storm-accompanied betrothal to the artist's final musical harmony?

Once again, recourse to a prophetic scheme outside the text provides a "key" to that obviously apocalyptic moment of union. And while Will and Dorothea must be presumed ignorant of the artist's musical scheme, that scheme is itself only a *quaternio* for a web that does become visible to them. According to Giuseppe Mazzini's little-known Romantic essay on the philosophy of music,

Filosofia della Musica, Will and Dorothea's betrothal represents a music that unites all nations and is "prophetic of Humanity." Although there is no direct proof that George Eliot read Mazzini's essay, she knew the Italian patriot well and published articles by him when she edited the *Westminster Review*.[44] The characterization of Will and Dorothea, however, provides strong evidence that Mazzini's musical prophetic scheme is, like Sir Thomas Browne's, woven into the tones of *Middlemarch*.

Mazzini's essay proposes music as the instrument of "synthesis." Since music "begins where poetry ends" and "is the algebra of the spirit that verifies and informs Humanity," music should be the force that unites Europe:

> Let our young artists elevate their hearts by the study of our national history, our national songs, the mysteries of poetry, and the mysteries of nature; let their glance embrace a vaster horizon than that afforded by their books and canons of art. Music is the perfume of the whole universe, and the artist who would seize that perfume must learn, by loving and faithful study of the harmonies that float over earth and heaven, to penetrate and identify himself with the Thought of the universe. (251)

The sacred purpose of music is to unite the two primary opposing elements of humanity: the individual idea and the social idea. In music, these two opposing elements are represented by melody and harmony, and these in turn are identified with Italian music and German music. The music that is "prophetic of Humanity" and identified with "the Thought of the universe," therefore, combines the two great national schools of music, Italian and German.

Will's many associations with Italian art and music, even his name, take on new meaning when we read Mazzini's characterization of Italian music:

> Yielding to every dictate or caprice of an undisputed will, it follows the impulse of every desire. No rational and enduring law, no progressive unity of life, thoughtfully directed towards an aim, is there. There is in it strong feeling, rapidly and violently expressed.... Lyrical almost to delirium, passionate to intoxication, volcanic as the land of its birth, and brilliant as her sun ... it bounds from object to object, from affection to affection, from thought to thought; from the most ecstatic joy to the most hopeless grief.... Its inspiration is the inspiration of the tripod; eminently artistic, not religious.... "Art for art's sake" is

> its highest formula. Hence its want of unity, its fragmentary, unconnected, and interrupted character.... The fulcrum is wanting to the lever; a connecting link is wanting to the myriad sensations its melodies embody and represent. (248–49)

Mrs. Cadwallader's description of Will as an "Italian organ-grinder with white mice" seems even more than customarily prophetic in light of this description.

But if Will seems a rather comical embodiment of Italian music, Mazzini's description of German music provides an even more suggestive source for Dorothea. German music is "profoundly religious, yet with a religion that has no symbol, and therefore no active faith translated in deeds, no martyrdom, no victory." Although it surrounds and cradles the listener "upon a wave of chords," the listener falls back again into "reality, into the prosaic life that hums around, with the consciousness of another world revealed afar off, not bestowed" (250). Representing a mystical sense of harmony, German music nevertheless lacks the "formula" of a mission to fulfill, the melody by which its harmony can be given shape and purpose. German music resembles, in fact, a hopelessly aspiring maiden:

> German music is eminently elegiac; it is the music of remembrance, of desire, of melancholy hopes, of sorrows which no human lip can console, a Music as if angels lost to heaven were hovering around. It aspires toward the Infinite, its country.... One might liken it to a maiden born for smiles, but who has met no smile in response to her own; whose soul is full of love, but who has found nought worthy of love on earth, and dreams of another sky, another universe, wherein she shall see the form of that being that will return her love and answer her virgin smile—the being whom, unknown, she adores. (249–50)

Such descriptions make it easy to conceive of Will and Dorothea's betrothal as destined to provide a "connecting link" for Will's disconnected melodies, a "formula" for Dorothea's ineffable sense of a mission to fulfill, and inevitably, a harmony that will unite humanity. Dorothea's first response to the musical emerald as a penetrating "scent" seems long ago to have predicted her capacity to "seize" the "perfume" of music and the "Thought of the universe," while Will's little Sunday songs indicate his "delirious lyricism" and his "caprice of an undisputed will." For George Eliot, that seer of far less "capacious credulity" than Sir Thomas Browne, Mazzini's scheme could serve as a supremely witty musical "fiction"—an unseen *quaternio* for the grandiose expectations of the Romantic symphony, here suitably reduced to a mere "middle march."

If Will and Dorothea's marriage will not quite succeed in uniting Europe, it will, after all, relate them to nearly everyone in Middlemarch. Through certain "hidden facts" not revealed until the moment when Will too rejects a dubious inheritance, we discover that Will is related to Bulstrode, and therefore to the Vincys and the Garths and the Featherstones. The group of apparently unrelated individuals at the Grange party has turned out, by connections so distant and motions so imperceptible as not to be detected even by Mrs. Cadwallader, to be linked by a truly astonishing web of blood and marital relations. This, though only an uneven fragment of a web, is the historian's "quincunx"—a web that we see to be both eminently historical and eminently musical. The bond of betrothal that links this "Italian organ-grinder" descended from a Polish patriot to an Englishwoman with a puritanical Swiss education, and joins them in a web of relationships connected to nearly everyone else in town, is one of those instances in which a "delightful Truth" has been confirmed by "sense and ocular Observation." Will and Dorothea's betrothal *is* prophetic of the union of humanity, if on a small "scale," and in those peals of thunder and flashes of lightning, we *can* faintly hear the "sublime music" of Stone Court.

In *Middlemarch*, then, we find the apocalyptic harmonies of *Romola* transposed into the "key" of musical comedy. Both the numerology and the stages of the heroine's pilgrimage become part of a comic vision of Neoplatonic prophecy, a vision that reveals the risks of accepting without question the "truths" of an ancient inheritance. But the "keys" to this comic vision are not revealed simply to be rejected but instead to be modulated into a new Romantic key—a key that postulates the existence of a kind of quincunxial web, and prophesies, if it does not perform, the harmony of humanity.

Yet outside this completed composition stands the artist, fully aware that every completed form, every aspiration to "Totality," is only the fragment of an uneven web. Deliberately, *Middlemarch* does not conclude with a seventh, or apocalyptic, book but proceeds through a full octave, ending on a "keynote" that both resounds the tones of its beginning and is itself a new beginning. Dorothea, in her dawn vision of her part in "that involuntary, palpitating life" may feel that she has found the true key to the harmony of the universe, but the artist knows that such "conclusions" cannot be confirmed. The ends of novels do not imitate life, which is always in the middle of things. But the visionary web is not erased: phoenix-like, it rises again from its own ashes—for how can we explain what such a thing is, except by saying it is something else?

CHAPTER 5

The Apocalypse of the Old Testament

A small incident that occurs early in the course of *Daniel Deronda* has large implications for the reader of the novel. Mr. Middleton, an "unexceptionable young clergyman with pale whiskers and square-cut collar," whose tastes run to theological reading, persuades himself that Gwendolen's avoidance of him must actually be a sign of her favor. Convinced that her cousinly familiarity with Rex excludes the possibility of any passionate interest in her cousin, Mr. Middleton interprets her apparent lack of passion for him as evidence for it. The narrator, quietly explaining why Mr. Middleton pursues this erroneous way of thinking, comments that "all meanings, we know, depend on the key of interpretation."[1]

The narrator seems to anticipate a more sophisticated reader than Mr. Middleton—a reader who understands that a narrative, like the events it records, can be interpreted in a variety of ways, depending on the reader's "key." As in the literary history of *Romola*, however, critics have often faulted *Daniel Deronda* for its failure to fulfill traditional generic expectations: presuming George Eliot's assumed reader to be a Mr. Middleton, they critique the double plot for its lack of any easily perceived unity. Even if critical analysis can produce an abstract or "intellectual" unity in the narrative, that narrative must nevertheless fail in its effect on the reader, who will surely perceive it as an unsuccessful mimesis: a history fragmented into two unequal "halves," and polarized between didactic extremes of egoism and altruism.[2]

In a revealing deconstructive reading, Cynthia Chase further identifies conflicts in the narrative, pointing to contradictions in its representation of history. Chase proposes that the narrative deconstructs the concept of history on which it depends, ultimately representing causality as the product of its own operations, "the effect of a play of signs," rather than the "truth" of the "subject's origin and destiny in a history" (220). Although the reader feels that Deronda's Jewish birth should be a cause of his prophetic vocation, for example, the narrative represents his birth as an effect of his previously developed affinity for Judaism. Chase also shows how the narrative leads relentlessly toward an external referent—the unmentioned fact of Deronda's circumcision—on which it "goes aground," for although the plot can function only by disregarding the circumcision, "the novel's realism and referentiality function precisely to draw attention to it."[3]

Chase's reading thus produces deconstructive operations in *Daniel Deronda* similar to those J. Hillis Miller affirms in *Middlemarch*, as also to the subversive effects of chronology that I have described in *Adam Bede*. But the implications of her reading can be extended—and in one aspect corrected—if we assume that contemporary readers of *Daniel Deronda*, unlike Mr. Middleton, recognized the possibility of more than one "key of interpretation." I suggest that narrative structure in *Daniel Deronda* functions in part as an interpretation of interpretation, for its most responsive reading depends on a sophisticated hermeneutical awareness produced by a Victorian controversy about "the Apocalypse of the Old Testament," or the Book of Daniel. Although the Book of Daniel occasioned violently opposed interpretations during the 1860s and 1870s, all interpreters agreed on one premise: the writer of Daniel was the first to envision a philosophy of history.[4] George Eliot quoted in her "Oriental Memoranda" notebook, for example, a comment by the Dutch critic Abraham Kuenen that the writer of Daniel, whatever his true identity, was "the first who grasped the history of the world, so far as he knew it, as one great whole, as a drama which moves onward at the will of the Eternal One."[5] Exegetes considered the nature of prophetic vision in the Book of Daniel crucial not only to "prophecy fulfilled and unfulfilled" but to the origin and meaning of history, and the book consequently became the subject of an outspoken debate.

Daniel Deronda bears the imprint of that debate, for its double narrative both dramatizes prophetic history and explores the way prophetic vision shapes the past as much as the future. Just as it is not coincidental that the hero is a Jew named Daniel, so it is probably not coincidental that the narrator's example of erroneous interpretation is an Anglican clergyman. Mr. Middleton is not, after all, the only such clergyman in the novel: Mr. Gascoigne also significantly misinterprets the course of Gwendolen's future. The "key" to the Book of Daniel that the established church in England accepted was, to George Eliot's mind, entirely erroneous. Yet that traditional interpretation of Daniel everywhere informs George Eliot's new interpretation of prophetic history in *Daniel Deronda*. Like her Victorian readers, we need to know that traditional interpretation not only to infer the motive for her deliberate separation of the plot into two narrative strands but also to gain an insight into her famous statement that she "meant everything in the book to be related to everything else there" (*GEL*, 6:290). Finally, Victorian hermeneutics suggest that the "external," or unmentioned referent, of Daniel's circumcision functions like the name of God in exegesis of the Book of Esther: though never mentioned in the text, it is nevertheless central to the interpretation of the text, an essential key to the vision with which George Eliot means to unite narrative and history.

As Moses Stuart remarked in his 1850 commentary on Daniel, the interpretation of the Apocalypse led inevitably to the study of the earlier apocalyptic work.[6] George Eliot's acquaintance with interpretations of the "Apocalypse of the Old Testament" has already appeared both in *Felix Holt*, where the narrator refers to the "mistaken criticism" of the Book of Daniel, and also in the apocalyptic structurings I have described in both *Romola* and *Middlemarch*.[7] But the period between 1860, when *Essays and Reviews* was published, and 1876, when *Daniel Deronda* appeared, was in itself likely to turn attention to the Book of Daniel.[8] During this period English critics first publicly responded to German rationalist criticism of Daniel, finding it devastating to traditional beliefs. As E. B. Pusey stated in his *Daniel the Prophet* (1864), the interpretation of the Book of Daniel was a "battlefield," admitting of no half-measures: the book was either divine or fraudulent, and Daniel either a prophet or a liar.[9] Pusey's commentary, which held firmly to the principle of supernatural inspiration, was followed shortly by Philip S. Desprez's *Daniel; or, The Apocalypse of the Old Testament* (1865), based on the German higher criticism. Rowland Williams, in his controversial preface to Desprez's work, explained the inconsistencies between the "Jewish or rationalistic theory" and the traditional Christian interpretation of Daniel. Accusing Pusey of laboring to "throw back interpretation, and fix upon the Bible the seven seals of tradition," he concluded that only if "a certain class of interpretations" was surrendered would students or congregations "have any key to the profound moral significance of the Old Testament."[10]

Yet one of the most characteristic forms of the traditional class of interpretations, surprisingly, suggests a model for George Eliot's construction of *Daniel Deronda* in two clearly separable narrative strands. "Continuous historical" interpretations of the Book of Daniel often took the form of historical dualism: a division of history into two great branches or streams, such as Augustine's division between the city of men and the city of God. T. R. Birks, for example, in *The Four Prophetic Empires* (1845)—a work published in the Christian's Family Library, to which the young Mary Ann Evans had subscribed—interpreted the metal image of Nebuchadnezzar's dream (Daniel 2) as envisioning the double aspect of history. The descending order of metals in the image teaches us "the downward course of mere earthly greatness," while the stone cut without hands represents the ever growing inheritance of truth into which each successive age enters.[11] The division between worldly decadence and heavenly increase is obviously similar to, and probably based on, the *City of God*.[12] More important, however, it reminds us of the similar division between decadence and vision—that is, between the English and the Jewish spheres—in *Daniel Deronda*.

But another variation of dualistic Christian history, also popular in the nineteenth century, bears an even closer resemblance to the double narrative of *Daniel Deronda*: a division of history between Jewish and Christian prophecy. John Davison's *Discourses on Prophecy* (1825), first presented as Warburtonian Lectures, explicated a "mixed or double" aspect of history since the time of Abraham. Some of the prophecies made to Abraham and his descendants were for the Jews only, some for the Christians or Gentiles only, and some for the entire human race. The structure of history—synonymous with the structure of prophecy—therefore could be seen to diverge into two great streams, occasionally bridged by universal prophecy but never to be reunited until that apocalyptic event, the conversion and restoration of the Jews.[13]

The double aspect of *Daniel Deronda* obviously resembles this prophetic structure of history. Gwendolen's narrative represents the English or Christian stream of history, Daniel's the Jewish. Opening in medias res, at the gambling resort in Leubronn, the narrative immediately focuses on Daniel's judgment of Gwendolen: "Was she beautiful or not beautiful? . . . Was the good or the evil genius dominant?" Daniel's function here, as elsewhere in the novel, is to interpret the moral or spiritual value of Gwendolen's history. Like the Hebrew prophets, he pronounces judgment on this Gentile and later exhorts her to repentance and regeneration. Daniel's advice and counsel to Gwendolen repeatedly bridge the two narratives, which conclude with Gwendolen's humble acknowledgment of Daniel's transforming influence on her: "it shall be better with me because I have known you" (882).

The double-narrative structure of the novel, then, bears an interestingly close resemblance to this Victorian version of Christian dualistic history, traditionally associated with the Book of Daniel. The novel differs in one important respect, however: it reverses the moral position of Jew and Christian. George Eliot has ironized her historical model, for in the novel it is the English Christian stream that must be "converted" and restored to the great river of human history by Hebrew prophetic vision.[14] The narrative solidly identifies the downward progress of worldly empire with the English "half," whereas the Jewish "half," dominated by Daniel, Mordecai, and Mirah, represents visionary growth and progress. Although the Meyricks, for example, provide a refuge for Mirah, she converts *them* to a wider sympathy, exposing the narrowness of their Evangelical beliefs. And Mrs. Mallinger, who supports the Society for the Conversion of the Jews and devoutly hopes Mirah will embrace Christianity, lives instead to see her husband's adopted son embrace Judaism as well as this Jewish maiden (267).

Instructive and even amusing though it may be to compare

Daniel Deronda with this Victorian version of dualistic history, the comparison does not in itself suggest how we could read the novel, in the words George Eliot quoted, as "one great whole." If *Daniel Deronda* functions in part as an ironic allegory of traditional Christian history, then its two plot lines come together only in the last chapter, and then only in prophetic types of an eventual "restoration" of the Jews and "conversion" of the Gentiles. The narratives, like Davison's structure of prophetic history, would not coalesce until some "apocalypse" beyond their time frame. This aspect of Danielic commentary, though it suggests a model and a rationale for George Eliot's separation of the narrative into two plot lines, fails to explain how the reader might be expected to relate everything in the novel to everything else—at least within its temporal realm.

Further investigation of the Victorian literature on Daniel, however, suggests a more complex conception of dualistic history that not only unites the two streams within a "universal history" but also points to the presence of an "apocalypse" in the text—a symbolic conversion that identifies Christian with Jew and bonds future with past. George Eliot produces that universal history in the text of *Daniel Deronda* through her appropriation of the Prophecy of the Seventy Weeks. The Old Testament prophecy serves as the dominant structuring metaphor in this novel, in contrast to its more limited narrative functions in *Romola* and *Middlemarch*. But to interpret this structure, the reader must first be familiar with the general features of "continuous historical" and typological interpretation of the seventy weeks—the interpretation traditional in the Victorian Anglican church.[15]

Since the time of Joseph Mede, scholarly exegetes had attributed great significance to the Prophecy of the Seventy Weeks in Daniel, for together with the prophecy of the Four Empires, it constituted the "SACRED KALENDAR AND GREAT ALMANAC OF PROPHESIE," signifying all time "from the beginning of the captivity of Israel, until the mystery of God should be finished."[16] In the early nineteenth century, George Stanley Faber's *The Sacred Calendar of Prophecy* (1828) worked out Mede's interpretation in an extraordinarily elaborate "continuous historical" exposition of "the grand master-number of seven times ... hitherto almost universally over-looked."[17] Faber's work, which became a classic in "continuous historical" exposition, combined prophecies from the Book of Revelation and the Book of Daniel into one grand chronological scheme reaching from 2325 B.C. to 3200 A.D. The "grand master-number of seven times" extended the seventy weeks into the period from the foundation of the First Empire to the final end of time.

Although Faber's was the most extensive "continuous historical" exegesis of Daniel, other exegetes also considered the Prophecy of the Seventy Weeks one of the most important chronological prophecies, and it was rarely omitted from Victorian works on prophecy. The prophecy, spoken by the angel Gabriel, stated that "seventy weeks are determined upon thy people and upon thy holy city, to finish the transgression, and to make an end of sins, and to make reconciliation for iniquity, and to bring in everlasting righteousness, and to seal up the vision and prophecy, and to anoint the most Holy" (Dan. 9:24). Interpreters identified this prophecy with Jeremiah's prophecy of seventy years of captivity for Israel (Jer. 25:12), explicating it both as the seventy years of the Jewish exile in Babylonia and as the simultaneous duration of the Babylonian Empire, the first of the Four Empires.

The seventy weeks thus symbolized the history of both exile and empire. But for Christian exegetes the seventy weeks was also a principal messianic prophecy of the Old Testament, because it predicted that the Messiah would be "cut off, but not for himself" after "threescore and two weeks" (62 weeks), that Jerusalem would be restored to the Messiah in 69 weeks, and the covenant confirmed for one week (Dan. 9:25–27). Consequently, in a third chronological interpretation, the seventy weeks became seventy "weeks of years," or 490 years, between the Jewish exile and the Crucifixion and Resurrection of Christ. Edward Bickersteth, for example, interpreted the 490 years as the period from "the decree of Artaxerxes given to Ezra, 458, to the death and resurrection of our Lord in A.D. 33."[18]

As Mede's comment implies, the prophecy also was interpreted as a type of the entire history of the "church" in exile, incorporating all the wanderings and exiles of the Hebrews as well as the long history of the Christian church before the glorious restoration of the Second Coming. Faber's *Sacred Calendar*, in fact, illustrates the "continuous historical" interpretation of the typological interpretation, for he attempts to demonstrate the entire period of exile for both Jews and Christians in precise historical terms.

In both the typological and the extensive "continuous historical" interpretation, it is important to note that the citizens of "empire" are as much exiled as the Jewish "church," for the rulers of worldly empires are spiritually exiled, while the Jews are exiled from their promised land. The Jews in turn served as a type of all true Christians exiled from their "promised land," or heavenly kingdom. The Prophecy of the Seventy Weeks unites the double plot lines of *Daniel Deronda*, first, in this typological interpretation of history as exile for both Jews and Christians.

Jean Sudrann has pointed out that Gwendolen and other English characters, as much as the Jewish characters, seem to be exiled. Sudrann suggests that "to a striking degree, *Daniel Deronda* is a novel of rootless human lives, lives lacking 'homestead,' 'native land,' and a family relation to the heavens."[19] Sudrann relates this rootlessness in the novel to George Eliot's personal experience of isolation and suggests that the novel presents a landscape more familiar to the twentieth than the nineteenth century in its sensitive depiction of alienation. But the landscape of exile, though indeed a twentieth-century paradigm, is also a familiar biblical trope. However deeply George Eliot's personal experience of isolation may inform the emotional tone of *Daniel Deronda*, the novel takes its epic "machinery" from the biblical literature of exile.[20]

Obviously, both Deronda's name and "love of universal history" suggest the Book of Daniel, traditionally seen as the major prophecy of the Babylonian exile (220).[21] Like Daniel the prophet, Deronda lives in "exile"—an exile from knowledge of his origin—and like the prophet, he becomes adviser to a Gentile, interpreter of a "dream" or vision that causes great spiritual turmoil. Modern readers are less likely to realize that Mordecai is also an exilic name, for in the Book of Esther a Jew named Mordecai advises his niece to marry the Persian ruler and thus enables her later to save her people from destruction. The Book of Esther may in fact have contributed more than the name of a character to the novel, for in the tale gambling, or the casting of lots, represents at first the

The Apocalypse of the Old Testament 139

seemingly haphazard fate of those disinherited or "exiled" but later the prophetic destiny attained through active choice of one's heritage—an obvious parallel to the emblematic theme of gambling in the novel.

Mordecai's other name, Ezra, has even stronger links to the literature of exile, for Ezra led the Jews in their return from the Babylonian exile. Names from earlier exiles also appear in the novel. Both Mordecai and Klesmer are compared to Elijah, the prophet whose forty-day exile in the desert exegetes read as a type of Christ's forty days of temptation in the wilderness. Both Mirah and Lydia Glasher are similarly compared to Hagar, Abraham's disinherited wife, who was driven into the desert with her son, Ishmael. Even the angelic machinery of this novel suggests a subtle link to the literature of exile, for not only is the angel Gabriel—mentioned twice in the novel—the angel in the Book of Daniel, but Daniel is the first biblical work to name angels.[22]

George Eliot's "landscape of exile" thus draws on names, characters, and even themes from the biblical literature of exile. That landscape, as Sudrann has demonstrated, characterizes both plot lines, for Daniel and Gwendolen are each exiled from their origins: lack of a "homeland," of a known birthplace, deprives them of a spiritual inheritance that would give shape and moral significance to their own lives. But George Eliot primarily exploits the numerological symbolism of exile to write Daniel and Gwendolen's individual histories as a united, prophetic history of humanity in exile. As in *Romola* (and to a lesser extent in *Middlemarch* and *Adam Bede*), the numbering of chapters becomes an integral part of the hermeneutic design of the narrative. But whereas in the earlier novels the numerological implications of chapter numbers chiefly reflect exegesis of the Book of Revelation, in *Daniel Deronda* they seem to allude specifically to interpretations of the Book of Daniel. To begin with, the seventy chapters of the novel suggest a structural analogue to the Prophecy of the Seventy Weeks.

I have shown that the Prophecy of the Seventy Weeks figures in both *Romola* and *Middlemarch*. But following Romola's return to Florence—her "New Jerusalem"—in the seventieth chapter, the narrative continues for two additional chapters during which she questions the value of both prophet and prophecy. The larger prophetic structure of the novel, patterned on the Apocalypse of the New Testament, thus frames or subordinates the Prophecy of the Seventy Weeks. In *Middlemarch* also the ironic "fulfillment" I have noted in the seventieth chapter is only a part of a larger apocalyptic structuring that seems to draw primarily on New Testament hermeneutics. But the entire, seventy-chapter narrative of *Daniel Deronda* appropriates interpretation of the seventy weeks as the prophecy of exile and messianic restoration.

The narrative opens in the gambling den at Leubronn, a scene of "universal" exile. The double plot lines may be seen as separate histories of "empire" and "exile," or as a vision of universal exile, as I have shown. The opening scene, moreover, symbolizes the particular nature of Daniel and Gwendolen's exiles as exiles from history. Gwendolen's loss of inheritance in the opening scene dramatizes her "exile" from her father or her heritage, while Daniel's redemption of her chain—the single object remaining from that inheritance—suggests his potential to redeem history for both Gwendolen and himself.[23] The seventieth, or concluding chapter, in turn, suggests symbolic equivalents of the Prophecy of the Seventy Weeks. Both Mordecai and Daniel resemble messianic figures, for Mordecai's death suggests the prophecy that the Messiah would be "cut off" after seventy weeks, while Daniel's marriage to Mirah and plans for his journey east suggest a symbolic "restoration" of Israel to Jerusalem. Gwendolen's humble acknowledgment of Daniel's influence and her promise to try to be a better woman, again, hint at a "conversion."

But this reading of the seventy chapters as a structural analogue to the Prophecy of the Seventy Weeks appears unsatisfactorily one-sided. The relationship of Mordecai's death and Daniel's "restoration" to the English or Christian realm in the novel remains unclear. And whereas Daniel has recently been given the key to his father's chest, suggesting a restoration of history for him, Gwendolen seems to have received no inheritance but that of a penitential existence at Offendene. If the separation of the two narratives may be seen as an ironic inversion of Christian prophetic history, the union of the narratives in a history of humanity in exile still suggests a romantic fulfillment only from the Jewish perspective.

Examined in its most visible similarities to the novel, exegesis of the Prophecy of the Seventy Weeks suggests that *Daniel Deronda* is simply George Eliot's Jewish apocalypse—another interpretation that fails to satisfy demands for either narrative or historical unity.

But by turning from the beginning and end of the narrative to its middle we may read a "universal" interpretation of the seventy chapters, for Daniel's restoration of Gwendolen's spiritual heritage emerges most clearly "in medias res"—the prophetic center of the novel's history from which both past and future can be re-visioned or reinterpreted. Here, the chapter number forty symbolizes the beginning and end of exile, just as the seventy chapters in their entirety function as an analogue for the seventy weeks of exile. But more important, George Eliot re-creates in this chapter the beginning and end of prophetic vision itself—its origin and its function in history—and so suggests a restoration of history to Gentile as much as to Jew.

George Eliot's notebooks mention that the Hebrew word for forty also means "a great number"—a fact on which she commented that "this is doubtful."[24] For her, the number undoubtedly recalled its pervasive typological and liturgical associations as the number of exile and temptation—such as Israel's forty years in the desert, Christ's forty days of temptation, or the forty days of Lent—for in *Daniel Deronda*, chapter 40 is both the end of Mordecai's exile and the beginning of Daniel's temptation. In this chapter Daniel appears to Mordecai in what Luther Harry Kriefall sees as an obvious dramatization of the well-known "Son of Man" prophecy in Daniel: "behold, one like the Son of man came with the clouds of heaven, and came to the Ancient of Days" (Dan. 7:13).[25] Daniel, coming down the river with the clouds of the golden sunset behind him, appears to Mordecai as the "fulfillment" of his "inward prophecy" (550). The fulfillment ends Mordecai's exile, for as the narrator later remarks, Mordecai's interpretation brings Daniel near to this "spiritual exile" (605). Daniel will become not only the "hand" to plant Mordecai's "banner" but the soul to share and perpetuate Mordecai's vision.

But the incident also marks the beginning of Daniel's "temptation," for he must decide whether to accept or reject Mordecai's identification of him as visionary heir and how to interpret this prophetic inheritance. The enigmatic image of Mordecai's face—significantly, in the *east* for Daniel—is as crucial for Daniel as his own image is for Mordecai. As in Daniel's earlier thought, this moment suggests two exiles on passing ships each suddenly recognizing the other's face. Reference to the exegetical debate concerning the "Son of man" prophecy in the Book of Daniel further enlarges the significance of this incident in the narrative.

The "Son of man" prophecy presented many problems to Christian exegetes, for just as in George Eliot's re-creation, both the "Son of man" and the "Ancient of Days" required interpretation. Most critics interpreted the "Son of man" as Christ, and the "Ancient of Days" as God the Father, and read the text itself as a major Christian prophecy in the Old Testament. But Christian exegetes were far from unanimous, and Jewish commentators, of course, had an entirely different view.[26] The "prophecy" as represented in the novel raises even more questions, for George Eliot places it in the context of rational or scientific inquiry. Whether Daniel is a Christian or Jewish "Messiah" is only one of the questions posed. The scene serves as focus for a scientific inquiry into the nature of prophetic vision itself and for the even more difficult problem of its proper influence on those living in a culture dominated by scientific or rational thought.

George Levine has shown how George Eliot's representation of Mordecai's prophetic vision resembles George Henry Lewes's consideration of scientific hypothesis in *Problems of Life and Mind*.[27] But contemporary rationalist biblical exegesis approached the problem of prophetic vision much more directly and provides an even more suggestive source for George Eliot's fictional construction. For example, as the Dutch critic Abraham Kuenen, whose *Religion of Israel* appears to have strongly influenced George Eliot's thought, explained:

> The vision is one of the distinguishing characters of ecstasy, and arises when the lively and excited imagination acts upon the nerves of sight (and sometimes of hearing also), in the same manner as the reality would in other cases, so that the person who is in this state does not doubt the existence of the objects which he imagines he beholds (and

of the person whose voice he thinks he hears). There is therefore nothing miraculous in such visions and dreams."[28]

Kuenen further stated not only that visions were fully explained by the bodily constitutions and intellectual milieux of the prophets but that such visions revealed nothing that was really new: "all the elements of which they were formed were already present before."[29]

In chapter 38, which begins "'Second-sight' is a flag over disputed ground," George Eliot's construction of Mordecai's prophetic vision seems to dramatize Kuenen's explanation. Because Mordecai's mind—like that of any poet—"wrought so constantly in images," his deep longing for a soul mate to end his exile comes to be expressed as a "figure" or image (530). Gradually that figure takes on a typical form expressive of "a man who would have all the elements necessary for sympathy with him, but in an embodiment unlike his own" (529). Finally, this figure with its typical form is seen against a golden sky. "The reason of the golden sky," we learn, is Mordecai's fondness for sunsets seen from the bridge. We further learn that Mordecai thought he recognized his "long-conceived type" on his *first* sight of Deronda and that the more he saw Deronda the more the resemblance struck him (536). We also read that Mordecai yearns for the vista of the bridge at sunset and goes there as often as he can, and we already know that Daniel enjoys rowing. Daniel's "fulfillment" of Mordecai's "prophecy" thus seems not merely rationally explicable but almost inevitable. As in Kuenen's explanation, the vision has arisen because of Mordecai's constitution and the sphere of ideas in which he moves, and none of the elements in it are new. They are in fact a clearly recognizable example of poetic or artistic vision, and the reader who turns back to the earlier scene of Daniel rowing on the river will discover comparable examples of the artistic power of foreshadowing. But as Kuenen suggested, the prophet himself always felt such "prophetic" images were "extraordinary." Mordecai sees Daniel's appearance as an extraordinary fulfillment of his prophecy—and this occasions a hermeneutic problem for Daniel, who finds the vision extraordinary in another sense.

Daniel ponders not only the nature and origin of Mordecai's vision but the response he should make to it. Should he take Mordecai's messianic interpretation seriously, or should he, like any "man of the world," merely indulge the prophet a little but ascribe no real value to Mordecai's visionary habits? Appropriately recalling the words of Christ in *Paradise Regained*—for the temptation of George Eliot's Daniel strongly resembles that of Milton's Christ—Daniel wonders whether the prophets and dreamers of dreams are "'Great benefactors of mankind, deliverers,'" or merely "devotees of phantasmal discovery" (569). Milton's Christ considers during his forty days' temptation not only which messianic interpretation is correct but also how he should define his own role in relation to that body of hermeneutics. George Eliot's Victorian "Messiah," however, must consider an even more difficult question: the validity of prophecy in a scientific age. Unlike the theologically conservative Mr. Middleton, Daniel recognizes the existence of more than one interpretive key. On what rational basis, he wonders, can he accept prophetic vision as a key to the universe, when another man was convinced he held the "mathematical key to the universe," and another the "metaphysical key?" (568).

Daniel's consideration probes much more widely and subtly than does Romola's similar consideration of her brother Dino's prophecy, suggesting George Eliot's acquaintance with an ever-increasing body of exegesis between the two novels. Examples such as the "forecasting ardour" of scientific hypothesis, or Columbus's "passionate patience of genius," even though combined with superstition, finally make Deronda resolve not to rule out the possibility of an important relation between Mordecai and himself simply because Mordecai has "clad it in illusory notions" (573). For the time being, he postpones a decision on how a rational or scientific individual should define himself in the light of prophetic vision. But in chapter 42, Daniel receives a fuller interpretation of messianic prophecy, one that both fulfills the demands of rational thought and reaches beyond its boundaries.

I have already demonstrated George Eliot's varying allusions in chapters numbered 42 to the interpretations of that apocalyptically significant number. In *Adam Bede* the chapter number 42 "crosses" Adam's resolve to witness for Hetty with that of the hermeneutic "history" of the two witnesses who prophesied for "a thousand two hundred and threescore days," or forty-two months (Rev. 11:3). Romola first appears as "visible madonna" in the forty-second chapter, appropriating interpretations of the apocalyptic "woman clothed with the sun" and her sojourn in the wilderness for the same period (Rev. 12:1–6). And in *Middlemarch* the forty-second chapter marks the end of Casaubon's hopes for his "Key to All Mythologies," an ironic anti-apocalypse for the prophetic work first named in chapter 7—the number said to signify prophetic fulfillment and completion.

In *Daniel Deronda*, chapter 42 functions—as in *Romola*—as an interpretation of the "wilderness" or exile prophecy, but here the interpretation specifically applies to exegesis of the Old Testament Apocalypse. Exegetes considered the number forty-two as prominent in the Book of Daniel as in the Revelation of St. John, and interpreted the "time, times and an half" during which "the power of the holy people" was to be scattered as synonymous with the three and one-half years, the 1,260 days, or the forty-two months in the later work (Dan. 12:7). Mordecai's speech in chapter 42 of *Daniel Deronda* obviously relates directly to this prophecy, interpreted as the dispersion of the Jews. In his impassioned speech to the "Philosophers," Mordecai insists on the preservation of Israel as a national entity in which its prophetic seed can continue to provide vision and fire for all nations. Though Mordecai claims, like Gideon, "to be a rational Jew," rationalism is for him "the light of the divine reason" that reveals more and more of the hidden bonds of connection (587). His interpretation, though specifically that of a Hebrew prophet, nevertheless suggests invisible bonds between Jews and Christians.

The lengthy debate at the "Hand and Banner" has bored countless readers, seeming less than relevant to Gwendolen's story. But it is essential to George Eliot's hermeneutical purpose, which is to unite Jewish and Gentile histories. Like Hans Meyrick's letter, however, the chapter at first appears to conflict with the ecumenical drive of the narrative, for Gideon and some of the other "Philosophers" class Mordecai's interpretation with the most reactionary, religiously divisive readings. They consider it both more rational and more progressive to advocate the amalgamation of the Jews into the nationalities among which they live. In arguing instead for the establishment of a Jewish homeland, Mordecai opens himself to association with the "heap of nonsense" concocted by both Jews and Christians who believe in "the restoration to Judea by miracle." As the "genial and rational Gideon" expresses it:

> "And as to the connection of our race with Palestine, it has been perverted by superstition till it's as demoralising as the old poor-law. The raff and scum go there to be maintained like able-bodied paupers, and to be taken special care of by the angel Gabriel when they die. . . . The most learned and liberal men among us who are attached to our religion are for clearing our liturgy of all such notions as a literal fulfillment of the prophecies about restoration, and so on. Prune it of a few useless rites and literal interpretations of that sort, and our religion is the simplest of all religions, and makes no barrier, but a union, between us and the rest of the world." (593)

Hans Meyrick and Gideon, it would seem, are kindred souls: canting rationalists exist among the Jews as well as the "Germans." According to Gideon, the most rational path to the union of Jews with Gentiles lies in dissolving Jewish identity and in discarding traditional interpretations of the "restoration" as an actual return to Israel. Mordecai, however, insists that he does not believe in miracles yet argues for an interpretation that is both rational and visionary. Citing the prophet Micah against such degenerate prophets as Gideon—"the sun is gone down over the prophets"— he insists that his people must have an "organic centre" and urges them to unite "in a labour hard but glorious like that of Moses and Ezra."[30] The true bond of unity, he believes, will be achieved only through a restoration of the Jews, because the Jewish religion must serve as "organic centre" for those of other faiths as well as the Jews themselves.

In the succeeding chapter, Mordecai reveals to Daniel that his full name is *Ezra* Mordecai Cohen. As a result of this revelation, Daniel discovers Mordecai's relation to Mirah, but the name signifies far more than a family relationship. As Chase has pointed out, not only are Mordecai and Deronda "engaged in a kind of reading, a hermeneutic practice," but also the narrative plays on "the notion of an act of naming" that she suggests operates in default of the hermeneutic model.³¹ This act of naming, however, has a subtle hermeneutic significance, for the name Ezra places Mordecai in a conservative, priestly tradition that both counteracts the conception of him as a fanatic with illusory notions and symbolizes his capacity to envision the past in such a way as to shape the future. The revelation of Mordecai's other name, in fact, lies at the heart of George Eliot's conception of how prophetic vision functions in a scientific age to end the individual's "exile" from history and the Christian's exile from Judaism.

In his detailed treatment of Ezra, Kuenen commented that "a parallel is drawn in the Talmud between him and Moses."³² Discussing Ezra's role in the restoration of the Jewish people after the Babylonian exile, Kuenen goes far beyond the traditional Christian conception of Ezra as a mere "scribe"—an orthodox Jew who reinstated the Law in its most rigorous and ritualistic form, even to insisting that the Jews put away their "strange wives." Kuenen considered Ezra remarkable as a leader in the restoration of his people—and probably as an author—for he concluded that Ezra had written down the Law for the first time. In revealing at this point in the narrative that Mordecai bears the name "Ezra," George Eliot suggests that he is both prophet and "priest" of the restoration. He symbolizes the prophetic vision of the future and the priestly conservation and restoration of the past. The surname Cohen further bears out this interpretation, for in her "Oriental Memoranda" notebook George Eliot noted that the name "Cohen" had originally signified "*diviner*," but that "afterwards, the word was taken in the sense, *minister of God*, and applied to the priests of Jehovah."³³

More than this, the name Ezra symbolizes Mordecai's ability to re-create the past and, in so doing, to shape the future. In her notebook George Eliot quoted a long section from Kuenen on what he called the "Book of Origins." This was a collection of laws together with historical narratives that Kuenen believed had been written during the Babylonian exile, most probably by Ezra. The collection, in Kuenen's opinion, was crucial to the restoration of Judaism precisely because the writer, dissatisfied with the existing (prophetic) conception of Israel's early history, had decided to "recreate the past" and hold up what he believed to be "a truer picture of that past" than had previously been written. To this author, Kuenen ascribed the first story of the creation as well as many passages in Exodus, Leviticus, and Numbers. George Eliot's quotation, cited here only in part because of its length, emphasizes the importance of that re-creation of the past:

> The author of the Book of Origins succeeded in his undertaking: the conception of the past which he advocated, gradually became a part of the consciousness of the Jewish nation, and has remained the traditional account down to the present day; we all begin by picturing Israel to ourselves as he has drawn it; it is only with difficulty that historical criticism has freed itself from the prestige which he exercised over his contemporaries and posterity. Such a success may be of no value as evidence for the historical truth of the picture which he designed, yet it must avail as proof of the power of his mind. And therefore I spoke, in the second place, of the presage which the Book of Origins contains. The priesthood which produces such a book is capable of great things. It is ready to pass to practical ground and there to assume the command. He who is able so to recreate the past, certainly possesses the power to reform the future. The Book of Origins is an achievement and the prophecy of other achievements.[34]

The "complete ideal shape" that Mordecai gives to Hebrew history has the power to reform Daniel's future. But it is through a re-creation of the past that Ezra Mordecai Cohen accomplishes Daniel's reformation. The past becomes an "effect" of present needs or "causes"—the need to rewrite the history of the Jews in light of the restoration Mordecai believes should take place. Thus the narrative does not require that Deronda discover a Jewish origin but rather gives that discovery when it does happen to occur an ideal shape.

The alert reader will surely have noticed that Ezra's name is now also identical with that of the Jewish pawnbroker. Again, the doubling of names dramatizes Kuenen's reinterpretation. In the two "Ezra Cohens," George Eliot has reformed the customary Christian interpretation of the Jewish people. Daniel Deronda first meets Ezra Cohen the stereotypical Jewish pawnbroker, always ready to profit from others, the orthodox Jew, who has apparently banished his sister because she married outside her religion. Later Daniel comes to know Mordecai well and finally to hear his visionary interpretation of the role of Israel in the world. Ezra the "scribe" is now linked with Ezra the prophetic reformer and restorer of Judaism. As Mrs. Meyrick remarks to Daniel, "There are Ezras and Ezras in the world" (628). In her deliberate pairing of "Ezras," George Eliot seeks to reform the reader's interpretation of Judaism, just as Daniel's original conception of the "Ezra Cohens" of London has been reformed by his knowledge of Ezra Mordecai Cohen.

The revelation of Mordecai as Ezra Cohen foreshadows and parallels the revelation of Daniel as a Jew. The hermeneutical model is identical: interpretation reforms history, or as Hans Meyrick expresses it, "present causes" have "past effects." Meyrick's phrase accurately expresses the formation of history through poetic vision. Only his entirely rational and skeptical perspective would prevent him from seeing that Daniel's present affinity for Judaism does, in fact, "cause" his Jewish "origin." Had Mordecai's vision not reformed Daniel's interpretation of Judaism, the revelation of his birth would have had either a different, probably negative, significance, or perhaps—if he had adopted Gideon's "rational" view—no significance at all. But in the words of the narrator, Daniel has received from Mordecai "the complete ideal shape of that personal duty and citizenship which lay in his own thought like sculptured fragments certifying some beauty yearned after but not traceable by divination" (571). That "complete ideal shape," as the narrator's comment indicates, results not from divination of the future but rather from the prophetic or "priestly" recreation of the past.

The same hermeneutic model suggests a solution to the problem of Deronda's circumcision—that unmentioned fact that seemingly embarrasses both the plot and its author. Just as the facts of Judaism probably meant little to Deronda until reinterpreted by Mordecai, so the slightly variant appearance of his penis might have had little importance in the absence of its interpretation as a religious symbol.[35] Kuenen, in fact, suggests precisely this explanation in his discussion of the practice of circumcision among the Jews. Moses found the custom of circumcision already current among the people and, as with other pagan rituals, simply "adopted it as a part of Jahvism," giving it a new interpretation as the sign of Jahveh's covenant with his people.

If the reader, after the revelation of Daniel's origin, applies this "key" to the historical past of the narrative, Daniel's circumcision proves an essential link to a "universal" prophetic significance in the narrative. This is not to suggest, however, that the Victorian reader was previously unaware of the "circumcision" in the text, but only that its significance was most probably limited to its appropriation in Christian liturgy. At the numerical midpoint of the novel, in chapters 35 and 36, the Feast of the Circumcision—though never named—is obvious by its very omission from scenes that dramatize its Christian interpretation. As in her earlier novels, George Eliot appropriates apocalyptic midpoint division, dividing the first half of both Gwendolen and Daniel's histories from the last half in such a way that the "latter prophecy" later interprets the former, revealing the hidden bond between the two.

Henry Alley points out that in *Daniel Deronda* the turning point of the narrative occurs in chapters 35 and 36, or the exact numerical center of the seventy-chapter sequence.[36] In these chapters, Gwendolen decides to begin a new life, and Daniel's condemnation of her changes to sympathy as he learns of the "empire of fear" that her marriage has become. As Savonarola served as human angel to Romola, teaching her a "higher truth" than any she had yet known, so Daniel becomes the "angel," or apocalyptic prophet, of Gwendolen's reformation. Romola's prophetic encounter takes place on Christmas Eve—the eve of a symbolic birth of Christianity—and her "Protestant" reformation is dramatized, appropriately, on the day when Luther would nail his ninety-five theses to the door, October 31. The apocalyptic encounter between Daniel and Gwendolen happens, equally appropriately, on a day symbolic of Hebrew as much as Christian prophecy: New Year's Day, or the Feast of the Circumcision.

The division between the two chapters dramatizes the division between the "old year," or decadent vision of Christianity, and the new year, when Hebrew "priestly" vision reforms history. The Grandcourts first arrive at the Abbey on December 29, in chapter 35. They tour the Abbey and view the conversion of the chapel into a stable—a powerful architectural emblem both of the decay of Gwendolen's proud hopes for her marriage into her humiliating subjection to Grandcourt and the decay of English Christianity into worldliness such as Mr. Gascoigne also represents. Characteristically, Daniel takes off his hat as if he had really entered a church, while Grandcourt sneers, "'Do you take off your hat to the horses?'" (474). Daniel perceives and reverences the historical vision, while Grandcourt sees only the beautiful, pedigreed symbols of wealth and power.

In chapter 36 time moves on to New Year's Day, and Daniel comes to a new understanding of Gwendolen's misery. On New Year's Eve, Gwendolen begs him to tell her what to do, confessing her remorse for having injured others. She has done something even worse than that first act of gambling, which Daniel criticized because she had tried to make her gain from another's loss (500). Daniel urges her to "try to care for what is best in thought and action," something beyond the gratification of her own selfish desires—a general, humanistic counsel that suggests Arnold's *Culture and Anarchy* more than any specifically religious tradition. But on New Year's Day, when Gwendolen comes to him a second time and insists on her remorse, Daniel not only urges her to see the "higher, the religious life" but to "take the present suffering as a painful letting in of light" and to take her fear "as a safeguard."

In this counsel, Victorian readers might have recognized an allusion to Keble's poem for the Circumcision of Christ, written for New Year's Day. Taking the suffering of the Christ child at circumcision as an image of the penitence necessary to begin a new life, or new year, Keble wrote:

> Look here, and hold thy peace:
> The Giver of all good
> E'en from the womb takes no release
> From suffering, tears, and blood.
>
> If thou wouldst reap in love,
> First sow in holy fear:
> So life a winter's morn may prove
> To a bright endless year.[37]

Even more than as an image of the pain and fear necessary to moral regeneration, however, Keble interprets the circumcision as symbolizing the union of the two "churches," Jewish as well as Christian. The "few precious drops" of the child's blood, shed at circumcision, are not only a type of the Crucifixion but also a mark of the grace imparted to Jewish hearts:

> They are the pledge and seal
> Of Christ's unswerving faith
> Given to His Sire, our souls to heal,
> Although it cost His death.
>
> They to His Church of old,
> To each true Jewish heart,
> In Gospel graces manifold
> Communion blest impart.

In Keble's interpretation, the Circumcision symbolizes both covenants, Christian and Jewish, and serves as a "bond of union" that unites history, or saints "parted by a thousand year."

To an unsuspecting Mr. Middleton, Daniel's advice to Gwendolen on New Year's Day appears simply to paraphrase the Christian interpretation of the Circumcision of Christ. In the words of the text for Keble's poem, it dramatizes the "circumcision made without hands"—a painful penitence that can lead to a new life. At this point in the narrative Daniel is presumably, after all, a Christian just like Gwendolen. But if, instead of applying the key of established Christian interpretation to the narrative past, the reader applies the "key" of Daniel's origin—which is not supplied until the fifty-first chapter—both narrative and history will reveal themselves as reshaped by this "present cause." The encounter between Daniel and Gwendolen becomes an emblem of the bond between the circumcision made with hands and the circumcision made without hands. Daniel's advice to Gwendolen confers the spiritual heritage of the Jew on the Christian. The reader now sees that the encounter dramatizes Keble's interpretation of the Feast of the Circumcision in a wider, more "universal" sense as a bond that not only unites Jew and Christian but past and future. We may read the encounter, in fact, as that which relates everything in the book to everything else there.

George Eliot's last novel repeats the lesson of her first: history is not a truth but a fiction, and a fiction dependent on the "key" of interpretation. Neither the traditionalist "Mr. Middletons" nor the rationalist "Hans Meyricks" and "genial Gideons" can lay claim to the truth of history, but the visionary artist may refictionalize the past and so hope to change the future. *Daniel Deronda* is George Eliot's last midrash, a narrative interpretation of interpretation, in which she critiques those "keys" that deny or obscure the hidden bonds of connection. But it is also her Old Testament apocalypse of history—her "Book of Origins" in which she seeks to reinterpret and ultimately to reclaim a prophetic heritage.

Critical history tells us readers have failed to appreciate this visionary aim, but *Daniel Deronda* should finally and radically reform our estimate of George Eliot's sophistication in both historical thought and narrative structure. In this novel she gives prominence to the treatment of causality, not as a given truth, but as a construction of the present. Past "causes" are indeed what present "effects" make them appear to be, and history is seen to be not a divine scheme but the product of human interpretation. As the "origin" must be constructed by the historian, so the text must be constructed, and even deconstructed, by the reader if the writer's interpretation of Jewish history is to emerge from it. Ultimately, the interpretation of everything present in the text depends on the reader's discovery of the crucial element missing from it: the hermeneutics of circumcision. Only if the reader writes into the text the "hidden letters" of this discourse will George Eliot's statement that she meant everything in the novel to be related to everything else seem even remotely comprehensible.

But if the reader "remembers" this quintessentially Victorian key of interpretation, then the text of *Daniel Deronda* emerges as George Eliot's last apocalyptic interpretation—an interpretation of the landscape of time as a common landscape of exile. Homelessness, disinheritance, and alienation, she suggests, are the universal condition unless bridged by a prophetic vision that perceives invisible connections and reinterprets ancient texts by the dim light of our common "night-school." In rewriting the Apocalypse of the Old Testament, George Eliot reaffirms prophecy as both necessary and human.

CHAPTER 6

Revising The Christian Year

George Eliot's 1874 volume of poetry, *The Legend of Jubal*, is little known and even less esteemed among twentieth-century critics.[1] Gordon Haight has commented that readers are hard pressed "to find something to say" about the ten poems in the collection (*GEL*, 6:28, n.4). But recently critics have considered some of the poems individually for the insights they may contribute to our understanding of George Eliot's art, and one critic has proposed that the order of poems in the volume may be thematic.[2] I suggest, however, that the order of the poems derives from and rewrites the Christian liturgical year, especially as John Keble's poems in *The Christian Year* interpret certain feasts and fasts. The resulting collection not only replaces Christian doctrine with humanist ideals but also revises Keble's patriarchal and elitist perspectives with poems that reexamine the value of womanhood and celebrate the community rather than the progress of the individual soul.[3]

In each of the poems selected for the volume, music symbolizes the power of visionary art to give meaning and purpose to an existence limited by death. Although many of Keble's poems exploit the Romantic identification of music and poetry, music is the controlling image for visionary art in all of the *Jubal* poems. Beyond this general thematic and metaphoric coherence, however, George Eliot appears to have created a subtler structure through arranging her poems to respond to Keble's interpretation of Anglican feasts and fasts. *The Legend of Jubal* thus becomes a humanist—and in a certain sense, a feminist—critique of Keble's *Christian Year*.[4] Where Keble's poems manifest a male-oriented, hierarchical, and otherworldly perspective, George Eliot's celebrate the common lot of mortal humanity and particularly praise the "feminine" element designated by the Positive movement as the affective nature of "mankind." As W. M. W. Call explained it, woman's nature had a natural affinity for the Positive system, for the "social instinct" dominated over the selfish in woman, and it was the accepted mission of women to subordinate the most brilliant activities to the purification and regulation of society through the affections.[5] I have already described George Eliot's appropriation in *Romola* of a Comtean interpretation of the apocalyptic "woman clothed with the sun" as a prophetic image of a "new age" to be characterized by feminine values, in contrast with the old age characterized by the masculine values of individualism and heroism.[6] The poems reprinted in *The Legend of Jubal* are miniatures of these new-age apocalyptics, a collection of secular myths and hymns so arranged as to revise the Christian year into a new landscape of time.

The available evidence suggests that George Eliot herself chose the order of the poems—some of which had been published separately—for the 1874 edition, though there is no explicit proof that she did so.[7] In proposing that she rearranged a group of poems written at different times—and probably with no single intention—into a collection intended to be not only thematically but structurally unified, however, I suggest what critics have already proposed concerning other Victorian poetic works, as well as what Keble is known to have done.[8] As James Kilroy comments, readers of Tennyson's *In Memoriam* consistently report "a single, coherent effect and an impression of careful architectonics" despite Tennyson's scattered composition of the lyrics.[9] A. Dwight Culler directly compares *In Memoriam* to Keble's *Christian Year*, suggesting that they differ primarily not in whether individual lyrics were rearranged in a thematically and structurally coherent order but only in the kind of order chosen. Keble arranged his previously written poems according to the liturgical year, while Tennyson arranged his "according to that inward calendar of what he actually felt."[10]

Critics have advanced similar hypotheses about artistic structures achieved through a meaningful arrangement of separate poems in works by Dante Gabriel Rossetti, Christina Rossetti, and Robert Browning.[11] Even the changes made in the 1878 Cabinet edition of *The Legend of Jubal* need not disprove the structure

I perceive in the 1874 edition, for the four poems added at Blackwood's request to the later edition were placed in the section where the 1874 *Jubal*'s correspondence to the Christian calendar seems weakest—the section corresponding to Holy Week. I shall discuss only the earlier edition, however, for I believe George Eliot's intention can be most plainly discerned there.

George Eliot was, in fact, most deeply concerned about this collection of poems, and her remarks about it supply some clues to her conception of the work. On first sending it to Blackwood on March 6, 1874, she remarked that every one of the poems "represents an idea which I care for strongly and wish to propagate as far as I can" (*GEL*, 6:26). Her prophetic motive was equally obvious to Blackwood, who rather cuttingly replied, "if you have any lighter pieces written before the sense of what a great author should do for mankind came so strongly upon you, I should like much to look at them" (*GEL*, 6:37). Not surprisingly, George Eliot made no reply to this comment, confining herself instead to such technical details as price and the placement of commas.

But even her persistent concern about the physical appearance of the volume suggests a part of its poetic lineage. George Eliot wanted *The Legend of Jubal* to resemble the "delightful duodecimo" edition of Keats's *Lamia, Isabella, The Eve of St. Agnes, and Other Poems* (1820). Indeed, the similarities between the two collections are apparent. Like the Keats volume, George Eliot's collection comprises several long poems on mythological and medieval subjects, including one based on a tale from Boccaccio, as well as a number of shorter lyrics. But the differences between the volumes are even more striking. The poems that George Eliot included in her collection are as much indebted to Wordsworth and Browning as to Keats, while one of those she omitted from *Jubal*—"In the South"—seems clearly inspired by Keats's "To Autumn."[12]

An even more significant difference between the two collections, however, derives from the apparent absence of any coherent formal or thematic structure in the Keats volume.[13] After the first three long poems in this collection, a second title page entitled "Poems" is inserted before the remaining group of lyrics. And the volume is completed, if it can be called such, with the fragment of "Hyperion," which ends in the middle of a phrase and was published over Keats's protests. The thematic symmetry of *Jubal*, by contrast, immediately strikes the reader. Beginning with a poem on Jubal's discovery of music—the immortal art created by the mortal artist—the collection ends with the hymn, "O May I Join the Choir Invisible," in which the poet aspires to "that purest heaven," to be to other souls "the cup of strength in some great agony." The order thus begins with the creation and proceeds to the apocalyptic "end," or purpose, of both visionary art and artist.

George Eliot also expressed the desire to have her volume be, like the Keats volume, just the size to slip in the pocket (*GEL*, 6:26). She seems to have wanted it to be something the reader could carry about and delve into, much as she herself may have carried about the little volume of Keble's poems that she received in March 1840 (*GEL*, 1:46). And as the beginning and end of the volume not only readily demonstrate a thematic symmetry, they can also be seen to correspond to the opening and closing of the Anglican liturgical year (omitting the long Trinity season that fills in the calendar from Pentecost to Advent): the awakening of the individual to thoughts of immortality by the apocalyptic trumpet call in Advent and the believer's spiritual ascension with Christ in the Resurrection and Ascension. The second and next-to-last poems also suggest fairly obvious correspondences to Christmas and Good Friday, the former ending with a carol to an "aged mother-maiden," and the latter describing Arion's willing sacrifice of his life for his art. To the reader familiar with Keble's *Christian Year*, only one of the ten poems in George Eliot's collection appears of somewhat dubious relation to the liturgical scheme; the majority are so arranged as to resound in classic harmony with the feasts and fasts of the Christian year.

George Eliot specifically demurred constructing a Positivist liturgy (*GEL*, 6:387), and that is not what I propose she attempted here. Yet it is not surprising that *Jubal* should take the shape of the Christian liturgical year, and in many cases even seem to respond directly to phrases in Keble's poems for the appropriate seasons. For all Anglicans as devout as Mary Ann Evans had been, the system of collects, epistles, gospels, and proper lessons in the *Book of Common Prayer* formed a visionary structure of time, one that not only commemorated the events of a particular history (the life of Christ) but encouraged the believer to participate spiritually in those events, thus endowing the most prosaic individual life with the poetry of history. By following this yearly cycle, especially as interpreted by Keble, the believer united historical past and prophetic future with the present. In imagination, mortality put on immortality. Like countless other Victorians, the young Mary Ann Evans read Keble's poems Sunday by Sunday. When the mature George Eliot selected poems for her own pocket-sized volume, she may have rediscovered the prophetic patterning of *The Christian Year* written among the poetic "scraps" she pieced together in this new tapestry—she may even have recognized hidden threads drawn from certain of Keble's poems. By comparing the poems in the 1874 *Jubal* with those of Keble's to which they appear to respond, both the submerged structure and the distinctively "feminine" and feminist vision of George Eliot's work can be brought into a new and informative perspective.

The poem placed first in the volume, "The Legend of Jubal," was the product of one of George Eliot's most painful experiences: the protracted and painful death of Lewes's son Thornie in the summer of 1869. Unable to concentrate on *Middlemarch*, George Eliot put away the beginnings of the novel and began "Jubal" while nursing Thornie.[14] She finished it in the weeks immediately after his death. Like Milton and Tennyson before her, George Eliot was moved to confront the problem of the poet-prophet's vocation in a world limited by death, but for her there could be no ultimate faith in a divine plan, whether revelationary or evolutionary. In her poem, the justification of visionary art against the fact of death itself lies in its capacity to arouse and express human feeling. Though each "little pulse of self" must die, the ability to participate in a universal harmony of human feeling is a kind of immortality.

But George Eliot gives to her opening poem the form of an advent epic, for "Jubal" restructures the little-known Genesis myth of the creation of the arts into a parallel to the Advent theme of awakening to immortality (Gen. 4:19–24). Following the discovery of death, Jubal creates the art of music through which he awakens his people to "music their larger soul." Immortality springs directly from the knowledge of mortality, as in the epistle for Advent Sunday: "And that, knowing the time, that now it is high time to awake out of sleep: for now is our salvation nearer than when we believed. The night is far spent, the day is at hand: let us therefore cast off the works of darkness, and let us put on the armour of light" (Romans 13:11,12). Keble's poem for Advent Sunday opens with a similarly musical conception of the urgent need to awaken to eternal life:

> Awake—again the Gospel trump is blown—
> From year to year it swells with louder
> tone,
> From year to year the signs of wrath
> Are gathering round the Judge's path,
> Strange words fulfill'd, and mighty works
> achiev'd
> And truth in all the world both hated and
> believ'd.

While "Jubal" takes the same theme as Keble's Advent Sunday poem, however, George Eliot's subject differs substantially. Keble's poem sketches a history of man's errors from the early Christian era onward, while George Eliot returns to the myth of man's original sin, or the inception of mortality. We should note, in passing, that although "Jubal" necessarily begins with reference to the Fall, George Eliot's version cancels the misogynist implications of the biblical myth. Man dies not because of woman's temptation but because of accidental male violence. This significantly feminist reinterpretation of the Fall, however, only serves as prelude to the subject of art, its origin and immortality. And George Eliot's final conception of art's transcendent function suggests her debt to Keble's poem for the Fourth Sunday in Advent even more than for Advent Sunday. Moreover, "Jubal" clarifies George Eliot's major distinction in poetics not only from Keble but from Wordsworth, whose Immortality Ode plainly inspired Keble's poem for the Fourth Sunday in Advent, or "Dimness."[15]

In this poem, Keble dwells on his inability to "read" Nature's book properly—to see divine glory or hear heavenly music with mortal eyes and ears. This Wordsworthian theme receives an un-

Wordsworthian resolution, for the poet concludes by directing the soul to persevere both in "upward looks" and in humble contentment with "one simple strain"—

> Till thou art duly train'd, and taught
>   The concord sweet of Love divine:
> Then, with that inward Music fraught,
>   Forever rise, and sing, and shine.

Keble's resolution is characteristically otherworldly: though the individual must be content with a humble life on this earth, eventually he will "rise," singing that "inward Music" of love, and join the divine concord of the Second Coming. The closing lines of "Jubal" might almost be an expansion of this apocalyptic concert of love:

> The words seemed melting into symphony,
> The wings upbore him, and the gazing song
> Was floating him the heavenly space along,
> Where mighty harmonies all gently fell
> Through veiling vastness, like the far-off bell,
> Till, ever onward through the choral blue,
> He heard more faintly and more faintly knew,
> Quitting mortality, a quenched sun-wave,
> The All-creating Presence for his grave. (41)

Clearly, Jubal also "rises," "sings," and "shines." Yet George Eliot's resolution is not identical with Keble's. The important difference lies in the question of what she meant by the "All-creating Presence."

That "Presence," I would suggest, though it does not correspond to Keble's "Love divine," differs significantly from Wordsworth's creative power also. Karen B. Mann, in comparing "Jubal" to Wordsworth's "On the Power of Sound" (1835), suggests that for both poets "sound" connotes the "power of mind" to perceive and create harmony between the mind and the universe. "It seems apparent," she states, " that Eliot means for music to symbolize mental power of a particular sort."[16] Although George Eliot's use of "music" may at first seem to incorporate the Wordsworthian sense of unity between mind and universe, I shall propose that she emphasizes far more a humanist and Comtean sense of feeling, meaning that power that unites human beings with one another.

"Nature," in George Eliot's poetry, frequently functions as a metaphor for the "inmost deep" of human feeling only. Her poetry almost seems a humanistic inversion of Keble's poetic use of the Doctrine of Analogy, interpreting the "music" of the universe as the tones and rhythms of human, not divine, love.[17]

When Jubal discovers music, for example, the strains he hears may at first suggest the Romantic harmony between man and universe:

> To Jubal such enlarged passion brought,
> That love, hope, rage, and all experience,
> Were fused in vaster being, fetching thence
> Concords and discords, cadences and cries
> That seemed from some world-shrouded soul
>   to rise,
> Some rapture more intense, some mightier
>   rage,
> Some living sea that burst the bounds of
>   man's brief age. (15–16)

But after building his lyre, Jubal uses it to call forth human passions:

> Touching his lyre to full harmonic throb
> And measured pulse, with cadences that sob,
> Exult and cry, and search the inmost deep
> Where the dark sources of new passion sleep. (23)

His listeners find themselves stirred by their own memories of the past and visions of the future, and they are moved by mysterious passions to rise and dance:

> Then Jubal poured more rapture in his psalm,
> The dance fired music, music fired the dance,
> The glow diffusive lit each countenance,
> Till all the circling tribe arose and stood
> With glad yet awful shock of that mysterious
>   good. (24)

As the circle image of the dancing people implies, it is the sphere of human feeling that the poet celebrates. Rather than a vision that half creates, half perceives the unity between individual man and Nature, George Eliot's poet-prophet half-hears and half-creates the music of the human community—the dance of a "circling tribe."

When Jubal sets out in search of "higher mountains," his journey does not lead to an apocalypse of meaning like that of Wordsworth's in the Alps.[18] Jubal's search for higher mountains instead seems to signify his poetic ambition—an individualism represented as opposed to his art—for his song grows weaker as he travels, and eventually he becomes unable to "Tell what the earth is saying unto me" (29). Apart from his people, Jubal can no longer hear earth's harmony; his search for higher peaks and newer songs represents an unproductive direction for poetic development.[19]

Yet when, unrecognized by his own people, Jubal lies down to die, he finds himself once again surrounded by "great Song" (38). In the midst of his music, a vision—which we note is that of a human face—appears and explains Jubal's great joy and the immortality of his music as his power to give that music to others:

> But thy expanding joy was still to give,
> And with the generous air in song to live
> Feeding the wave of ever-widening bliss
> Where fellowship means equal perfectness. (40)

His lot has been "to feel, create, bestow" and to shine "in man's soul," though his own fleshly self must shrivel and die. The "All-creating Presence," therefore must represent the harmony that one human being gives to another, the music of fellowship and "equal perfectness," differing both from the Romantic emphasis on the visionary perception of Nature and Keble's on the restoration of divine harmony in the "Second Advent."

George Eliot's unpublished poem on a female poet, "Erinna," seems to pose even more definitively the origin of poetry from human feeling rather than from Nature.[20] In this most interesting poem, George Eliot describes the classical poet Erinna who, according to a preceding note in her poetry notebook, died in early youth when chained by her mother to her spinning wheel. Isolated from the world of action and "primal" work, Erinna seeks some pattern to shape her song of "lonely pain." This pattern she cannot take from the "piercing flute" of Cybele, the earth mother, because Cybele is "deaf to human care" and impartial to good and ill alike. It is from Pallas Athena, "Master in loving!," that Erinna finds "the pattern thy sweet love hath set," suggesting, as Bernard J. Paris comments, that Athena's love and intelligence are necessary for Erinna's poetic design of a "human, moral order."[21]

Both "Erinna" and "Jubal," then, posit the origin and function of visionary poetry chiefly within the sphere of humanity—a humanity seen under its "feminine" or social aspect, regardless of the gender of the poet. For George Eliot, as other poems in the *Jubal* collection will demonstrate, this humanist and Comtean interpretation of poetics is distinctively nonelitist: it divests the individual poet of the special authority Romanticism accorded him. As Michael H. Bright has pointed out, the Romantic poet's paradoxical claim both to "an extraordinary ability to commune with the spiritual world" and to an egalitarian brotherhood with the common man veered more and more toward an elitist authority in the Oxford Movement's conception of the priestly role.[22] George Eliot's poems on the origin of visionary art may thus be seen as a critique of Keble's (Romantic) elevation of the poet-prophet's privileged vision.

"The Legend of Jubal" not only reinterprets the Advent theme of awakening to the apocalyptic trump but seems to transform Keble's treatment of that theme from a heavenly to a human music. The second poem in *Jubal*, "Agatha," appears to respond even more directly to Keble's poem for Christmas Day. In this poem, Keble develops a typological interpretation of the Nativity. As Charlotte Yonge expressed in her *Musings over the Christian Year and Lyra Innocentium*, the reader should mark "at what words of the message the Angels broke into rejoicing; namely, at the revelation that the Deity had become Incarnate, and was actually tabernacling among men. . . . He is verily born in the heart of the faithful Christian, enthroned in the pure virgin bosom."[23] In short, Keble's poem represents the birth of Christ to the Virgin Mary as a type of Christ's indwelling in pure hearts.[24] Allusion to the Virgin Mary legend pervades "Agatha," but more importantly, Agatha herself manifests the birth in a "pure virgin bosom" of a Christ-like love for others. In addition, George Eliot's poem ends with a pastoral carol that, as we shall see, precisely fulfills Keble's concluding exhortation.

"Agatha" is set in the rural village of "Sanct Margen," or as the poem translates the name, "Holy little Mary." Both setting and subject actually derive from a spot the Leweses visited from May to July of 1868. George Eliot later commented that "there was really an aged woman among those green hills who suggested the picture of Agatha" (GEL, 6:49). The poem, however, was probably written either in December 1868 or January 1869, as George Eliot inscribed a copy given to Mrs. Cross in January 1874, "Christmas, 1868," thus strongly suggesting her own association of the poem with Christmas.[25]

The poem opens with an Annunciation-like episode in which Agatha's simple goodness and loving care for others are revealed in a dialogue with an "angel"—the Countess Linda. The poet then speaks, describing the mixture of jesting and reverence with which the local people speak of Agatha and the other two elderly women for whom she provides a home. The song with which the poem closes strikes the reader as indeed a curious, almost macabre mixture, singing both of the accidental death of "Toni," and of the "little maidens old.... Mothers ye, who help us all." The closing couplets clearly designate the song as a Christmas carol, saluting the Virgin Mary, the Holy Babe, Joseph, the Virgin's mother, and the angel Gabriel. But it can also be seen that the carol responds directly to the closing lines of Keble's poem, "So shall ye tread untir'd His pastoral ways, / And in the darkness sing your carol of high praise." The singers in George Eliot's rural idyll are literally treading a pastoral way in the darkness, returning home from a feast after midnight. Their carol mingles praise of the biblical saints with praise and prayers for the living saint, the "aged mother-maiden," in their midst.

In "Agatha," George Eliot transposes a type of Christ-like humility and love into the terms of musical humanism. Like Dorothea in *Middlemarch*, Agatha is conceived as a poem or "song." As she describes her life of charity and prayer, the Countess Linda comments: "That is your way of singing, Agatha ...," though the old woman demurs, "Nay I cannot sing" (54). George Eliot's poetic conception echoes Browning's in "Transcendentalism: A Poem in Twelve Books":

> So come, the harp back to your heart again!
> You are a poem, though your poem's naught.[26]

As John Joyce points out, "The message is that poets must 'sing' to create the magic of their art.... Browning saw the dramatic monologue form as a vehicle which allows a poet the opportunity to avoid 'dry' philosophizing and to 'sing.'"[27] Here, the poem of old Agatha's life is finally given the shape of an actual song—a simple, pastoral carol meant to embody the simple virtue of her life.

But George Eliot's "carol," while both imitating Keble's typological example and fulfilling his closing exhortation, may also be seen as a humanist and even feminist response to his. Keble's poem, like all Christmas literature, celebrates the Virgin's motherhood. George Eliot's "Christmas" poem, however, deliberately celebrates the life of a spinster. (There are, in fact, no poems on motherhood in *Jubal*.) The life George Eliot finds worthy of poetic praise is truly that of the "least of women": Agatha has neither "primal" work nor marriage to justify her existence. She typifies the most restricted domesticity of women: their confinement to small worlds, trivial tasks, and inevitable poverty. Yet Agatha manages not only to maintain herself independently but to nurture others—she is a perfect type of those "feminine" values elevated in Positivism, "the purification and regulation of society through the affections," while contrasting with the Christian celebration of marriage and motherhood for women.

If old Agatha is herself a "song," a human lyre, "Armgart" is a music-drama, a small "opera" that plays subtly on the conventions and innovations of the very musical form it dramatizes. The conflict between art and the artist that forms the subject of the poem takes on added meaning from Gluck's *Orfeo ed Eurydice*, the opera most frequently referred to in the poem. Moreover, the placement of the poem in *Jubal*, by suggesting its relation to the post-Christmas commemorations of martyrdom, illuminates the significance of Armgart's loss of her voice as a sacrifice necessary for a greater good.

The three poems immediately following that for Christmas Day in *The Christian Year* commemorate three kinds of martyrdom. As Keble explains in a footnote to the poem for St. Stephen's Day (December 26), the first is in both will and deed (St. Stephen), the second in will but not in deed (St. John the Evangelist), and the third in deed but not in will (Holy Innocents). It is to the third—and to Keble's poem for Holy Innocents—that "Armgart" seems to respond, for Armgart suffers a martyrdom comparable to that of "Rachel," the collective name for the mothers of infants killed by Herod in an attempt to murder the infant Christ. Armgart's voice, the vehicle for her art, is itself a "holy innocent"—a supreme gift that I shall argue the poem defends as not only "divine" but "natural" for a woman. Yet through accepting her loss like a bereaved mother, burying her "little corpse" and learning "to love / Another's living child" (135), Armgart becomes part of a greater "song." Her fate demonstrates George Eliot's insistence on an egalitarian poetic—the singer is not greater than the song.

The great interest of "Armgart" for the modern reader lies in its convincing presentation of the conflict, not just between art and the artist but specifically between the *woman* artist and her art. The poem suggests comparison to Elizabeth Barrett Browning's *Aurora Leigh* (1857), which also questions (and defends) the validity of the woman artist's vocation.[28] But the circumstances of "Armgart" suggest its more immediate connection to music—and to death. In March 1870, the Leweses embarked on a two-month trip to Germany and Austria, during which they attended many concerts and operas. George Eliot's idea for a poem concerning a woman artist's loss of her voice came to her following this trip. The timing of the poem suggests a deeply personal aspect, for since Thornie's death in the summer of 1869, she had not been able to return to the writing of *Middlemarch*. Perhaps in "Armgart," she was able to work through the fear that she herself might lose her "voice," and with it her very identity. It seems significant that shortly after writing "Armgart," she began work on the "Miss Brooke" section of *Middlemarch*.

Whatever motivation we may speculate lies behind the poem, however, Armgart's defense of her art as "supreme vocation"—

against Graf's various arguments of its unwomanliness—is persuasive. Not only does the singer protest her lack of "mean vanity," but the intensity of her feeling about her art startles, and tends to convince, the reader. As Walpurga explains to Graf in the first scene:

> For herself,
> She often wonders what her life had been
> Without that voice for channel to her soul.
> She says, it must have leaped through all
>   her limbs—
> Made her a Maenad—made her snatch a brand,
> And fire some forest, that her rage might mount
> In crashing roaring flames through half a land,
> Leaving her still and patient for a while.
> "Poor wretch!" she says, of any murderess—
> "The world was cruel, and she could not sing:
> I carry my revenges in my throat;
> I love in singing, and am loved again." (73)

Poetic feeling seems much closer here to Keble's theory, which Stephen Prickett describes as more like the safety valve on a steam boiler, than to the mere spring or fountain of Wordsworth's poetics.[29] Armgart *must* have the vent of music or she may go mad, become a pyromaniac or a murderess.

This intensity of poetic feeling typically characterizes George Eliot's female artist figures. The Princess Halm-Elberstein, for example, remarks bitterly to her son Daniel Deronda: "you can never imagine what it is to have a man's force of genius in you, and yet to suffer the slavery of being a girl."[30] The Princess's almost equally convincing defense of her art is introduced by a stanza from "Erinna" that also presents forcefully the woman artist's pent-up feeling:

> She held the spindle as she sat,
> Erinna with the thick-coiled mat
> Of raven hair and deepest agate eyes,
> Gazing with a sad surprise
> At surging visions of her destiny—
> To spin the byssus drearily
> In insect-labour, while the throng
> Of gods and men wrought deeds that poets wrought in song.

Each of these three female artists describes her need for self-expression in art as deep and compelling—a need that strongly suggests its sincerity, or "naturalness."

In addition, Armgart's rebuttal of her suitor's arguments that she should give up her art for the sake of others seems far more defensible than the Princess Halm-Eberstein's. Armgart has not, after all, deserted a child. It is rather her suitor whose motives appear somewhat questionable. When Graf attempts to persuade Armgart to subordinate her art to marriage because "A woman's rank / Lies in the fulness of her womanhood: / Therein alone she is royal," her scornful reply reveals his own hypocritical egotism:

> Yes, I know
> The oft-taught Gospel: "woman, thy desire
> Shall be that all superlatives on earth
> Belong to men, save the one highest kind—
> To be a mother. Thou shalt not desire
> To do aught save pure subservience:
> Nature has willed it so!" (92–93)

Again, Armgart's argument that since nature gave her her voice, her singing can hardly be considered unnatural, seems unarguable. As Kathleen Blake comments, at this point "the poem seems to be with her," despite the apparently contradictory outcome in which Armgart, instead of triumphing as an artist, loses her voice.[31] If the arguments for the woman artist's need for self-expression are as convincing as we think they are, then we must conclude—as do Sandra M. Gilbert and Susan Gubar—that although George Eliot sympathized with her "Satanic Eve," she was unable to integrate passionate poetic feeling with a woman's role and could devise no other fit reward for her female artist than a "fall into gender."[32]

But "Armgart" has a subtle ironic resonance detectable only in relation to the music referred to in the poem. This musical clue suggests that the artistic problem concerns the conflict between poetic elitism and humanistic egalitarianism as much as art and the woman's role. The very part chosen by Armgart—that of Orfeo in Gluck's opera—both adds to her defense of the woman artist's vocation and undermines her personal claim to "supreme vocation." After her triumphant performance as Orfeo, Armgart crowns the bust of Gluck with a wreath, insisting that her song was so passionate the composer himself "sang, not listened: every linked note / Was his immortal pulse that stirred in mine" (75). She refuses to take seriously her teacher's scolding for her unnecessary trill which, she protests, was added "At nature's prompting, like the nightingales" (76).

But Gluck's opera *Orfeo ed Eurydice* was written specifically to reform the Metastasian Italian opera, with its unnecessary and undramatic ornamentation. Calzabigi, who wrote the libretto for the opera, is said to have begged Gluck to banish "*i passagi, le cadenze, i ritornelli* and all the Gothic, barbarous and extravagant things that have been introduced into our music."[33] By introducing a trill wholly for artistic embellishment, Armgart contravenes the artistic identity she claims to feel with Gluck and reveals both her ambition and her lack of artistic depth. The wreath she places on his bust would probably have been rejected by the composer.

On the other hand, the specifics of the opera strongly confirm Armgart's defense of the naturalness of her voice and therefore of the rightness of her singing. When she tells Graf that Nature gave her a voice "Such as she only gives a woman child," and that

> Men did not say, when I had sung last night,
> "'Twas good, nay, wonderful, considering
> She is a woman"—and then turn to add,
> "Tenor or baritone had sung her songs
> Better, of course: she's but a woman spoiled" (93)

she doubtless alludes to the fact that Gluck originally wrote the part of Orpheus for a *castrato* contralto. When the opera was translated into French, the part was rewritten for a tenor, since the French opera did not employ *castrato* singers. But since many listeners felt the part sounded better in its original contralto range, in 1859 Berlioz rearranged the Paris version of the opera into a key suitable for a contralto rather than a tenor, and the part of Orfeo was sung by a woman in this version.[34] Armgart's words thus take on a double force in reference to the part she has just sung, for Orfeo was definitely not better sung by a tenor, and indeed only a most unnatural male voice—that of a "spoiled" man—could sing the part as it was originally conceived by the composer.

The operatic undertones of this little drama make it clear that the problem of the woman artist's vocation was not a simple one for George Eliot. The demands of the music itself suggest that Armgart's ambition is unacceptable: in the eyes of the poet, personal ambition conflicts with "supreme vocation" in art, as Gluck's operatic reform perfectly exemplifies. The egotistical artist cannot transcend ego through her art. But the demands of the music also prove that women's voices are essential, and men's cannot be substituted. How then can the woman artist resolve this dilemma?

Just as Armgart's raptures about her art tend to convince the reader and successfully obscure the evidence of her ambition, so her later protests about the awful state of womanhood without the gift of artistic vocation are too persuasive. Her description of the ordinary woman's lot as "a dog's life! / A harnessed dog's . . ." is as intense as her earlier description of her need to sing—and as deceptive. Armgart has wrongfully believed that her song lifted her apart from her sisters, who were "empty of divineness" (115). The loss of her voice is not a good thing in itself, but as Walpurga teaches her, it can lead to "new birth—birth from that monstrous Self" (129). It is not accidental, I think, that Armgart's original statement, "I love in singing, and am loved again," was spoken by Walpurga, for it has really been Walpurga whose "song" was "loving, and being loved again." Now, in her painful discovery of kinship with others who, like Walpurga and Leo, have no personal artistic success to buoy them up, Armgart can accept her part in the common lot of humanity. Through giving up one small voice —like those "Rachels" who suffered the loss of their innocent infants—Armgart joins in the universal chorus of humanity.

The poem revises Keble's theme, "Oh, joy for Rachel's broken heart!," because Armgart's martyrdom—though not desired—accomplishes a greater good. The singer can learn to love "another's living child"—and to benefit from hearing someone else sing the great theme of freedom and fellowship in Beethoven's *Fidelio*. And though George Eliot accords her a kind of artistic martyrdom, the resolution of the poem does not contradict Armgart's earlier statement that she can "live unmated, but not live / Without the bliss of singing to the world, / And feeling all my world respond to me." Armgart is now able to feel the world's response, and therefore to truly experience "the bliss of singing to the world." She will also probably live unmated, for Graf's final letter suggests his fickleness more than anything else.[35]

As Blake suggests, the conclusion of the poem "takes careful sorting," for no simple conflict between art and a woman's role is proposed. Rather, the poem presents a convincing and subtle defense of the woman artist's need for self-expression as wholly comparable to that of the male artist's—as natural, as strong, and as irresistible as Keble's description of the very essence of poetic feeling. But the poem presents this defense in the context of the larger conflict between poetic elitism and George Eliot's conception of the egalitarian nature of visionary art. Armgart's conflict bears comparison with Jubal's as much as with the Princess Halm-Eberstein's or Erinna's. In George Eliot's poetics, the attempt to scale personal peaks of ambition means that the artist, whether male or female, will cease to hear the "earth's" music.

The next poem in the volume, "How Lisa Loved the King," exhibits no obvious relationship to major liturgical feasts or fasts. The subject of the poem does appear, however, to parallel Keble's poem for the First Sunday after Christmas, or the last Sunday in the year. The theme of Keble's poem, as Charlotte Yonge points out, is that "love—one moment of sincere love, outweighs in God's balance all that world of folly and sin behind. Such love as *she* brought to whom 'much was forgiven because she loved much,' is the love here meant" (38). In "How Lisa Loved the King," a king forgives the folly and presumption of a young girl's love for him because, like Mary Magdalene, she "loved much." The poem thus appears to be, like "Agatha," a secular and humanistic revision of the celebration of divine love. But the circumstances of "Lisa" also suggest that the poem corrects the conceptions of both art and womanhood in Keats's poem "Isabella."[36] Where music is the medium for the knowledge of death in "Isabella," it communicates the knowledge of love in "Lisa." And where Isabella's love becomes the focus of male violence and eventually leads to her own insanity and death, the purity of Lisa's love breaks through patriarchal perceptions of social rank and restores her to health and happiness.

George Eliot never detailed her motives for writing "Lisa"—

completed in February 1869 after the writing of "Agatha"—other than to state that the poem was begun "simply with the longing to fulfil an old intention, and with no distinct thought of printing" (*GEL*, 5:16). But her emphasis on the 1820 Keats volume that included "Isabella," and the fact that both poems rewrite a Boccaccian tale, suggest that she may have intended to respond to Keats's poem.[37] Although admittedly speculative, this intention seems particularly likely when we see how similar the two poems are in certain details and how precisely opposed in their implications.

Boccaccio's macabre tale—the story of a young woman who hears the ghostly music of her dead lover in a vision, disinters his skull and replants it in a pot of basil, only to pine away when her basil pot is stolen—seems to have intrigued George Eliot as much as Keats. At the conclusion of *Middlemarch*, Lydgate calls Rosamond his basil plant, remarking bitterly that "basil was a plant which had flourished wonderfully on a murdered man's brains."[38] But the poem "Lisa" suggests George Eliot may have judged "Isabella" much as Matthew Arnold did, considering its main action far from the Aristotelian ideal despite its "vivid and picturesque turns of expression."[39] In Keats's poem, music carries a pervasively melancholic and even funereal connotation, Isabella's love for her dead lover has disturbing erotic implications, and her behavior after her lover's death is morbid if not insane. The poem, in fact, seems to revel in its own morbidity. "Lisa," by contrast, is so full of sweetness and light as to stand convicted of Victorian healthy-mindedness. But the narrative circumstances of "Lisa" are similar enough to those of "Isabella" to suggest the former was written to balance the latter with a neatly paired opposition.

In both narratives, a young Florentine woman of a rich, mercantile family threatens to pine away because of a love deemed socially inappropriate by her family. And in both narratives, music becomes the medium of communication for that love. There, however, the similarity between the two narratives ends and opposition begins, for in Keats's poem music communicates the knowledge of death and violence while in George Eliot's it communicates the purity and idealism of Lisa's love. Isabella responds to the ghostly music of her dead lover by digging up his skull and subsequently reburying it, thereafter sitting beside it and weeping, while Lisa's song not only results in the restoration of her health but confers a measure of egalitarianism on the society by winning the king's respect for a commoner. Music, or visionary art, has only an aesthetic function in Keats's poem but a moral function in George Eliot's. In addition, where Keats's heroine passively accepts her brothers' violence and is reduced to self-destructive acts, George Eliot's actively works to regain her health and freedom. Though not a poet herself, Lisa seeks out music written by another to express her feeling and to communicate with her loved one.

Most significantly of all, the two poets attribute radically opposed conceptions of love to their female protagonists. Keats dramatizes the erotic and guilty implications of Isabella's love for a man who is of lower status than she, while George Eliot emphasizes the purity of Lisa's love for a king:

> Who was it felt the deep mysterious glow,
> The impregnation with supernal fire
> Of young ideal love—transformed desire,
> Whose passion is but worship of that Best
> Taught by the many-mingled creed of each young breast? (141)

The expression of Lisa's love in Minuccio's song not only brings the king to Lisa, restoring her to health but has an effect upon her society that is supposed to be at once ennobling and egalitarian. The king and queen accept Lisa's love as a kind of "standard," symbolized by the king's wearing of Lisa's colors. In this instance, ambitious, or "high flown," love is fully acceptable, since it has no thought of personal elevation but aspires only to its own purity.

"Lisa" thus appears to revise both misogynistic and aesthetic readings of Keats's poem. But it can also stand as an appropriate humanistic version of Keble's poem for the last Sunday of the year, for the latter is based on the Isaiah text in which divine love restores a king to health (Isa. 38). In George Eliot's poem, the purifying love of a young girl restores a king to moral and social health, giving him a new sense of the worth of a socially unexalted subject, and informing his whole society with a new and higher standard of love. Finding in secular history a counterpart to biblical history, the poem provides a humanist example of Keble's theme that "what cannot be, Love counts it done," as well as what Call described as the "feminine" purification and regulation of society through the affections.

As the first three poems deal with the great theme of love as related to Keble's poems for Christmas and year-end feasts and fasts, it is appropriate that the next poem in *Jubal* should correspond to the Epiphany theme, or the manifestation of the divine. Of Keble's seven poems for the Epiphany season, Charlotte Yonge commented that the poem for the Sixth Sunday after Epiphany— "The Benefits of Uncertainty"—was one of his most "poetical" and most frequently reprinted (64). The poem, like the collect, epistle, and gospel for Sixth Epiphany, concerns Christ's final epiphany in the Second Advent. Keble, however, seems to turn his poem into an attack on one of the most popular aspects of Evangelical Christianity: fervent expectations and precise predictions of the Second Advent. George Eliot's poem "A Minor Prophet" also criticizes apocalyptic "prophets" but proceeds to present a major defense of prophetic vision on the same grounds for which Keble attacks it— its human origin.

The speaker in Keble's poem first deems "unwise" those who long for the "dawning morn," for initial uncertainty makes every victory more precious. He continues, as Yonge notes, with analogies to a number of things made more precious by their very frailty or uncertainty: "the frail flower, the changeful spring, the last-born babe," and, finally, the fate of our immortal souls. He then asserts the inadequacy of human visions of heaven because of their derivation from images of earthly existence:

> What is the heaven we idly dream?
> The self-deceiver's dreary theme,
> A cloudless sun that softly shines,
> Bright maidens and unfailing vines,
> The warrior's pride, the hunter's mirth,
> Poor fragments all of this low earth:
> Such as in sleep would hardly soothe
> A soul that once had tasted of immortal Truth.

> What is the Heaven our God bestows?
> No Prophet yet, no Angel knows;
> Was never yet created eye
> Could see across Eternity;

> Not seraph's wing for ever soaring
> Can pass the flight of souls adoring,
> That nearer still and nearer grow
> To th'unapproached Lord, once made for them so low.

The poem closes with an image of the anonymity of "souls adoring" who daily lose themselves in hope and whose earthly growth is "unseen, unfelt" like the lowly violet, yet who will one day be wakened by the breath of God into "od'rous bloom." The unheroic, unknown character of Christian lives on earth thus becomes an image for the unknowability of the final apocalypse: as only God sees the soul's earthly growth, so only God sees heaven. Keble's message is clear: since all human attempts at prophetic vision are but "poor fragments all of this low earth," visions and dreams are best relegated to the mysteries of God.

"A Minor Prophet" begins with a theme similar to Keble's: the absurdity of some varieties, at least, of apocalyptic prophecy. George Eliot left no clues about her motivation for this poem other than to suggest its matter had first been written in prose three or four years earlier and had originally been entitled "My Vegetarian Friend" (*GEL*, 4:174). In a gently humorous vein, the speaker in the poem proceeds as if describing an actual visit to "Elias Baptist Butterworth,"

> A harmless, bland, disinterested man,
> Whose ancestors in Cromwell's day believed
> The Second Advent certain in five years. (175)

In Elias's millennial vision, the earth will become too perfect for anything as imperfect as animals—

> Earth will hold
> No stupid brutes, no cheerful queernesses,
> No naive cunning, grave absurdity.
> Wart-pigs with tender and parental grunts,
> Wombats much flattened as to their contour,
> Perhaps from too much crushing in the ark. (180)

Instead, "all these rude products" will disappear, along with "every faulty human type" because of "diet vegetarian."

But Elias's conception of earthly perfection disturbs George Eliot's prophet persona. Stating "bitterly" that change is bought only with sacrifice and that he cannot enter warmly into any joys save those of "faulty, struggling human kind," he identifies himself with Spenser's pastoral poet-prophet:

> Speaking in parable, I am Colin Clout.
> A clinging flavor penetrates my life—
> My onion is imperfectness: I cleave
> To nature's blunders, evanescent types
> Which sages banish from Utopia. (183)

Yet George Eliot's "Colin Clout" makes it clear that his faith does rest in a kind of perfection:

> I too rest in faith
> That man's perfection is the crowning flower,
> Toward which the urgent sap in life's great tree
> Is pressing,—seen in puny blossoms now,
> But in the world's great morrows to expand
> With broadest petal and with deepest glow. (185)

But this faith, and therefore his visions, are rooted in human imperfection, in unheroic and unsung human struggle—those "puny blossoms" that will someday expand in "the world's great morrows." Life presses toward human perfection, not an apocalyptic or millennial perfection of the earth.

But George Eliot then questions, in vein parallel to Keble's, whether even prophetic visions of human perfection are valid. Speculating on the vast distance between "the patched and plodding citizen" and the examples of "mighty men and mighty deeds" that can only hold out a hope to him "like the brilliant west / Telling of sunrise in a world unknown," Colin suggests that

> Maybe 'tis wiser not to fix a lens
> Too scrutinizing on the glorious times
> When Barbarossa shall arise and shake
> His mountain. (187–88)

Perhaps such visions are, even though more human than Elias Baptist Butterworth's, still too heroic, too perfect. The prophet then answers his own objection:

> Yet no! the earth yields nothing more Divine
> Than high prophetic vision—than the Seer
> Who fasting from man's meaner joy beholds

> The paths of beauteous order, and constructs
> A fairer type, to shame our low content.
> But prophecy is like potential sound
> Which turned to music seems a voice sublime
> From out the soul of light; but turns to noise
> In scrannel pipes, and makes all ears averse. (188)

George Eliot's Colin Clout defends prophetic vision for the same reason Keble disavows it—because it is composed only of "poor fragments all of this low earth." But from these images of "faulty, struggling human kind," the humanist prophet constructs a "fairer type, to shame our low content." Thus, in lines used as the motto for the final book of *Middlemarch*, and characterizing Dorothea Brooke,

> Full souls are double mirrors, making still
> An endless vista of fair things before
> Repeating things behind. (189)

Even from examples of apparent failure, the humanist prophet creates a prophecy, a "fairer type" of those who aspire to human perfection.

"A Minor Prophet" thus makes a major defense and interpretation of prophetic vision that seems to answer Keble's Sixth Epiphany poem, "The Benefits of Uncertainty." Prophetic vision is "potential sound," which can be either sublime music or noise from "scrannel pipes," but because absurd prophetic visions exist does not mean we should eschew prophecy in general and cultivate dimness of vision. Indeed, "A Minor Prophet" might almost be seen as a poem on Keble's text: "Beloved, now are we the sons of God, and it doth not yet appear what we shall be." Nothing is more "Divine," replies George Eliot, than the Seer's construction of "fairer types," those images of what humanity has struggled to be and therefore of "what we shall be." George Eliot's conception suggests Tennyson's *In Memoriam*, in which Arthur Hallam stands as a type of what mankind will become. But in George Eliot's scheme, no divine plan shapes this development, only human vision.[40]

Finally, George Eliot's poem ends with a secular image of unheroic and anonymous souls that nevertheless, as in Keble's poem, are part of a spiritual movement toward a great end. But where Keble's souls lost in hope are like violets that will one day bloom again in the breath of God, George Eliot's are part of the wide ocean that pushes the rushing tide "to the level of the cliff." They are like "patriots who seem to die in vain," but who make "liberty more sacred by their pangs." Where Keble makes the certainty of apocalypse a rationale for the uncertainty of apocalyptic visions, George Eliot defends prophetic vision as essential to human progress.

The first five poems in *Jubal* suggest themes from feasts and fasts associated with Christmas, the first major feast of the year. The second five poems similarly appear to cluster around Easter themes. The thesis of a collective correspondence to the liturgical year seems weakest, however, in relation to Holy Week. Only two poems can be clearly related to Holy Week themes, while another ("Two Lovers") is so slight that its importance to any poetic scheme is difficult to discern. As I have earlier suggested, this may explain the later insertion of four additional poems in this section of the volume—if it was, in fact, George Eliot who was responsible for the placement of poems in the 1878 *Jubal*.[41] Keble's *Christian Year* leans toward the liturgically more important Easter celebration, containing a poem for every day in Holy Week as well as for all the Sundays in Lent and the three Sundays preceding the Lenten season.

In any case, the sixth poem in the 1874 *Jubal*—a group of eleven Shakespearean sonnets entitled "Brother and Sister"—echoes and revises Keble's themes for the pre-Lenten Sundays called Septuagesima, Sexagesima, and Quinquagesima. As Charlotte Yonge commented, at this time "our Sunday year begins to adapt itself to the time of Easter—when following the old beginning of the year, the course of reading reverts to the opening record in the Bible" (67). Keble's poems for the three pre-Lenten Sundays accordingly treat the Creation, Fall, and the first and second Covenants in which God's love redeemed his people. Closely paralleling Keble's themes, George Eliot's sonnets of childhood describe her own creation as a poet and her early schooling in love. Yet these seemingly transparent lyrics resonate with undeclared reversals and oblique criticisms. In "Brother and Sister," George

Eliot seems to revise not only Keble's patriarchal view of woman but Wordsworth's poetic view of sisters.

George Eliot originally wrote the "Brother and Sister" sonnets in the summer of 1869, completing them just before she attempted the first beginning of *Middlemarch*, only to turn to another poem—"Jubal." She later described the "childhood of a brother and sister" as "one of my best loved subjects" (*GEL*, 5: 403), and the poem is certainly the most personal and moving in the volume. Although the similarity to incidents recounted in the *Mill on the Floss* almost startles the reader (since the poem was written nearly ten years after the novel), the poem suggests that time had wrought more than forgiveness for a still uncommunicative brother. In these images of a "little sister," George Eliot finds her own Wordsworthian "spots of time"—the seed time for a distinctively female poetic mind.

"Brother and Sister" at first seems derivative, even imitative, of Wordsworth's account of his poetic development in the opening books of the *Prelude*. For example, where Wordsworth hears "notes that are / The ghostly language of the ancient earth" (Book II, ll. 308–9), George Eliot hears "a happy strange solemnity, / A deep-toned chant from life unknown to me" (195). (Although this is the only explicit reference to music, the entire poem rests—as do the opening books of the *Prelude*—on the metaphor of early childhood experience as the primal notes of the poet's music.) Again, Wordsworth describes his childhood hours as "fair seed-time" for his soul; George Eliot states that "Those hours were seed to all my after good" (197). And Wordsworth's salute to "ye Presences of Nature" that "Impressed upon all forms the characters / Of danger or desire . . ." (Book I, ll. 464–73) seems rephrased in George Eliot's

> Thus rambling we were schooled in deepest lore,
> And learned the meanings that give words a soul,
> The fear, the love, the primal passionate store,
> Whose shaping impulses make manhood whole. (197)

Yet despite her inability even to escape the masculine gender for maturity here, George Eliot's attempt at her own poetic "spots of time" nevertheless contains fundamentally different emphases from Wordsworth's—emphases that are crucially female. As much as it echoes the *Prelude*, "Brother and Sister" suggests even more a reversed "Tintern Abbey," for poetic development is rooted first in the relationship between a brother and sister and only secondarily in that between child and nature. Wordsworth's tribute to his sister ends his poem—George Eliot describes her relationship with her brother as the spring of all her later "texts." Love and awe for her brother inform the little girl's perception of the natural world, whereas Wordsworth is characteristically solitary in his perception of Nature. George Eliot takes even her image of fear—the "dark smile" of a gypsy that startles the child at play—from the realm of human relations, in contrast with Wordsworth's description of solitary fear: the "grim" and unknowable shape that towers between the child and the stars (Book I, ll. 357–424). From her earliest beginnings, George Eliot's poetic re-creation suggests that love creates the female poet, that the sibling comes before the scene.

Secondly, "Brother and Sister" suggests that it is from her creation in love, and her consequent awareness of differences between the perception of the sexes, that the female poet learns irony. In the *Prelude*, Wordsworth describes his childhood education in the "forms" and symbolic meanings essential to poetry, but George Eliot speaks of learning

> ... chronicles which yield me many a text,
> Where irony still finds an image meet
> Of full-grown judgments in this world perplext. (199)

In this and the succeeding sonnet she describes how the little sister's guilt is turned to merit, and then to mere luck. The seemingly simple incident of catching the silver perch disguises ironic layers of differing male and female perceptions: where the little sister perceived only her guilt and disobedience, the brother has his eye on the fish and praises her for catching it. But again, where the gardener probably would have praised her brother's skill in fishing, he praises the little sister's luck. One cannot help suspecting that for the mature poet, the incident took on even more ironic implications from the consciousness of that dreamy little sister's "luck" in later life.

Indeed, the most Wordsworthian image in the poem—the moment when "sky and earth" merge in some "strange new light" and carry the child on toward "the vast unknown"—also becomes the crux of its irony, for the little sister's immersion in this poetic vision elicits her brother's anger rather than a great poem. The incident seems to deliberately upset Wordsworth's model of developing poetic vision, slyly suggesting that the mind of a future female poet might be distracted from the contemplation of Nature, rather than exhorted to it, by the imperious authority of an older brother.

In its entirety, then, the poem substitutes a social for a solitary model of poetic development, suggesting through undeclared but recognizable reversals of Wordsworthian imagery how differently the muse appears through the eyes of the little sister. Most notable is the characteristically feminine interest in social relationships, and the development of the female imagination in and through such a relationship.[42]

But if "Brother and Sister" offers a feminine contrast to the masculine poetic development in Wordsworth's poetry, the poem suggests a feminist critique of Keble's pre-Lenten poems, particularly the poem for Sexagesima. Although his poem for Septuagesima takes creation as its subject, Keble deals with the evidence of divine creation in the present natural world—a theme that broadly parallels both Wordsworth's and George Eliot's accounts of their own poetic creations. Similarly, Keble's poem for Quinquagesima, based on an interweaving of Paul's celebration of charity in 1 Corinthians (the epistle for the day) with the first and second Covenants of love, makes no quarrel with George Eliot's emphasis on love as essential to poetic creation. But in his Sexagesima poem on the Fall, Keble dwells almost from the beginning on woman's sin and woman's subsequent punishment, asserting this as a divinely ordained pattern:

> See here the fruit of wandering eyes,
> Of worldly longings to be wise,
> Of Passion dwelling on forbidden sweets:
> Ye lawless glances, freely rove;

> Ruin below and wrath above
> Are all that now the wildering fancy meets.
>
> . . . .
>
> If filial and maternal love
> Memorial of our guilt must prove,
> If sinful babes in sorrow must be born,
> Yet, to assuage her sharpest throes,
> The faithful mother surely knows,
> This was the way Thou cam'st to save the world
>   forlorn.
>
> If blessed wedlock may not bless
> Without some tinge of bitterness
> To dash her cup of joy, since Eden lost,
> Chaining to earth with strong desire,
> Hearts that would highest else aspire,
> And o'er the tenderer sex usurping ever most:
>
> Yet by the light of Christian lore
> 'Tis blind Idolatry no more,
> But a sweet help and pattern of true love,
> Showing how best the soul may cling
> To her immortal Spouse and King,
> How He should rule, and she with full desire
>   approve.

In the first of the eleven sonnets, the little sister speaker holds her brother in the same awe as Milton's Eve does her Adam: "I thought his knowledge marked the boundary / Where men grew blind, though angels knew the best" (193). But later she discovers his superiority is partly luck, and later still, she joins him in the "fellowship" of learning the "harder, truer skill." In an image that reverses the crucial Genesis incident, the brother picks the apple for the sister—"The fruit that hung on high beyond my reach / He plucked for me" (201). This image crystallizes George Eliot's reversal of the biblical significance of woman's relationship to man, for the little sister's difference from her brother actually furthers his spiritual growth:

> Thus boyish Will the nobler mastery learned
> Where inward vision over impulse reigns,

> Widening its life with separate life discerned,
> A Life unlike, a Self that self restrains.
>
>> His years with others must the sweeter be
>> For those brief days he spent in loving me. (201)

George Eliot thus completely inverts Keble's characterization of woman's disobedience of God's law, her subsequent punishment and sorrowful subjection to her husband's law. Perhaps it is significant that she employs a type of the Law—Moses' rod—anachronistically:

> For who in age shall roam the earth, and find
> Reasons for loving that will strike out love
> With sudden rod from the hard year-pressed mind? (197)

She here suggests that it would be as impossible for the adult who has not learned love in infancy to suddenly "strike out love" from the hardened mind as it would be for Moses to strike out water from the rock. Her use of the type assumes the reader will find the biblical miracle equally incredible, or at least that such miracles cannot be the source of love in the modern world.[43] In the poem, an entirely different model of love between male and female overturns that based on Old Testament law. The sexes are different, but each is important to the other's spiritual growth. Recognizing the primal importance of this early, loving relationship to her own poetic development, despite the traditional biblical and poetic subordination of "little sisters," George Eliot concludes:

> But were another childhood-world my share,
> I would be born a little sister there. (203)

If the parallel between George Eliot's "Brother and Sister" and Keble's pre-Lenten themes seems strong, that between "Stradivarius" and Keble's poem for Palm Sunday seems even closer. Indeed, this poem—which was not completed until September 1873—is one of the two poems in the volume that could have been written with the express intention of rounding out a correspondence to Keble's *Christian Year*. Keble's theme for Palm Sunday is not so much, as Charlotte Yonge puts it, on the "sacred vocation of the bard" as on the equally sacred vocation of those who lack the bard's gift for music but who can at least still hope to "listen well" or to join in childlike praise. "Stradivarius," which draws on the Leweses' acquaintance with the famed violinist Joachim, converts Keble's theme to the even more egalitarian praise of the craftsman who merely makes the instrument.

In this instance, George Eliot's somewhat lackluster treatment of the theme compares unfavorably with Keble's, which seems visibly inspired by Herbert's "Easter," as well as indebted to "Lycidas."[44] Keble's poem at first focuses on those "Heirs of more than royal race," the bards:

> Sovereign masters of all hearts!
> Know ye, who hath set your parts?
> He who gave you breath to sing,
> By whose strength ye sweep the string,
> He hath chosen you, to lead
>   His Hosannas here below;—
> Mount, and claim your glorious meed;
>   Linger not with sin and woe.

But it soon moves to those "of meaner birth":

> Lord, by every minstrel tongue
> Be Thy praise so duly sung,
> That Thine angels' harps may ne'er
> Fail to find fit echoing here:
> We the while, of meaner birth,
>   Who in that divinest spell
> Dare not hope to join on earth,
>   Give us grace to listen well.

In his final verse, Keble moves all the way down the Neoplatonic order, concluding with the praises that will be sung by the very lowest in creation, the "stones" of earth:

> Then waken into sound divine
> The very pavement of Thy shrine,
> Till we, like Heaven's star-sprinkled floor,
> Faintly give back what we adore:
> Childlike though the voices be,
>   And untunable the parts,
> Thou wilt own the minstrelsy,
>   If it flow from childlike hearts.

In "Stradivarius," George Eliot discards the hierarchical order of Keble's poem and instead focuses on the Romantic subject of the workingman's sacred vocation, contrasting it with the artist's hypocritical claim of a much higher vocation. Stephen Prickett has commented that in Keble's poetry, "poverty and humility are given their due as Christian virtues, but there is no active belief that greater truth is to be found in the low or rustic portions of society."[45] "Stradivarius" clearly aligns George Eliot with the Romantic tradition, providing a strong testimony to her criticism of Keble's implicit elitism.

Beginning, as does Keble, with praise of the true musician— "Your soul was lifted by the wings today / Hearing the master of the violin"—George Eliot's poem then immediately moves to the theme of those who are not musicians but whose work is equally important. Stradivarius, the maker of the violin, becomes an image for the sacred vocation of all workers or craftsmen. When Naldo the artist taunts him with the "petty kind of fame" that comes from merely making the violins, Stradivarius replies that his work is a way of helping God, since he makes the instruments on which God's musicians play. Naldo, on the other hand, is criticized for his slackness and failure to produce finished works from the grandiose inspirations he claims. The contradiction between artistic ego and the great "song" of humanity parallels the theme of "Armgart."

"Stradivarius" also compares with "Agatha" in its attempt at the Brownian mode in which the speaker's life becomes a "poem," though his poem's "naught." But George Eliot's poem, characterized by an oversimple moral earnestness, lacks the psychological interest and complexity of Browning's dramatic monologues. George Eliot's Caleb Garth in *Middlemarch* far more successfully exemplifies the workingman's nobility and dedication to his vocation. "Stradivarius," however, does serve as a particularly suggestive example of George Eliot's reliance on Keble's themes in *Jubal*, and of her conversion of those themes from Keble's Christian Neoplatonism to musical humanism.

While "Stradivarius" seems especially close to Keble's thematic order, the relation of the next poem, "Two Lovers," raises more doubts than any other. One of the earliest poems (1866) in the volume and of slight significance by almost any standard, its six short stanzas celebrate conjugal love from youthful betrothal to the shared solitude of old age. The theme of the poem, or love as the basis for lifelong "song," thus generally conforms to the theme of the volume. Conceivably, George Eliot saw the poem as a humanist version of Keble's theme for the Monday before Easter, in which the permanence of God's love is compared to the evanescence of human relationships, for in "Two Lovers," the love of the married pair continues after children have come and gone. This theme can be seen as a humanistic parallel to Keble's lines

> ... the time may come
> When the babe's kiss no sense of pleasure yields
> E'en to the doting mother: but Thine own
> Thou never canst forget, nor leave alone.

Significantly, "Two Lovers" does not praise the *mother's* love for the child, as Keble's poem does, but speaks always of the "two parents."

The relation of "Arion" to Keble's *Christian Year* is as clear as that of "Two Lovers" is dubious. George Eliot has not only altered details of the narrative from Herodotus so as to echo accounts of the Crucifixion, but seems to intend the poem to fulfill the same devotional purpose Keble sees in the Crucifixion: to draw spiritual power from the "darkest hour" of another. As "Stradivarius" responds to Keble's Palm Sunday theme, so "Arion" converts Keble's Good Friday meditation into yet another type of musical humanism.

In Herodotus's tale of Arion, the musician makes a miraculous escape from the sailors on the back of a dolphin who has been charmed by his music. The sailors, on the other hand, are later crucified for their attempt to murder Arion. George Eliot's revision of the narrative removes the element of miracle and transforms Arion's story into the account of a heroic death that echoes certain details from the gospel accounts of the Crucifixion. Arion, for example, at first fears and wishes to avoid his death; later, the sailors feel they are in the presence of some god; and finally,

Arion is said to fall to his death like a "pierced eagle." The poem becomes a classical counterpart for the story of the Crucifixion in which music, or visionary art, gives man the courage to face death. Arion's music is self-transcendent, enabling him to accept death without fear, and freeing him—so to speak—from the bonds of mortality. His song functions as an exemplum of the prophetic function of poetry as expressed in "O May I Join the Choir Invisible," the closing poem in *Jubal*—to be "to other souls / The cup of strength in some great agony."

Like "Stradivarius," this poem may have been written specifically to round out the structural scheme in *Jubal*, for although the subject was conceived as early as 1868, the poem itself was not written until the spring of 1873.[46] And the poem not only constitutes a conception in musical metaphor of art's ultimate purpose but seems to provide a precise humanist parallel to Keble's meditation on the Crucifixion:

> Is it not strange, the darkest hour
>   That ever dawn'd on sinful earth
>   Should touch the heart with softer power
> For comfort, than an angel's mirth?
> That to the Cross the mourner's eye should turn
> Sooner than where the stars of Christmas burn?

Similarly, "Arion" illustrates the theme—dominant in George Eliot's art—that the primary power of visionary art draws on images of "faulty, struggling human kind," rather than heroic conquest. Arion confronts what he fears the most and achieves an immortal heroism in that confrontation, even though he cannot conquer death itself.

"O May I Join the Choir Invisible" (1867), though written before "Arion," makes the obvious sequel to it, as well as the appropriate closing hymn for the entire volume. Here the poet defines her "undying music" as participation in the human choice of "immortal deed," whose memory makes the minds of others better. Their music is not the hymn of triumph, but the "yearning song" of struggles toward "our rarer, better, truer self." As George Eliot wrote to the translator Charles Ritter in 1878 (*GEL*, 7:56), she hoped to transform the history of failure into a "prophecy" of better things to come.

The poem also appropriately translates resurrection and ascension themes into humanist terms, seeming particularly close to Keble's vision in his poem for Ascension Day. In this poem, Keble contrasts his imaginative vision of ascending with Christ to Christ's concern for human sorrows:

> The sun and every vassal star,
> All space, beyond the soar of angel wings,
>   Wait on His word: and yet He stays His car
> For every sigh a contrite suppliant brings.
>
> He listens to the silent tear
> For all the anthems of the boundless sky—
>   And shall our dreams of music bar our ear
> To His soul-piercing voice forever nigh?
>
> Nay, gracious Saviour—but as now
> Our thoughts have trac'd Thee to Thy glory-throne,
>   So help us evermore with Thee to bow
> Where human sorrow breathes her lowly moan.

But where Keble sees a contradiction between heavenly bliss and sharing in human sorrow, for George Eliot it is all one. In "O May I Join the Choir Invisible," the poet aspires to Christ's function of a universal compassion for human sorrow, and defines heaven as the Christ-like capacity to strengthen others and become part of the "undying music" of humanity:

>   May I reach
> That purest heaven, be to other souls
> The cup of strength in some great agony,
> Enkindle generous ardor, feed pure love,
> Beget the smiles that have no cruelty—
> Be the sweet presence of a good diffused,
> And in diffusion ever more intense.
> So shall I join the choir invisible
> Whose music is the gladness of the world. (233)

The volume that began with the discovery of human mortality now closes with a hymn to human "immortality." "O May I Join the

Choir Invisible" exemplifies George Eliot's vision of the "music" that both inspires humanity in the face of inevitable mortality and itself takes on immortality, outliving its maker's death. As "The Legend of Jubal" images the creation of visionary art, so this poem represents its "apocalypse," or final unveiling.

I have endeavored to show that *The Legend of Jubal* corresponds to and revises Keble's *Christian Year*, its structure taking on the contours of the liturgical year from Advent to Ascension. Instead of meditating on the life and death of Christ, George Eliot meditates on the life and death of the visionary artist. Her poems proceed not only from the birth of the first artist to the transcendent death of another but from the first artist's discovery of music and mortality to a final hymn of immortality. *Jubal* is essentially a book about death. In poem after poem, George Eliot confronts the dual problem of death for the artist: loss of life itself and loss of the ability to create while alive—seemingly a "living death." In poem after poem, she strives to "put on the armour of light," to transcend her own mortality through her art. Taking the Christian year as pattern, she seeks to arrange both art and life into a new landscape of time that reforms "ecclesiastical history" and gives new meanings to earthly existence.

But large though this prophetic design is, *Jubal* becomes something even more visionary through its veiled dialogue with Keble and other poet-prophets of the patriarchal line. Hidden within the fabric of ostensibly "feminine" values lies a quiet pattern of feminist protest. And placed unobtrusively in the very center of the volume are George Eliot's two constructions of herself as prophet and poet: a latter-day Colin Clout and a "little sister." In the second of these, she begins to generate the separate mystery of the female poet's origin and poetics. It is unfortunate that she did not pursue her poetic experiments further than she did, for she seems to have been approaching a distinctively female "apocalypse" in this mode comparable to her earlier attempt in *Romola*. Like the novel, *The Legend of Jubal* may not be experimental enough to produce a radically female prophecy, yet its revision of a traditional and deeply conservative interpretation of history deserves a sympathetic reading. In the context of that exemplum of Victorian popularity, *The Christian Year*, George Eliot's "pocket-sized volume" appears a much more innovative landscape of time than we might otherwise judge it to be.

Notes

PREFACE

1. Jacques Lacan, *Écrits, A Selection*, trans. Alan Sheridan (New York: W. W. Norton & Co., 1977), p. 47.
2. For example, Hal Lindsey's *The Late Great Planet Earth*, a work that builds directly and uncritically on nineteenth-century British apocalyptics, was a best-seller throughout the 1970s. See also Martin, "Waiting for the End," on the popularity of millenarianism in the present decade.
3. Fairbairn, *Prophecy*, p. 203. Further quotations in this paragraph of my text are from pp. 27, 182, and 30, respectively.
4. Fairbairn, *The Typology of Scripture*, p. 2.
5. Ibid.; Fairbairn, *Prophecy*, p. 31. As Landow, *Victorian Types, Victorian Shadows*, and Sussman, *Fact into Figure*, demonstrate, typological symbolism was widely employed in Victorian art and literature. Fairbairn pointed out, however, that the treatment of typology by "our leading hermeneutical and systematic divines . . . is rather negative than positive," and opened his own substantial work on the subject with a detailed discussion of the reasons for its neglect in nineteenth-century hermeneutical discourse (*Typology of Scripture*, pp. 140, 2–45). Fleishman, *Figures of Autobiography*, p. 115, notes that "it is the absence of an over-arching form of his life that one misses in the local applications of typology by Browning and other poets," suggesting the appeal of an all-inclusive narrative of history in constructing fictions of the self.
6. I am indebted to Frank Kermode's discussion of "fictions of the End" in *The Sense of an Ending*.

CHAPTER 1

1. Studies of George Eliot's religious development include Jay, *The Religion of the Heart*; Wiesenfarth, *George Eliot's Mythmaking*, pp. 27–41; Haight, *George Eliot*, pp. 1–67; Knoepflmacher, *Religious Humanism in the Victorian Novel*, pp. 24–71; Paris, *Experiments in Life*, pp. 1–148; and Willey, *Nineteenth-Century Studies*, pp. 204–51.

2. Sandeen, *The Roots of Fundamentalism*, provides a historical analysis of the scholarly millenarian tradition in Britain during the time of George Eliot's youth; see especially chap. 1, "The Revival of British Millenarianism, 1800-1845," pp. 3–41. Tuveson, *Redeemer Nation*, deals with the contemporary but distinct millenialist tradition during the nineteenth century. Harrison, *The Second Coming*, erroneously assumes that only millennialists were "intellectually sophisticated" while millenarians were "largely self-educated," p. 5. Jay, *Religion of the Heart*, discusses millenarianism as a nonessential doctrine in Evangelical Anglicanism, pp. 88–97, and Chadwick, *The Victorian Church*, and Elliott-Binns, *Religion in the Victorian Era*, touch on Evangelical millenarianism around the time of the Catholic Emancipation Bill in 1829 and the Reform Bill of 1832.

For the origins of the school of "continuous historical" prophetic exposition in England, see Firth, *The Apocalyptic Tradition in Reformation Britain, 1530–1645*; Bauckham, *Tudor Apocalypse*; Fairfield, *John Bale*; Patrides, *The Grand Design of God*; and Hill, *Antichrist in Seventeenth-Century England*. Frei, *The Eclipse of Biblical Narrative*, discusses eighteenth-century exposition of the Old Testament as a prophetic scheme of history but does not place it in the context of the Protestant tradition of "continuous historical" prophetic exposition; see especially chap. 4, "Anthony Collins: Meaning, Reference, and Prophecy."

I have not chosen to use Sandeen's and Bauckham's term "historicist" for this tradition of prophetic exposition, but rather "continuous historical," because this was the term used by nineteenth-century expositors themselves. Biblical criticism that did not accept prophecy as a supernatural vision of time and confined itself largely to the determination of date, authorship, and circumstances of prophetic works, and to literary analysis of them, was more often referred to as "scientific" or "higher criticism," or lumped under the title "Praeterist."

3. Mill, *The Spirit of the Age*, p. 1.
4. Elliott, *Horae Apocalypticae*, 1:319.
5. Eliot, *Adam Bede*, p. 573.
6. Haight, ed., *The George Eliot Letters*, 1:11–12 (hereafter cited in the text as *GEL*).
7. Sandeen, *Roots of Fundamentalism*, chaps. 1 and 4.
8. Sandeen points out that while millenarianism in Britain is usually ascribed to the political developments associated with the Reform Act, the Millerite success in America at about the same time is attributed to the great revival of the 1830s, or connected to the panic of 1837 (ibid., p. 58). Victorian Evangelicals seemed to attribute the growth of millenarianism to European political events, which they tended to universalize. Perhaps a common pool of apocalyptics applied primarily to European political events, rather than either English or American, was a significant factor in the rise of millenarianism on both sides of the Atlantic.

9. Ibid., p. 8.

10. Alford, *The Greek Testament* (1861), commented "From Joachim's time we may date the rise of the continuous historic school of interpretation" (p. 246). Elliott included a detailed summary of Joachim's apocalyptic interpretation, emphasizing his "historical" approach and his prediction that Antichrist would occupy the papal throne (*Horae Apocalypticae*, 4:384–427).

11. Review of Keith, *Evidence of the Truth of the Christian Religion*, p. 290.

12. Haight, *George Eliot*, p. 24.

13. Knoepflmacher comments that the proposed chart reflected a sense of history as nothing but "a succession of conflicting doctrines, schisms, claims and counterclaims," and logically concludes that George Eliot's "developmental view of history" was constructed later in life (*Religious Humanism*, p. 47).

14. *Scripture Help* was apparently published in the Christian's Family Library among the first fifteen volumes (see *The History of the Church of Christ . . .*, abridged from the work of the Rev. Joseph Milner, ed. Rev. E. Bickersteth [London: Seeley & Burnside, 1834]). Whether an 1839 subscriber would have received it is therefore uncertain.

15. Woodhouse, *The Apocalypse*, p. 303; Faber, *Dissertations on the Prophecies*, 1:33. Reviews in the 1806 *Christian Observer* point out that Whitaker, *Commentary on the Revelation of St. John* (1802), agrees with Faber's view of the 1260 years, as well as with Woodhouse (September, p. 561; October, p. 616).

16. Faber, *Dissertation on . . . the 1260 Years*, 1:32–33.

17. Although Bishop Thomas Newton noted that "Mohammed first contrived his imposture in the year 606, the very same year wherein the tyrant Phocus made a grant of the supremacy to the Pope; and this might incline one to think that the 1260 years of the reign of Antichrist are to be dated from this time," he later rejected the conclusion on the grounds that though "they might rise together, yet they were not fully established together" (*Dissertations on the Prophecies*, p. 618).

18. *Jewish Expositor* 12 (1827): 244.

19. Sandeen, *Roots of Fundamentalism*, p. 22.

20. See Faber, *The Sacred Calendar of Prophecy*, 1:152, 342, 362.

21. Bickersteth, *Practical Guide to the Prophecies*, p. 253.

22. Haight identifies this as Bickersteth's *Practical Guide to the Prophecies*, 4th ed. (London: Seeley and Burnside, 1835; 6th ed., 1839), in *GEL*, 1:48, n. 6.

23. Chadwick, in *The Victorian Church*, pt. 1, describes the *Christian Observer* as the "focus and arbiter of instructed evangelican opinion" (p. 451). Elisabeth Jay places it midway between two other Evangelical organs, *The Christian Guardian*, which reflected the views of conservative Evangelical clergy, and the *Record*, characterized by "apocalyptic fervour

and zealous espousal of pre-millennialist doctrine" (*Religion of the Heart*, p. 23). Sandeen describes the *Christian Observer* as the "voice of the evangelical party" and points to this 1824 article as its first notice of the millenarian revival (*Roots of Fundamentalism*, p. 23).

24. *Christian Observer* (July 1825): 422–34, and (August 1825): 489–520.

25. See Birks, *Memoir of the Rev. Edward Bickersteth*, 2:39. See also Sandeen, *Roots of Fundamentalism*, p. 25.

26. Sandeen, *Roots of Fundamentalism*, p. 11.

27. A few examples: In the May 1828 issue of the *Christian Observer*, an inquirer asks whether the number of the beast might not be the year of its rise, or 666 A.D. (pp. 272–73). In October 1829, a correspondent argues that Christ's Second Advent would be premillennial (pp. 592–97). In the November 1827 issue, "Paulinus" writes that the 1260 years will be dated from the code of Justinian, or 529–34 A.D. (p. 667). In June 1828, "Family Sermon #144" suggests that Revelation 7:9–10 refers to the church triumphant, rather than a particular period in church history.

28. *Christian Observer* (March 1830): 129–42.

29. Frere, "On the Expectation of an Individual Antichrist," p. 658. Frere was the author of *A Combined View of the Prophecies of Daniel, Esdras, and St. John* and *On the General Structure of the Apocalypse*. Sandeen comments on the absence of articles concerning prophecy in the *Christian Observer* after 1830, noting that the millenarians turned to their own periodicals at this point. Since the early 1830s were a time of fervent growth in prophetic enthusiasm, the editors of the *Christian Observer* may have ceased publishing in sheer rebellion against the avalanche of material (*Roots of Fundamentalism*, pp. 22–26).

30. Chadwick, *Victorian Church*, 1:35–36.

31. "The Cholera at Sedgley," *Christian Observer* (January 1834), deals with the cholera as an opportunity for spiritual rebirth.

32. "On the Influence of Certain Doctrines upon Missionary Exertions," *Christian Observer* (October 1839): 598–603, and "The Rev. Mr. Goode on His Missionary Sermon:—With Remarks on His Letter," *Christian Observer* (December 1839): 722–45.

33. *Christian Observer* (January 1840): 63.

34. Bickersteth, *Memoir*, 2:39.

35. Tuveson, *Redeemer Nation*, pp. 25–51. Sandeen comments that, in contrast to the "imprudent millenarian of the seventeenth-century, the nineteenth-century millenarian was a political reactionary. Since the course of history led straight to judgment, change could only produce a crescendo of corruption. Catholic emancipation, the Reform Bill, democracy, industrialization—the millenarian opposed them all, but with a sense of resignation born of the knowledge that the world must grow more evil day after day" (*Roots of Fundamentalism*, p. 41).

36. Chadwick, *Victorian Church*, 1:442.

37. Bickersteth, *Practical Guide to the Prophecies*, pp. 286–87.

38. *Christian Observer* (January 1840): 38. The second Epistle of Peter is sometimes spoken of as the "prophecy of St. Peter," as in Mede's *Paraphrase and Exposition of the Prophesie of Saint Peter*.

39. Haight, *George Eliot*, pp. 32–36.

40. George Eliot's translations of Strauss's *Life of Jesus* (London, 1846) and Feuerbach's *Essence of Christianity* (London, 1855) are well known. Neither work addresses the problem of prophecy directly. By contrast, both Charles Hennell and Robert Mackay deal with prophecy at length, and Greg, in *The Creed of Christendom*, which George Eliot also read and reviewed, devotes a chapter to the prophecies.

41. George Eliot first read Hennell's *Inquiry* in 1842 (Haight, *George Eliot*, p. 39).

42. Pinney, ed., *Essays of George Eliot*, p. 30.

43. Mackay, *Progress of the Intellect*, 1:102–3.

44. Pinney, ed., *Essays of George Eliot*, p. 44.

45. Cumming, *Apocalyptic Sketches*, First Series, p. 13.

46. Pinney, ed., *Essays of George Eliot*, pp. 158–90.

47. Elliott, *Horae Apocalypticae*, 3:299–303.

48. Ibid., 2:1–200.

49. Cumming, *Apocalyptic Sketches*, First Series, p. 60.

50. Ibid., p. 311.

51. Ibid., p. 450.

52. Ibid., Second Series, p. 468.

53. Elliott, *Horae Apocalypticae*, 4:26.

54. Mackay, *The Rise and Progress of Christianity*, p. vi.

55. "The Time of the End," pp. 65–77.

56. Pinney, ed., *Essays of George Eliot*, pp. 158–90. It is interesting to compare George Eliot's attitude toward Dr. Cumming in this essay with that of Hal Lindsey in *The Late Great Planet Earth*. Lindsey speaks of Cumming with awed reverence, especially singling out Cumming's prediction of "Israel's physical rebirth as a nation and restoration of Palestine" (p. 39). Lindsey does not, however, mention Cumming's prediction that the Second Advent would take place in the 1860s.

57. Alford, *The Greek Testament*, p. 246.

58. Charles, *Studies in the Apocalypse*, pp. 1–79.

59. George Eliot is supposed to have asked John Chapman to send her "De Motte's Commentary on the Old Testament" (*GEL*, 2:209). Since no such author is listed in either the *Catalog* of the British Library or the *National Union Catalog, Pre-1956 Imprints*, while De Wette was a well-known German critic whose *Introduction to the Old Testament* (1843) was translated into English (3d ed., Boston, 1859), it seems likely De Wette was intended.

60. Sandeen, *Roots of Fundamentalism*, pp. 36–39. Dean Alford mentions

only Maitland, Todd, Burgh, and Isaac Williams as members of this school (*Greek Testament*, p. 248), but Elliott also states that four writers of the Oxford Tracts are futurists (*Horae Apocalypticae*, 4:597).

61. The narrator applies this phrase to "all those painstaking interpretations of the Book of Daniel" in *Felix Holt, the Radical*, p. 503.

62. McGinn, *Visions of the End*, p. 30.

63. Birks suggests "that great and sudden revolution which convulsed the whole of Europe, and seemed, even in England, to threaten the dissolution of the social fabric" as the change leading to Bickersteth's changed views on prophecy (*Memoir of the Rev. Edward Bickersteth*, 2:1, 38).

64. Abrams, "English Romanticism," pp. 53–72.

65. Collingwood, *The Idea of History*, pp. 49–52.

66. *Westminster Review*, o.s. 75, n.s. 19 (January 1861): 247.

67. Hennell, *The Early Christian Anticipation of . . . an End of the World*, p. 88.

68. Ibid., pp. 33–34.

69. See *GEL*, 2:125; 3:381 and n. 38; 4:104.

70. Maurice, *Lectures on the Apocalypse*, p. vi.

71. Ibid., pp. 10–11.

72. Ibid., p. 104.

73. Suzanne Graver provides a useful discussion of Comte's position on "The Woman Question" and its relation to George Eliot's views of women in *George Eliot and Community*, pp. 167–83.

74. Quotations in this paragraph of my text are from Maurice's *Lectures on the Apocalypse*, Lecture no. 12, pp. 207–29.

75. *Westminster Review*, o.s. 69, n.s. 13 (April 1858): 317.

76. Call, "The Apocalypse," pp. 448–87. For George Eliot's acquaintance with Call, see Haight, *George Eliot*, p. 242.

77. Eliot, Journal, July 1861–December 1877, p. 13, Yale MS IV.3.

78. Call, "The Apocalypse," p. 470.

79. Davidson, "The Apocalypse of St. John," p. 354.

80. Call, "The Apocalypse," pp. 486–87. The closing quotation is from Tennyson's *In Memoriam*.

81. Wittreich, *Visionary Poetics*, p. 52.

CHAPTER 2

1. Eliot, *Scenes of Clerical Life*. In "George Eliot: Feminist Critic," Carol A. Martin suggests that in this work George Eliot's "realism" acts "in the service of her feminism" (pp. 22–25).

2. Sadoff, "Nature's Language," p. 426.

3. George Eliot, *Adam Bede*, ed. Stephen Gill (Harmondsworth: Penguin Books, 1980), pp. 223 and 573. All further references in my text are

to chapter and page of this edition. Suzanne Graver illuminates some of the complexity of what "natural history" means in George Eliot's "credo of realism" in *George Eliot and Community*, pp. 28–79.

4. Palliser, "*Adam Bede* and 'The Story of the Past.'"

5. Harvey, *The Art of George Eliot*, pp. 115–21.

6. See chap. 8, "*Adam Bede* and *Henry Esmond*: Homo-social Desire and the Historicity of the Female," in Sedgwick, *Between Men*, pp. 134–60.

7. Clayton, "Visionary Power and Narrative Form," pp. 645–72.

8. Note Arthur Donnithorne's significant comment that he can "hardly make head or tail" of Coleridge's "Ancient Mariner" as a story (p. 109). The poem, which I suggest provides an important context for George Eliot's narrative, includes the following lines:

Since then, at an uncertain hour,
That agony returns:
And until my ghastly tale is told,
This heart within me burns.

I pass, like night, from land to land;
I have strange power of speech.
(Coleridge, *Selected Poetry and Prose*, p. 23, ll. 582–87)

9. Kincaid, "Coherent Readers, Incoherent Texts," pp. 781–802, and Garrett, *The Victorian Multiplot Novel*, especially the Introduction. Garrett summarizes the long tradition of narrative criticism that has insisted on a single narrative and on narrative coherence but himself postulates that Victorian novels do not represent a "secure and comprehensive vision but a continual, shifting, unstable, and unpredictable confrontation between single and plural, individual and social, particular and general perspectives" (p. 22). My emphasis on George Eliot's intellectual formation, however, obviously differs from Garrett's position, for I emphasize the author's exploitation of historical ambivalence and narrative incoherence.

10. Bonaparte, *The Triptych and the Cross*.

11. The prophecy is familiar to many through Handel's setting of its texts in the *Messiah*, a work that George Eliot loved. Gordon S. Haight notes that she and Lewes attended a performance very shortly after the publication of *Adam Bede* (*George Eliot*, p. 287).

12. August 18, 1799, should have been the fourth Sunday after Trinity in the Anglican calendar. Although George Eliot treats it as a working day, her later change of the day Saturday, November 2, to Sunday, November 2, suggests that she changes Sunday, August 18, to Monday, August 18, and thus moves calendar dates here one day ahead. Providing that is the case, then the Sunday following August 18 would still be the fifteenth Sunday after Trinity.

13. Poem for the twenty-fourth Sunday after Trinity, titled in the table

of contents "The Imperfection of Human Sympathy," in *The Christian Year*, pp. 237–40.

14. Clayton, "Visionary Power," p. 655.

15. Charles Palliser points out that *Adam Bede* parallels the "reading" of the landscape with other acts of interpretation ("*Adam Bede* and 'The Story of the Past,'" p. 62).

16. Clayton, "Visionary Power," p. 661.

17. In 1800 Easter fell on April 13, and the first day of Lent, or Ash Wednesday, on February 26. Since George Eliot has apparently advanced her chronology two days in this year, Ash Wednesday would have been February 24. This change makes Ash Wednesday coincide with the Feast of St. Matthias, for which the Epistle concerns the choice of a new disciple "to be a witness with us" from those who "went in and out among us, beginning with the baptism of John" (Acts 1:15–26), and the Gospel concludes with "Come unto me, all ye that labour and are heavy laden. . . . For my yoke is easy, and my burden is light" (Matt. 11:25–30).

18. In Chapter 3 I discuss in greater detail the "continuous historical" exegesis of the two witnesses.

19. John Olding testifies to finding the baby "a week last Monday," or on March 1 (p. 479). Sarah Stone testifies that Hetty had come to her house on Saturday evening, the 27th of February (p. 477). And the trial is held on a Friday (p. 489), therefore on Friday, March 12.

20. I refer here to the second lesson for Morning Prayer on March 12 (*Book of Common Prayer* [London: Barritt and Co., 1837]).

21. 1 Tim. 2:11–15. Note Seth's citation of another text from this Epistle (5:14) in his attempt to persuade Dinah to marry him (78).

22. Esther 4:13. The Book of Esther and its exegesis figures even more strongly in *Daniel Deronda*: see my Chapter 5, "The Apocalypse of the Old Testament."

23. The wedding apparently takes place on a weekday, so although very close to the day in the liturgical calendar on which Adam and Hetty were betrothed, it is not identical.

CHAPTER 3

1. *The Mill on the Floss* was published in April 1860; publication of *Romola* in serial form began in July 1862 and ended in August 1863. George Eliot's "English story," *Silas Marner*, was published in 1861, between the two longer works (Haight, *George Eliot*, pp. 321, 340–41, 360, 365).

2. U. C. Knoepflmacher comments that from *Romola* on George Eliot seems concerned with the "history of man" in some more universal sense than in her earlier "pastoral" novels (*George Eliot's Early Novels*, p. 5).

3. George Eliot, *The Mill on the Floss*, ed. Gordon S. Haight (Boston:

Riverside Edition, Houghton Mifflin Co., 1961). All further references in my text are to chapter and page of this edition.

4. Haight provides a helpful note on chronology in the Riverside Edition; he identifies all dates in the novel that can be determined while pointing out the many references to such indefinite dates as the occasion when Maggie meets Phillip in the Red Deeps on a day "far on in June" 1836 (pp. xxiii–xxiv).

5. Miller, "Emphasis Added," pp. 36–48.

6. Nineteenth-century editions of the Authorized Version frequently include not only a "chronological index" between the Old and New Testaments but printed headings for Archbishop Ussher's seven-age chronology (*Annales Veteris et Novi Testamenti*, 1650–54) on the relevant pages of the biblical text. Biblical narratives were thus always already framed by "prophetic history" for the Victorian reader.

7. In Jacques Lacan's reinterpretation of Freud's theory, the "Law of the Father" signifies the prohibition of the child's desire. Diane F. Sadoff analyzes "The Law and the Father" in *The Mill on the Floss* and reads both this novel and *Romola* as expressions of George Eliot's need to work through "problematic father-daughter material about desire and authority" (*Monsters of Affection*, pp. 78–88).

8. Marianne Hirsch also suggests that Maggie's bleak "social possibilities" resemble those of the witch whose picture she is asked to explain; see "Spiritual *Bildung*," in Abel et al., eds., *The Voyage In*, pp. 33–34. Elaine Showalter mentions the "witch" as one of the metaphors George Eliot employs to illustrate Maggie's position; see *A Literature of Their Own*, p. 125.

9. See section IV of this chapter, where I suggest that Temple's article in *Essays and Reviews* reinterprets Daniel's Four Empires prophecy as "The Education of the World."

10. Moers, *Literary Women*, p. 254.

11. McDonnell, "'A Little Spirit of Independence,'" p. 206. See also McDonnell's "'Perfect Goodness' or 'The Wider Life,'" pp. 379–402.

12. Eliot, Journal, August 1861, pp. 7 and 8; November 1861, p. 16; December 1861, p. 18, Yale MS IV.3.

13. Although a few readers have always thought highly of *Romola* (Robert Browning, for example, considered it a noble "prose poem," F. D. Maurice's compliments were so lavish George Eliot would not quote them on paper, and Henry James called it the most important of George Eliot's works), the novel has never matched the popular success of *Mill on the Floss* or *Middlemarch*. Most modern criticism agrees with George Levine's statement that "the initial and inescapable fact about *Romola* is that of its failure" ("*Romola* as Fable," in Hardy, ed., *Critical Essays on George Eliot*, p. 78). Gerald Bullet, for example, states that the novel fails to be "a tolerable piece of studied conventional fiction" (*George Eliot*, p. 199). Barbara

Hardy criticizes the "deadness" of the novel and George Eliot's overuse of "pure exposition" (*The Novels of George Eliot*, pp. 59–61). Carole Robinson tries to explain why *Romola* is "so remarkable a failure" ("*Romola*," p. 29). Lawrence Poston speaks of the failure of *Romola* to live up to George Eliot's other works ("Setting and Theme in *Romola*," p. 356). Avrom Fleishman feels George Eliot failed to organically unite background and characters in the novel (*The English Historical Novel*, p. 163). Joseph Wiesenfarth states that the only useful approach to the novel is to admit its faults while still attempting to show what George Eliot was trying to do (*George Eliot's Mythmaking*, p. 146). But if *Romola* is an experimental work, rather than an attempt at the conventional genre of historical fiction, it cannot rationally be judged a failure by conventional standards.

14. Bonaparte, *The Triptych and the Cross*, p. 3. Further references to page numbers of this work will be designated *Triptych* and included within parentheses in my text. Peterson, "*Romola*," pp. 49–62, has argued that the stages of the heroine's spiritual growth unify the novel. George Levine, despite his opening premise of *Romola*'s failure, nevertheless provides an imaginative and highly fruitful approach to the narrative as "romance" or "fable" ("*Romola* as Fable," in Hardy, ed., *Critical Essays on George Eliot*). Sullivan, "The Sketch of the Three Masks in *Romola*," pp. 9–13, suggests further that these stages are prophetically portrayed in Piero di Cosimo's sketch. Bullen, "George Eliot's *Romola* as a Positivist Allegory," pp. 425–35, although suggesting that the stages are based on Comte's philosophy of history, nevertheless feels that "the self-imposed task of giving substance to abstract Positivist theory" accounts for the "failure" of the novel.

15. De Jong, "*Romola*—A *Bildungsroman* for Feminists?," pp. 75–90.

16. George Eliot made the symbolic element of Romola's name quite clear in an 1871 letter to Alexander Main, in which she stated "You have been rightly inspired in pronouncing Romŏla, and in conceiving Romŏlo as the Italian equivalent of Romolus" (*GEL*, 5:174). In a later letter she clarified the pronunciation—and its obvious derivation from the name and the city—still further: "the correct pronunciation according to the Italian usage is Rōmŏla" (*GEL*, 9:215).

17. Weinstein, in *Savonarola and Florence, Prophecy and Patriotism in the Renaissance*, explores at length the development of the Florentine apocalyptic tradition, and his entire work is a study of how Savonarola's millenarianism and the city's grew together. George Eliot would have discovered this tradition through her reading of Giovanni Villani's *History of Florence (Historia universali de suo tempi)*, #2225 in Baker, ed., *The George Eliot–George Henry Lewes Library*, a copy of which she owned and studied in preparation for *Romola*. Weinstein describes Villani as the first to record the prophecy of the Second Charlemagne (which George Eliot alludes to in the novel) and its association with Florence as a formative part of the city's apocalyptic tradition (pp. 38–43).

18. Drummond, "A Popular Introduction to the Study of the Apocalypse," pp. 129–42; Elliott, *Horae Apocalypticae*, 2:142; *Jewish Expositor* (February 1816): 60. See also Cumming, *Apocalyptic Sketches*, First Series, Lecture 23, "The Church during the Effusion of the Vials."

19. Peterson, "*Romola*," and Sullivan, "The Sketch of the Three Masks," posit four-part allegorical structures.

20. Bullen, "George Eliot's *Romola* as a Positivist Allegory."

21. Frank E. Manuel points out that not only Comte's but Lessing's three ages of mankind are "virtual paraphrases of Joachim," (*Shapes of Philosophical History*, p. 44). George Eliot's allusion to the Joachimite myth of "Pope Angelico" (see Reeves, *Prophecy in the Later Middle Ages*) in the proem of *Romola* attests to her interest in Joachimite prophecy, as does her later purchase of a reprint of Ernest Renan's essay, "Joachim de Flore et l'Évangile Eternal" (*Revue des Deux Mondes* 64 [1966]: 94–142), #1797 in Baker, ed., *The George Eliot–George Henry Lewes Library*. Renan was one of the first modern scholars to study Joachim and in the essay suggests an affinity between the monk in George Sand's novel *Spiridion* and Joachim. E. B. Elliott was also much interested in Joachim and devoted a large section to describing his works in *Horae Apocalypticae*, 4:384–427, particularly his sevenfold concordance of Old and New Testaments and his division of the Apocalypse into seven visions. But there is no evidence George Eliot read Elliott's work directly, even though her study of John Cumming's *Apocalyptic Sketches* meant she was familiar with its main tenets.

22. Sullivan, "The Sketch of the Three Masks"; Bullen, "*Romola* as a Positivist Allegory;" and Bonaparte, *Triptych*.

23. Lewes, "A Word about *Tom Jones*," pp. 333–34.

24. Sadoff argues that George Eliot's difficulty in writing *Romola* arose because her material "forced her to confront her traumatic memories of father and brother," but that she was not successful in resolving the trauma created by memory (*Monsters of Affection*, p. 98).

25. Haight, *George Eliot*, pp. 362, 396–97. I employ the now common distinction between "feminine" and "feminist" attitudes as that between a position that celebrates women and the values believed to be peculiarly their own but implicitly accepts the separate spheres of the sexes in traditional patriarchal society, and a position that challenges patriarchal society, seeking to identify and resist the sources of sexual oppression in it. The question of George Eliot's "feminism" is a complex one and highly resistant to such pat categories. Mary Gosselink de Jong provides a balanced, searching consideration of the nature of "feminism" represented by Romola's progress in "*Romola*—A *Bildungsroman* for Feminists?"

26. George Eliot, *Romola*, ed. Andrew Sanders (Harmondsworth: Penguin Books, 1980), p. 391. All further references in my text are to chapter and page of this edition.

27. Since the terms "fellow-feeling" and "sympathy" do not carry the

significance of the biblical and hermeneutic origins I wish to suggest here, I substitute the word "charity" for the community-oriented ethic that governs Romola at this point. I do not mean to imply, however, any dramatic difference in the meaning of these terms but only to underline the subtle shading lent by different discursive origins.

28. Mede, *The Key of the Revelation*, p. 13.
29. Newton, *Dissertations on the Prophecies*, p. 262.
30. Ibid., p. 525.
31. Bonaparte, *Triptych*, pp. 178–79. Bonaparte later recognizes that Romola enters "the Protestant era" but associates this with her rebellion against Savonarola (pp. 203–25). Later, she also suggests Savonarola "is a Protestant without knowing it" (p. 226), but seems unaware of the Protestant tradition explicitly identifying him as such. Gezari, "*Romola* and the Myth of the Apocalypse," points out Savonarola's identification as a Protestant by Luther and the German Protestant tradition (pp. 77–102). Despite her title, Gezari does not draw any connection between *Romola* and the Apocalypse.
32. Villari, *The History of Girolamo Savonarola*, 1:xiii–xix.
33. Meier's biography of Savonarola is #1430 in Baker, ed., *The George Eliot–George Henry Lewes Library*.
34. Villari, *The History of Girolamo Savonarola*, 1:315.
35. Pinney, ed., *Essays of George Eliot*, p. 44.
36. Ibid.
37. Mackay, *The Rise and Progress of Christianity*, p. 3.
38. Bickersteth, *Practical Guide to the Prophecies*, chap. 16.
39. Mede, *Key of the Revelation*, p. 33.
40. Sullivan, in "The Sketch of the Three Masks in *Romola*," first demonstrated that the briefly described mural is a complex allegory depicting the stages of Romola's life. Peterson, in "*Romola*," had earlier identified four distinct stages in Romola's spiritual journey but did not associate these with Piero's prophetic sketch. Barbara Hardy passes over the sketch with the brief suggestion that the masks are "a faint image of the three faces of Tito, Romola, and Savonarola," while "the child, the hope, and the Golden Age are there at the end" (*Novels of George Eliot*, p. 176). Hugh Witemeyer discusses Piero di Cosimo chiefly as a "Ruskinian" artist with penetrating insight into human nature, the ability to paint the "reality ... behind the veil of appearances," and relegates his explanation of the sketch as an "allegory" of "three phases of western religious sensibility" to his footnotes. Witemeyer points out Tito's misinterpretation of the child as the Golden Age or philosophy of Epicurus, suggesting that Tito fails "to see that these stages of mind are represented by the masks of the satyr and the Stoic" (*George Eliot and the Visual Arts*, pp. 56–60, 198–99).
41. Sullivan, "The Sketch of the Three Masks," p. 12.
42. Bonaparte discusses the sketch and its prophetic significance at

length in Chapter 2, "The Greek, Roman and Christian Worlds," but see also Chapter 9, "The Birth of Modern Man," especially pp. 235 ff.

43. William Cuninghame, in commenting on Mede, states that it is a prophetical method to begin with "a general sketch or outline, and afterwards give a more complete and finished colouring of events" (*A Dissertation on the Seals and Trumpets of the Apocalypse*, p. 40). Cuninghame here quotes from Woodhouse and extends the principle to the Book of Daniel.

44. See Chapter 5, "The Apocalypse of the Old Testament," and n. 5.

45. In a letter to Mrs. Richard Congreve, October 16, 1860, George Eliot commented: "We were glad to hear that the well written article in the 'Westminster' on the 'Essays and Reviews' was by your friend Mr. Harrison. Though I don't quite agree with his view of the case, I admired the tone and style of the writing greatly" (*GEL*, 3:353). The comment indicates her familiarity with *Essays and Reviews*, as well as Harrison's critique.

46. Weinstein, *Savonarola and Florence*, pp. 144, 161–62.

47. Ibid., p. 162.

48. Mackay, *Progress of the Intellect*, 1:395–98. Comparison of the Four Empires to Hesiod's Four Ages and also to the "Hindoo" scheme was evidently conventional: George Stanley Faber also does so in *The Sacred Calendar of Prophecy*, 2:4.

49. Mackay, *Progress of the Intellect*, 1:4, 6.

50. Temple, "The Education of the World," in Hedge, ed., *Recent Inquiries in Theology*, pp. 1–56.

51. Harrison points out that this concept, in which the human race is seen as a "colossal man," is adopted "without acknowledgement and possibly unconsciously" from Auguste Comte ("Neo-Christianity," p. 300).

52. Temple, "The Education of the World," in Hedge, ed., *Recent Inquiries in Theology*, pp. 17–22; Harrison, "Neo-Christianity," pp. 305–6.

53. For example, this is Bishop Newton's interpretation in *Dissertations on the Prophecies*. Charles Hennell, in *An Inquiry concerning the Origin of Christianity*—a work that George Eliot read several times, always with admiration—proposed an original interpretation, suggesting that the first kingdom is Babylon, but the second Media, the third Persia, and the fourth Macedonia (pp. 278–82).

54. Although some expositions consider the first three chapters of the Apocalypse a "vision," it seems to be more common to speak of these chapters as an "introductory part" or "prologue," and the closing verses of the last chapter as an "epilogue," as does Call ("The Apocalypse," pp. 464–65).

55. Bickersteth, *Practical Guide to the Prophecies*, p. 254. See also the reproduction of this chart in my text.

56. James Martineau, in an article published shortly after *Romola*, also suggests this dialectic: "It is the peculiarity and the glory of the Hebrew faith that, in its view, all history fell into the form of a moral problem on

the sublimest scale, and appeared not simply as the play of human passions, but as the stately march of a Divine thought.... The Timaeus,—the Greek book of Genesis,— exhibits the origin, the harmony, the movement of the universe,—not omitting to find a place in it for human souls: but such as it is at first, such is it for ever; changing only with an eternal periodicity, and with no life able to break the cycle of alternate birth and death" ("Early History of Messianic Ideas," pp. 554–55).

57. Quotations in the preceding sentence are from Mackay, *Progress of the Intellect*, pp. 428, 429, 431, 423–24, and 426. Since the lion is also the emblem of Florence, Tito's rings sustain a double interpretation of evil as identified with Florence, or more probably, with the Platonist revival in Florence.

58. George P. Landow discusses this typological interpretation in Victorian literature in "Bruising the Serpent's Head," pp. 11–14.

59. "The Prophetic Sentence Denounced against the Serpent," pp. 711–12.

60. Bonaparte comments that "among the many remarkable things that have never been noticed in *Romola* is the fact that the events of the book follow a very strict symbolic calendar" (*Triptych*, p. 78). She discusses the symbolism of Advent, Christmas Eve, Easter, the Nativity of the Virgin and of John the Baptist, and the Martyrdom of John the Baptist, among others. The phrase "Gospel and Revelation" is from one of George Eliot's letters: "And besides that, I have—Roman History!... But this too, read aright, has its Gospel and Revelation" (*GEL*, 4:106).

61. Since Pico della Mirandola is a minor character in *Romola*, it is not at all unlikely that George Eliot—with her usual thoroughness—familiarized herself with his works. Henry Hallam's *Introduction to the Literature of Europe*, which George Eliot read as part of her preparation for the novel, particularly mentions the *Heptaplus*, describing it as "a cabbalistic exposition of the first chapter of Genesis" (1:162). If she did read *Heptaplus*, it would have furnished her with a particularly striking example of septenary structure, for it consists of seven expositions on Genesis, each of which is divided into seven chapters—"the whole corresponds to the seven days of creation" (Mirandola, *Heptaplus*, p. 84). Although noting his "excessive tendency to belief," Hallam speaks favorably of him on the whole, describing him as "justly called the phoenix of his age," and a "superior" and "wonderful" person who should not be forgotten (*Introduction to the Literature of Europe*, p. 163).

62. Milman, "Savonarola," p. 14.

63. Villari, *History of Girolamo Savonarola*, 1:113.

64. The division between four and three is a commonplace of apocalyptic exposition, as when Call notes that "in accordance with the mystical principle of numbers which our prophet adopts, the first four seals are distinctly separated from the last three" ("The Apocalypse," p. 468).

65. Bonaparte notes that the exact date of the Feast of John the Baptist is not mentioned in the novel, perhaps because George Eliot "did not trust her source" (*Triptych*, p. 135). The Feast has been variously celebrated on June 24th, 25th, and 26th.

66. Keble, *The Christian Year*, pp. 277–78.

67. Mackay, *Progress of the Intellect*, 1:396.

68. These sermons are called "Advent Sermons" in Villari's biography, but Advent did not begin until November 30th in 1494 (see *History of Girolamo Savonarola*, 1:220). Weinstein points out that Savonarola's preaching at this time is based on the Second Charlemagne prophecy, and capitalizes on the civil apocalyptic tradition that expected to see its fulfillment in Florence (*Savonarola and Florence*, pp. 65–66).

69. For example, in a review of *Armageddon* (1858), the reviewer notes, "it is supposed by him that the beast under its 'septimo-octave' head, which is identified with Louis Napoleon, will personally enact the part of the last and great Antichrist" ("Prophecy, Its Interpretation, and Our Place in It" [*Christian Observer* (January 1860)]: 45). The reviewer later notes that the author of *Armageddon* "follows Mr. Faber; and so also Mr. Frere; and, though with ideas, and on grounds, quite peculiar, Mr. Trevillian" (p. 51). Faber's thesis led to much "bitterness of spirit" between him and E. B. Elliott. George Eliot's castigation of Cumming for his "minute identification of human things with such symbols as the scarlet whore, the beast out of the abyss, scorpions whose sting is in their tails, men who have the mark of the beast, and unclean spirits like frogs," indicates her awareness of this aspect of Victorian prophecy ("Evangelical Teaching," in Pinney, ed., *Essays of George Eliot*, p. 180).

70. Bonaparte infers the date of Tito's "last supper" as December 23, which is also the winter solstice, or darkest day of the year. However, it is on December 23 that Tito tells Romola he has already been called to Rome "about some learned business for Bernardo Rucellai" (388). In Chapter 38, we are told that Tito's journey to Rome "had been resolved on quite suddenly, at a supper, only the evening before" (402). I believe this places the supper on December 22—but since December 22 is the eve of the winter solstice, the Rucellai supper would still take place on the darkest *night* of the year.

71. In Mede's words, synchronism of prophecies occurs "when the things therein designated run along in the same time," encompassing "an agreement in time or age" (*Key of the Revelation*, p. 1).

72. Faber comments: "Those, who, like myself, profess to work upon Mr. Mede's PRINCIPLE, are at full liberty to doubt, whether that great father of apocalyptic interpretation has satisfactorily established *all* his synchronisms: but no person, who values the praise of intellect, will ever venture to reject the PRINCIPLE *itself*. That *principle* is, in fact, an eternal abstract truth.... In short, if the principle of ABSTRACT SYNCHRONISATION

be rejected, the Apocalypse forthwith becomes a mere chaos" (*Sacred Calendar*, 1:xii–xiii).

73. Elliott, like Faber, disagrees with the particulars of Mede's synchronisms, especially the division of the Apocalypse into two parts interpreted as being chronologically parallel but accepts the principle of synchronism as a distinct advance in apocalyptic interpretation (*Horae Apocalypticae*, 4:488).

74. Mackay, *Progress of the Intellect*, 1:102–3.

75. Bonaparte also suggests that Romola's betrothal to "Bacchus" foreshadows her later "marriage to Christ" but infers this from symbolic details of Romola and Tito's costumes (*Triptych*, pp. 96–100).

76. The additional biblical references in Bickersteth's chart reinforce the symbolic identification of the fifth day with judgment, as in Daniel's vision of the stone "cut out without hands, which smote the image" (Dan. 2:34), Ezekiel's vision of the river and its many fishermen (Ezek. 47:9–11), and Christ's call to Simon Peter and Andrew to become "fishers of men" (Matt. 4:19) (*Practical Guide to the Prophecies*, p. 252).

77. Temple, "The Education of the World," in Hedge, ed., *Recent Inquiries in Theology*, p. 11.

78. Peterson, "*Romola*," p. 57.

79. Haight, *George Eliot*, p. 365.

80. Jacobus, "The Law of/and Gender," p. 57.

CHAPTER 4

1. George Eliot, *Middlemarch*, Norton Critical Edition, ed. Bert G. Hornback (New York: W. W. Norton & Co., 1977). All further references in my text are to chapter and page of this edition.

2. In an interview with Robert Coover, Larry McCaffery queries the novelist about his recurrent interest in number "and its inevitable companion, numerology," suggesting that these seem to be "a perfect example of what you described earlier as fictions man used to navigate through the world." Coover replies: "Yes, or to stumble through it. It's one way among many that the mind gets locked into fixed distorting patterns. Silly stuff. But it was an important element in the Christian apocalyptic vision, so it had to be part of the *Brunists*. Then, once I started working with it, I found it useful in a lot of secondary and ironic ways. Especially in the formal design" ("Robert Coover on His Own and Other Fictions," p. 54). Like her latter-day counterpart, I suggest, George Eliot discovered how "useful" the apocalyptic scheme could be in "secondary and ironic ways," most especially in her "formal design."

3. Miller, "Optic and Semiotic in *Middlemarch*," in Buckley, ed., *The*

Worlds of Victorian Fiction, p. 143. See also Hertz, "Recognizing Casaubon," pp. 24–41, which extends Miller's thesis.

4. Miller, "Narrative and History," p. 464.

5. Stump, in *Movement and Vision in George Eliot's Novels*, also discusses the web image in *Middlemarch*; see especially pp. 136–71.

6. Browne, *Pseudodoxia Epidemica*, in *Sir Thomas Browne: The Major Works*, ed. C. A. Patrides (New York: Penguin Books, 1977), p. 234. All further references to Browne's works are to this edition except where otherwise identified and are hereafter cited as *Major Works*.

7. The gender of the *Middlemarch* narrator is debatable. Gilbert and Gubar, in *The Madwoman in the Attic*, make the interesting suggestion that the weaving of social webs in George Eliot's novels is largely a feminine preoccupation. Yet they propose that in *Middlemarch* "Eliot makes such gender-based categories irrelevant" and that the narrator "becomes an authentic 'we,' a voice of the community that is committed to accepting the indeterminacy of meaning, as well as the complex kinship of people and things" (p. 523). Since I believe that the author distinguishes between several different webs in the novel and that the narrator is identified only with the predominantly masculine image of the prophet-historian weaving a web of prophecy and history, I use the masculine pronoun in reference to this "belated historian." Other critical discussions on this issue include Hardy, *The Novels of George Eliot*, pp. 155–84; Miller, "Optic and Semiotic," in Buckley, ed., *The Worlds of Victorian Fiction*; Knoepflmacher, "*Middlemarch*," pp. 53–81; Isobel Armstrong, "*Middlemarch*: A Note on George Eliot's 'Wisdom,'" in Hardy, ed., *Critical Essays on George Eliot*, pp. 116–32; and Stange, "The Voices of the Essayist," pp. 312–30.

8. Browne reveals the Platonic derivation of his figure at the end of his fourth chapter (*Major Works*, p. 378). Since George Eliot was at this time reading Joseph Bertrans, *Les Fondateurs de l'astronomie moderne* (Paris, 1867), which describes the work of five Renaissance scientists, Browne's was probably only one of the musical prophetic schemes known to her (Pratt and Neufeldt, eds., *George Eliot's Middlemarch Notebooks*, pp. 65 and 149). S. K. Heninger, Jr., *The Cosmographical Glass*, describes a number of Renaissance musical and prophetic schemes of the universe, such as Robert Fludd's monochord extending from "silent stones" to "angelic choirs," in chap. 4, "The Pythagorean-Platonic Tradition," pp. 81–143.

9. Miller, "Narrative and History," p. 467. Miller implies George Eliot's closeness to poststructuralist perspectives on history and narrative, though he notes that history is not "chaos" for her. But as Anne K. Mellor states, it is important to differentiate the modern deconstructionist from the romantic ironist, for the latter is as much an enthusiast as an ironist: "Having ironically acknowledged the fictiveness of his own patternings of human experience, he romantically engages in the creative process of life

by eagerly constructing new forms, new myths.... They too die to give way to new patterns, in a never-ending process that becomes an analogue for life itself" (*English Romantic Irony*, p. 5).

10. Henkle, *Comedy and Culture*, p. 13.

11. Miller, in "Optic and Semiotic," in Buckley, ed., *The Worlds of Victorian Fiction*, points out this important comment in *The Mill On the Floss*, Book II, chap. 1.

12. The reader should also note the statement in chap. 37: "Will had—to use Sir Thomas Browne's phrase—a 'passionate prodigality' of statement both to himself and others" (Eliot, *Middlemarch*, p. 249). The phrase "passionate prodigality" is from *Urn Burial*.

13. Pratt and Neufeldt, eds., *George Eliot's Middlemarch Notebooks*, p. xxviii.

14. *The Works of Sir Thomas Browne*, ed. Simon Wilkin, 3 vols. (London, 1852). A copy of this work, underlined and annotated, is #320 in Baker, ed., *The George Eliot–George Henry Lewes Library*. Baker points out that quotations from Browne's *Pseudodoxia Epidemica* appear in *Felix Holt* and *Daniel Deronda*, as well as in *Middlemarch*, and that George Eliot also refers to Browne in essays as widely separated in time as the 1851 review of Robert Mackay's *Progress of the Intellect* and the 1865 review of William Lecky's *Influence of Rationalism* (p. xlvii).

15. See Pratt and Neufeldt, eds., *George Eliot's Middlemarch Notebooks*, pp. 64–67, or pp. 120–26 in the original notebook pagination.

16. As Ruth Vande Kieft has commented in an article linking Melville and Browne, Thomas Browne's literary reputation was a Romantic and nineteenth-century phenomenon: his prose style was lauded by Lamb, Coleridge, Hazlitt, Southey, and De Quincey, and was a major influence on American transcendentalists. Kieft not only suggests Browne had a highly significant influence on Melville, but comments that "Browne's innumerable applications of the quincunx may be compared with Melville's finding in the visible and invisible universe a symbolic representation of many facets of whaling" ("'When Big Hearts Strike Together,'" pp. 39–50, especially p. 46). Coleridge not only cites Browne's "genuine idiom" but in a letter to Sara Hutchinson recommends the reading of *Urn Burial* "above all." In the same letter, however, he also calls *The Garden of Cyrus* the "interesting, though far less interesting, Treatise on Quincuncial Plantations of the Ancients" and closes the letter with a quotation from the wonderful final paragraphs of *The Garden of Cyrus*, beginning "But the Quincunx of Heavens runs low . . ." (Brinkley, *Coleridge on the Seventeenth Century*, pp. 414 and 448–49). Interestingly, Emily Dickinson seems also to have linked the Apocalypse of St. John and Browne's works, as I have suggested is the case in *Middlemarch*, though Dickinson merely saw them both—along with Ruskin—as exemplars of prose style (Childs, "Emily Dickinson and Sir Thomas Browne," pp. 455–65).

17. Greenberg, in "Plexuses and Ganglia," pp. 33–52, discusses a number of historical physicians whose lives or work seem relevant to Lydgate's and who are mentioned earlier in the text of the novel or in George Eliot's *Quarry* and other notes. W. J. Harvey, in "Casaubon and Lydgate," in Hardy, ed., *Middlemarch*, had earlier suggested, however, that George Eliot meant to characterize Lydgate and Casaubon as "fundamentally mistaken in the nature of their research"—a proposal that makes a crucial distinction between Lydgate and all the physicians known to history because of their scientific accomplishments.

18. "The Influence of Rationalism," in Pinney, ed., *Essays of George Eliot*, p. 409.

19. Huntley, *Sir Thomas Browne*, pp. 204–23. In "*The Garden of Cyrus* as Prophecy," in Patrides, ed., *Approaches to Sir Thomas Browne*, pp. 132–42, Huntley argues that *The Garden of Cyrus* is a prophecy or vision springing from the prototype of the Book of Revelation. Margaret A. Heideman had earlier suggested that the urn-womb symbol unites Browne's two essays ("*Hydriotaphia* and *The Garden of Cyrus*," pp. 235–46).

20. In the 1852 edition, *The Garden of Cyrus* appears at the end of vol. 2, and *Urn Burial* at the beginning of vol. 3.

21. There are some fifteen separate notes on *Urn Burial*. See Pratt and Neufeldt, eds., *George Eliot's Middlemarch Notebooks*, pp. 66–67 and 150–51.

22. Knoepflmacher, "Fusing Fact and Myth," in Adam, ed., *This Particular Web*, p. 45.

23. Pratt and Neufeldt, eds., *George Eliot's Middlemarch Notebooks*, pp. xx, 4–8, 96–99.

24. Thomas Warton, *History of English Poetry* (London, 1824), 2:363–66. Pratt and Neufeldt, eds., *George Eliot's Middlemarch Notebooks*, p. 6.

25. Knoepflmacher, "Fusing Fact and Myth," in Adam, ed., *This Particular Web*, p. 53. Pratt and Neufeldt, eds., *George Eliot's Middlemarch Notebooks*, p. 85. According to this edition, George Eliot's remark about Isaac Casaubon as Shakespeare's contemporary appears on p. 160. Wilson, "The Key to All Mythologies," pp. 27–28, further suggests Isaac Casaubon's *Dittionario*, a work that dealt with true and false myths, as model for the *Middlemarch* "Key to All Mythologies." But see n. 28 below.

26. *Major Works*, p. 289. *Brampton Urns* is not included in this edition. In the 1852 edition, Browne's references to M. Casaubon and to Dr. Casaubon appear in 3:25 and 55.

27. Jacob Bryant's *A New System, or an Analysis of Ancient Mythology*, 3 vols. (1774–76), is often thought of as a model for Edward Casaubon's proposed "Key to All Mythologies." Will Ladislaw indeed suggests to Dorothea that her husband may be merely "crawling a little way after men of the last century—men like Bryant" (p. 154). Bryant is mentioned in George Eliot's essay on "The Progress of the Intellect" (Pinney, ed., *Essays*

of George Eliot, p. 36), and notes from the *New System* appear in the Folger notebook (Pratt and Neufeldt, eds., *George Eliot's Middlemarch Notebooks*, p. 48). It is interesting to note, however, that George Stanley Faber's *The Origin of Pagan Idolatry*, 3 vols. (London, 1816), is a precise example of a nineteenth-century work patterned *on* Bryant's, devoted to yet another quest after the common origin of all pagan myths. W. D. Paden, in *Tennyson in Egypt*, has shown how *The Origin of Pagan Idolatry* influenced Tennyson's earlier poetry. Though I have no evidence that George Eliot read this particular work by Faber, his discussions of such myths as the "great mother" as an "Ark," or the "fish-god" Dagon suggest a possible source for imagery in both *Romola* and *Middlemarch*.

28. "Some finde sepulchrall Vessels containing liquors, which time hath incrassated into gellies" (*Major Works*, p. 286). The "liquors" in this case refer to tears, thickened by time into jelly.

29. Browne himself frequently acknowledges his indebtedness to Plato, but George Yost's "Sir Thomas Browne and Aristotle" describes the predominance of Aristotle in seventeenth-century curricula and Browne's heavy indebtedness in scientific writing to Aristotle's "Book of Animals."

30. See George P. Landow's discussion of the "reality of types" in his *Victorian Types, Victorian Shadows*, pp. 51–63.

31. John R. Knott, Jr., in "Sir Thomas Browne and the Labyrinth of Truth," in Patrides, ed., *Approaches to Sir Thomas Browne*, pp. 19–30, illuminates Browne's figurative reading of scripture, but this interpretation of Browne's phrase, "sense and ocular Observation," suggests that Browne considered this rather than observation and generalization the surest path to truth. I must disagree with Knott's emphasis here.

32. Barricelli, "Romantic Writers and Music," states that the organ was "the instrument favored by the Romantics as the 'whole' or 'complete' instrument, hence the instrument of Totality" (p. 117, n. 39).

33. Cumming, *Apocalyptic Sketches*, First Series, p. 43.

34. Miller, "Optic and Semiotic," in Buckley, ed., *The Worlds of Victorian Fiction*, pp. 139–40, n. 10.

35. Rey M. Longyear suggests that many of Beethoven's "surprising modulations, tonal shifts, and unexpected resolutions of dominant harmonies can only be considered puns in music, with the same effect on the hearer." The restatement of musical ideas "in the wrong key" and a "humorously sudden modulation achieved by the irregular resolution of dominant harmony" are other examples of Beethoven's Romantic irony ("Beethoven and Romantic Irony," pp. 152, 154, 158, and 159).

36. George Eliot was an ardent amateur musician herself. Since girlhood she had played the piano, and well enough to attempt Beethoven sonatas. In a letter to Charles Lee Lewes in 1859, she mentioned owning "about eighteen sonatas and symphonies of Beethoven" (*GEL*, 3:177). Frederick Lehmann, who played "every piano and violin sonata of Mozart

and Beethoven" with her during the winter of 1866, commented that George Eliot was "a very fair pianist, not gifted, but enthusiastic, and extremely painstaking" (ibid., 8:386). Beethoven's music figured prominently also in the musical evenings that were a regular part of social life in the Lewes household.

In addition, George Eliot seems to have been particularly drawn to the Romantic emphasis on the "twin birth" of music and poetry during the period before and after the writing of *Middlemarch*. Many of the most "musical" (thematically speaking) poems later published in *The Legend of Jubal* were written at this time. Among the general works she read as part of her encyclopedic preparation for *Middlemarch*, also, was Dr. Charles Burney's *General History of Music* (1776), which not only contained an extensive discussion of ancient music but explicitly stated what later became the familiar Romantic theory of poetry: "Music, Poetry, Prophecy, and the Priesthood, seem inseparable employments in high antiquity" (1:337). George Eliot would seem to have been well prepared, then, to undertake an elaborate and subtle musical discourse at this time.

37. Although it is true that George Henry Lewes first suggested in a letter to George Eliot's publisher that dividing the novel into eight half-volume sizes would be wise for economic reasons, Jerome Beaty has also concluded that the eight-volume format was designed to fit the fiction, not vice versa, and that the half-volume form is fundamentally an artistic, not an economic, form (*"Middlemarch" from Notebook to Novel*, pp. 45 and 49).

38. Pratt and Neufeldt, eds., *George Eliot's Middlemarch Notebooks*, p. 39.

39. Cumming, *Apocalyptic Sketches*, Second Series, p. 50.

40. Pinney, ed., *Essays of George Eliot*, p. 163.

41. Cumming, *Apocalyptic Sketches*, Second Series, p. 50.

42. Pratt and Neufeldt, eds., *George Eliot's Middlemarch Notebooks*, p. 64.

43. Abrams, *The Mirror and the Lamp*.

44. According to Haight, *George Eliot*, "Mazzini was one of the few refugees Marian found acceptable as a contributor; she had long admired his efforts to unite Italy under a republican government" (p. 99). Mazzini is cited in chap. 42 of *Daniel Deronda* as a model of the prophetic vision of nationality. An abridged English translation of Mazzini's essay appears in N. Gangulee, ed., *Giuseppe Mazzini: Selected Writings* (1945; reprint, Westport, Conn.: Greenwood Press, 1974), pp. 245–51. All quotations in my text from Mazzini's works are from this edition. Barricelli's essay, cited above, analyzes Mazzini's philosophy of music and places it in the larger context of Romantic writings on music.

CHAPTER 5

1. George Eliot, *Daniel Deronda*, ed. Barbara Hardy (Harmondsworth, England: Penguin Books, 1967), p. 88. All further references in my text are to chapter and page of this edition.

2. Since F. R. Leavis's dictum, in *The Great Tradition*, that *Daniel Deronda* would be a much better novel if the entire plot relating to Daniel was simply cut away, critics have attempted to demonstrate how the two plot lines can be seen as an organic whole. For example, Maurice Beebe, in "'Visions Are Creators,'" argues that "*Daniel Deronda* is a novel of ideas, and only by reading it on the ideological level rather than the narrative level alone may we see that everything is indeed related. The one story is commentary on the other, and the two stories are counterpointed variations of a single theme" (p. 168). However, Jerome Beaty responds that, though "there is a convincing case for the thematic unity of *Daniel Deronda*," the reader's response confirms a long tradition of critical opinion that the novel "falls inevitably into two unwelded parts" ("*Daniel Deronda* and the Question of Unity," pp. 16–19).

3. Chase, "The Decomposition of the Elephants," pp. 215–27. Although critics have traditionally criticized the "failure of realism" in *Daniel Deronda*, Chase is representative of a recent critical stance that asserts the impossibility of realism in fiction and uses George Eliot's own novels to deconstruct her statements of intended fidelity to it. J. Hillis Miller's "Narrative and History" suggests that George Eliot deliberately deconstructs traditional conceptions of history and narrative in *Middlemarch* (pp. 455–73). Other critics have attempted to explore in a larger frame of reference what George Eliot meant by "realism." E. S. Shaffer, in "*Kubla Khan*" and the Fall of Jerusalem, suggests that "'realism' is a shibboleth that prevents us from understanding the functioning of this novel" (p. 227) and that *Daniel Deronda* was intended to be an "epic poem in modern terms" that "adheres to a new set of epic roles and epic 'machinery' based on the nature of Biblical history" (p. 250). Other works in this vein are U. C. Knoepflmacher's "Fusing Fact and Myth: The New Reality of *Middlemarch*," in Adam, ed., *This Particular Web*, and *George Eliot's Early Novels: The Limits of Realism*; John P. McGowan's "The Turn of George Eliot's Realism"; and Catherine Gallagher's "The Failure of Realism: *Felix Holt*."

4. An example of this opinion is Arthur Penrhyn Stanley's comment that "there may be many innocent questions about the date, or about the interpretation of the Book of Daniel, and of the Apocalypse. But there can be no doubt that they contain the first germs of the great idea of the succession of ages, of the continuous growth of empires and races under a law of Divine Providence, the first sketch of the Education of the world, and the first outline of the Philosophy of History" (*The Jewish Church*, 1:518). Interestingly, modern historians agree with this Victorian assess-

ment of Daniel as the origin of the philosophy of history. See, for example, Collingwood, *The Idea of History*; Lowith, *Meaning in History*; and Manuel, *Shapes of Philosophical History*.

5. Eliot, "Oriental Memoranda," Pforzheimer MS 710, fol. 14. The quotation is from Kuenen, *Religion of Israel*, 3:111. See n. 28 below concerning Kuenen's possible influence on *Daniel Deronda*.

6. Stuart, *A Commentary on the Book of Daniel*, p. iii.

7. Eliot, *Felix Holt, the Radical*, p. 503. William Baker, in *George Eliot and Judaism*, has discussed George Eliot's interest in Jewish writers and attempted to relate it to *Daniel Deronda*. E. S. Shaffer, in *"Kubla Khan" and the Fall of Jerusalem*, has analyzed the novel in relation to the German criticism that George Eliot had translated earlier in her career. My approach is intended to complement the work of these two critics, placing *Daniel Deronda* in the context of English Protestant exegesis, both traditional and contemporary.

8. The first essay in *Essays and Reviews*, "The Education of the World" by Frederick Temple, may be seen as a reinterpretation of the Four Empires scheme in Daniel (Boston, 1861). (See Frederic H. Hedge, ed., *Recent Inquiries in Theology*, commonly referred to as *Essays and Reviews*.) Other commentaries on Daniel which appeared between 1860 and 1876, in addition to those cited in my text, are Bosanquet, *Messiah the Prince; or, the Inspiration of the Prophecies of Daniel*; Boyle, *The Inspiration of the Book of Daniel*; Darby, *Studies in the Book of Daniel*; Faber, *The 70 Weeks of Daniel*; Fuller, *An Essay on the Authenticity of the Book of Daniel*; Goode, *Fulfilled Prophecy a Proof of the Truth of Revealed Religion*; Kelly, *Notes on the Book of Daniel*; Sawyer, *Daniel, with Its Apocryphal Additions*; Thurman, *Our Bible Chronology Established, the Sealed Book of Daniel Opened*; Zöckler, *The Book of the Prophet Daniel*.

In addition to commentaries specifically on Daniel, works on Jewish history usually contained significant commentary on the Book of Daniel. Prominent among such works were Kuenen, *Religion of Israel*; Milman, *History of the Jews*; Stanley, *Lectures on the History of the Jewish Church*; Ewald, *History of Israel*.

9. Pusey, *Daniel the Prophet*, p. 75.

10. Desprez, *Daniel*, pp. viii, lxi, and lxvii.

11. Birks, *The Four Prophetic Empires*, pp. 86–87.

12. Interestingly, Marcus Dod's translation of *City of God*—the first English translation to appear since the early nineteenth century—was published in 1871. I have not been able to discover any evidence, however, that George Eliot read Augustine's *City of God* either at this time or earlier.

13. Davison, *Discourses on Prophecy*; see especially Discourse III. Davison's work went through many editions and was cited frequently in other works on prophecy throughout the century. It became a standard reference in "continuous historical" exegesis.

14. Brian Swann, in "George Eliot's Ecumenical Jew," pp. 39–50, points out that *Daniel Deronda* is much like a morality play "in which traditional terms are reversed," since Deronda is Christ-like and Grandcourt is Satanic. However, Swann suggests missionary novels, such as Mrs. Ogden's *Into the Light*, as Ur-forms for George Eliot's novel (p. 44).

15. Landow, *Victorian Types, Victorian Shadows*, and Sussman, *Fact into Figure*, discuss typology in the Victorian era.

16. Mede, *The Apostasy of the Latter Times* (1642), p. 69. Although this work is subtitled "A Treatise of 1 Timothy Chap. 4 ver. 1,2," Mede's determination of the date of the "latter times" rests on the Book of Daniel, and much of the work is devoted to interpretation of the seventy weeks. The *Apostasy* was reprinted several times in the nineteenth century, in editions by T. D. Gregg (London, 1836), J. H. Brown (London, 1840), and Rev. T. R. Birks (London, 1845, 1855).

17. Faber, *The Sacred Calendar of Prophecy*, p. vii.

18. Bickersteth, *Practical Guide to the Prophecies*, p. 133.

19. Sudrann, "*Daniel Deronda* and the Landscape of Exile," p. 436.

20. I have already referred to Shaffer's point that *Daniel Deronda* is an "epic poem" utilizing the "machinery" of biblical history, but she has not specified the predominance of references to the biblical literature of exile.

21. Even the higher criticism only relegated Daniel to a later period of "exile," i.e., the persecution of the Jews under Antiochus Epiphanes in the second century B.C. Kuenen, for example, dated the Book of Daniel sometime after 165 B.C. (*Religion of Israel*, 3:106).

22. Kuenen states that "the author of the book of Daniel . . . is the first who mentions the names of angels," a practice that Kuenen ascribes to Persian influence (ibid., 3:38). George Eliot's "Oriental Memoranda" notebook demonstrates her interest in angelic names, for under the heading "Angel," she notes "Biblical Special Names: Michael, Gabriel, Raphael, Uriel." The entry also lists angelic names found in apocryphal and Talmudic literature (Pforzheimer MS 710, [fol. 5]).

23. It may be pertinent here to point out that "chain" was a very common metaphor for prophetic history, connoting particularly its elusiveness and obscurity, and the need for prophetic vision with which to unite its separate links. For example, Faber, in referring to the "chronological chain of prophecy," comments that "one of the principal chains, which in such manner binds together the detached prophecies of numerous inspired writers, is the yet future predicted restoration of Judah" (*The Sacred Calendar of Prophecy*, 1:xvii).

24. Eliot, Notebooks, Pforzheimer MS 711, [fol. 29].

25. Kriefall, "A Victorian Apocalypse," p. 123. Although Kriefall calls the passage in *Daniel Deronda* a "realization" of the "Son of Man" vision in Daniel 7, he is not primarily concerned with the relationship between the novel and the Book of Daniel but rather with what he feels is George

Eliot's embodiment of Strauss's concept of Christ in the character Daniel Deronda.

26. Birks, *The Four Prophetic Empires*, epitomizes the traditional interpretation when he states that the Son of Man is "plainly" Christ, although he represents also "the whole body of his ransomed people." John Cumming, whose *Lectures on the Book of Daniel* was included among the books George Eliot read in preparation for her critique of Cumming in 1855, concluded that the "Ancient of Days" must refer to Christ, since God the Father was never pictured in the Bible. Since the "Son of Man" was also Christ, Cumming found himself in an exegetical position that he confessed he could not explain (p. 243). Pusey, in *Daniel the Prophet*, reaffirms the traditional interpretation that the "Son of Man" prophesied the coming of the Messiah and that this prophecy was fulfilled by Christ (p. 130). Desprez, in *Daniel, or the Apocalypse of the Old Testament*, comments that, while "unable to endorse the traditional opinion that the writer saw the glories of our own Messiah, and spake directly of him, we would admit that the symbols of Daniel may have contributed to give shape to the messianic conceptions of the Christian period" (p. 241).

27. Levine, "George Eliot's Hypothesis of Reality," pp. 1–28.

28. Kuenen, *Religion of Israel*, 3:204–5. George Eliot's many quotations from the English translation of this work—not all of which are identified as such—in her "Oriental Memoranda" notebook (Pforzheimer MS 710), demonstrate its importance to her thought. The exact relationship of Kuenen's work to her conception of *Daniel Deronda*, however, cannot be decisively stated, as neither the notebook nor its contents are dated. The notebook (which has not yet been published) consists of a sort of dictionary of material on "Oriental," chiefly biblical, subjects, with a page allotted to each letter of the alphabet and material arranged alphabetically according to subject. The first page of the notebook contains a list of works consulted, and since the next to last of these works—Sayce's *Babylonian Literature*—was not published until 1877, William Baker concludes that the notebook must be "relatively late"—i.e., not finished until after *Daniel Deronda* (*Some George Eliot Notebooks*, 1:12 [MS 707]). However, some of the material in the notebook quoted from the first two volumes of Kuenen's work—most notably, the lengthy quotation concerning the "Book of Origins"—seems so integral to the conception of *Daniel Deronda* as to make it likely that these two volumes were read before or during the writing of the novel. The dates of publication make this a distinct possibility: the first volume of *Religion of Israel* (in the English translation quoted by George Eliot) appeared no later than July 1874. (Baker's assertion that the English translation of "Kenan's [sic] *Religion of Israel* was published in 1873 appears to be an error.) The second volume had been published by April 1875. George Eliot was working on *Daniel Deronda* during the summer of 1874 and mentions in her journal in January 1875

that she is just now "beginning the part about Deronda," or chapter 16 (Haight, *George Eliot*, p. 476). She did not deliver the first volume (chaps. 1–18) to Blackwood until May 1875. The third volume of Kuenen's *Religion of Israel*, from which she quoted the comment on Daniel (Eliot, "Oriental Memoranda," Pforzheimer MS 710, fol. 14), was not published until October 1875. The novel itself was published in eight parts from February to September 1876. Volume 1 could thus have been seminal to George Eliot's conception of *Daniel Deronda*. Volume 2, however, could either have shaped her conception in progress or been quoted later because it provided such an extraordinary parallel to her own thought. While the former seems more probable to me, especially in view of the remarkable similarities between Kuenen's characterization of Ezra and George Eliot's use of the name in the novel, the latter is possible. Whether made before or after the writing of the novel, however, George Eliot's quotations from Kuenen provide new insight into *Daniel Deronda*.

29. Kuenen, *Religion of Israel*, 1:205.

30. In one of her notebooks, George Eliot quoted a passage from Micah 3:6, King James version: "Therefore night shall be unto you that ye shall not have a vision; & it shall be dark unto you that ye shall not divine; & the sun shall go down over the prophets, & the day shall be dark over them" (Baker, ed., *Some George Eliot Notebooks*, 1:119 [MS 707]). Baker does not point out that Mordecai's speech in chapter 42 of *Daniel Deronda* contains a paraphrase of this quotation: "'What wonder? The night is unto them, that they have no vision; in their darkness they are unable to divine; the sun is gone down over the prophets, and the day is dark above them; their observances are as nameless relics'" (Eliot, *Daniel Deronda*, p. 591). The quotation is in MS 707, not MS 710, in which George Eliot recorded her quotations from Kuenen, but it is interesting that Kuenen also quotes this passage from Micah (*Religion of Israel*, 1:83), although not in the King James translation. Kuenen quotes the passage as an example of the prophet's denunciation of the "false prophets" of his time.

31. Chase, "The Decomposition of the Elephants," p. 221.

32. Kuenen, *Religion of Israel*, 2:232. Much of this volume focuses on Ezra, whom Kuenen regarded as the probable author of the *priestly* (as opposed to the *prophetic*) narratives in the Old Testament. See pp. 147–73, 212–50, 286–95.

33. Eliot, "Oriental Memoranda," Pforzheimer MS 710, fol. 12, italics George Eliot's. Under the spelling "Kohen," George Eliot notes "Arabic *Kahine*. Seer. Hence it came to mean in Heb. priest. Munk says Kohen means black man i.e. clothed in black" (ibid., [fol. 23]).

34. Ibid., fol. 30.

35. Newton discusses the prevalence of circumcision in the Victorian era in "*Daniel Deronda* and Circumcision," pp. 313–27.

36. Alley, "New Year's at the Abbey," pp. 147–49.
37. Keble, *The Christian Year*, pp. 35–37.

CHAPTER 6

1. George Eliot, *The Legend of Jubal and Other Poems* (Boston: James R. Osgood and Co., 1874). All further references in my text are to this edition, which was printed from advance sheets and appears to be identical in the texts and ordering of the poems to the 1874 London edition published by William Blackwood and Sons. The poems in *The Legend of Jubal* were also published, with four additional poems, in the 1878 Cabinet edition of George Eliot's works, as is discussed in my text.

2. See Blake, "*Armgart*—George Eliot on the Woman Artist" and Mann, "George Eliot and Wordsworth." Prior to these essays, Cynthia Ann Secor's "The Poems of George Eliot" suggested the possibility of a meaningful order of poems in both the 1874 and 1878 editions of *Jubal* (Appendix A). As summarized, Secor proposed that "Jubal" opens the collection with a statement that the knowledge of death leads to purposeful activity—labor and creation, industry and culture. The next three poems are about loving and productive lives. The fifth poem is in effect a prophecy for the future, in which the image of static identity is opposed to that of dynamic union. In "Brother and Sister," dynamic union is followed by change. "Stradivarius" argues the necessity of self-sacrificing labor. "Two Lovers" portrays an idealized human union, a couple pursuing willing and loving labor. "Arion" balances this union with an image of isolated heroism, and "Choir Invisible" describes a heaven resulting from labor and art. Secor believes the later four poems were added to the 1878 volume in such a way as to reinforce this ideational order.

3. Keble, *The Christian Year*. Page numbers are not given for this text, as pagination in many editions varies widely, and allusions to the rather short poems can be fairly easily located.

4. Elaine Showalter, in *A Literature of Their Own* and also in her more recent essay "Towards a Feminist Poetics," has distinguished three historical periods of the female tradition in British literature as Feminine, Feminist, and Female. Showalter places George Eliot in the Feminine period, characterized by the use of a male pseudonym and by internalization of male assumptions about female nature. Particularly in relation to *The Legend of Jubal*, I would underline Showalter's statement that "the feminist content of feminine art is typically oblique, displaced, ironic and subversive; one has to read it between the lines, in the missed possibilities of the text" ("Towards a Feminist Poetics," p. 35). That is precisely the case with the private, unannounced relationship I postulate between George Eliot's

poetic work and Keble's. Her very celebration of feminine values at times functions as a veiled, but nonetheless real, feminist critique of patriarchal religion. I would further suggest that in "Brother and Sister" George Eliot reaches into the female phase, exploring the female experience itself as the "source of an autonomous art" (ibid., p. 36).

5. Call, "The Religion of Positivism," pp. 305–49. This article is a review essay of Auguste Comte's *Catechism of Positive Religion*, trans. Richard Congreve (1858). See especially p. 317 for Call's discussion of the influence of women in the Positive movement.

6. See my discussion in Chapter 1 and in Chapter 3, section III, of F. D. Maurice's appropriation of the Comtean distinction between "masculine" and "feminine" values in his interpretation of the "woman clothed with the sun."

7. As Secor points out, an author so careful with "the placement of every comma" was not likely to have allowed her publisher to arrange the poems ("The Poems of George Eliot," p. 425). In addition, Blackwood's urging that George Eliot restore the dates she had removed from the manuscript not only suggests that she was responsible for the nonchronological order of the poems but that she had at first intended to remove all evidence of their chronological order, thus heightening the implication of some kind of order (*GEL*, 6:37).

8. Tennyson, in *Victorian Devotional Poetry*, states for example that "Keble rearranged a gathering of poems written over a long period to correspond to the Church year. Likewise, there are poems attached to a particular Sunday or holy day referring to some other season of the year than the one in which the day falls" (p. 83).

9. Kilroy, "The Chiastic Structure of *In Memoriam, A.H.H.*," p. 358.

10. Tennyson, *The Poetry of Tennyson*, p. 156.

11. See Baker, "The Poet's Progress," pp. 1–14; Kent, "Sequence and Meaning in Christina Rossetti's *Verses* (1893)," pp. 259–64; Joyce, "Music's Principle of Retrograde Motion as a Structuring Element for Browning's *Men and Women* (1863, 1968)," pp. 468–83.

12. "In the South" has been published in Paris, "George Eliot's Unpublished Poetry," pp. 539–58. Secor, who dates the manuscript 1867, notes that the poem is reminiscent of Keats and comments that this and "Ex oriente lux" are as "lovely as anything she wrote" ("The Poems of George Eliot," p. 54).

13. Recent criticism has suggested the possibility of meaningful structure in Keats's volume, however; see especially Fraistat, *The Poem and the Book*.

14. Haight, *George Eliot*, p. 421.

15. Keble's general debt to Wordsworth's early poetry is well known, as is Wordsworth's left-handed compliment that *The Christian Year* was so good he wished he had written it himself so that he could rewrite it and make it

even better (as quoted in Prickett, *Romanticism and Religion*, p. 92). Prickett comments on the shallowness of Keble's Wordsworthian echoes in the poem for the Fourth Sunday in Advent, as well as its "straightforward" otherworldliness (ibid., p. 104).

16. Mann, "George Eliot and Wordsworth," p. 685.

17. Tennyson discusses Keble's use of the Doctrine of Analogy in his chapter "Tracterian Poetics," *Victorian Devotional Poetry*, pp. 12–71. Prickett's chapter, "Keble's 'Two Worlds'" in *Romanticism and Religion*, pp. 91–119, focuses on the difference between Wordsworth's "Nature" and Keble's "Two Worlds."

18. Wordsworth, *The Prelude*, Book VI, ll. 638–40, in *Selected Poems and Prefaces*, p. 269. This and other references to *The Prelude* in my text are to the 1850 edition.

19. Karen B. Mann suggests that Jubal's "first expectation of ever higher personal success" is exemplified in the poem "in the climbing of higher and higher mountains which will eventually allow him to hear the true music of the spheres." She concludes, however, that it is "Jubal's sense of the largeness of the world embodied in the roaring of the sea, and the growing weakness of his personal power to order what that sea speaks to him" that brings a "crippling paralysis" ("George Eliot and Wordsworth," p. 685). Mann's emphasis on the poetic function of creating order seems to me to distort George Eliot's primary emphasis on the expression of feeling.

20. "Erinna" has been published in Paris's article, "George Eliot's Unpublished Poetry," pp. 545–49. The date of this poem is uncertain, although it must have been written prior to the publication of *Daniel Deronda* in 1875, since lines 5–12 appear as the motto for chapter 51 in the novel. As Secor comments, the poem looks as if it belongs in the *Jubal* collection, yet George Eliot chose not to include it even in the later 1878 edition ("Poems of George Eliot," p. 78). Secor suggests that the poem "does not contain the emphasis on futurity that characterizes her most ambitious works" and that George Eliot may have thought the poem in some sense incomplete. Certainly, the final stanza of the poem does not encompass a resolution for the problem of the artist's mortality that it raises, and George Eliot may have thought "Jubal" a more complete working-out of a similar poetic theme.

21. Paris, "George Eliot's Unpublished Poetry," p. 548, n. 14.

22. Bright, "English Literary Romanticism and the Oxford Movement," p. 389.

23. Yonge, *Musings over the Christian Year*, p. 23. Yonge is the only author who comments on each of Keble's poems individually. Although I have no evidence that George Eliot had read this particular work of Yonge's, I cite Yonge's comments to illustrate what was probably a characteristically Victorian Anglican response to Keble's poems. In addition, Yonge had been

Keble's pupil at Confirmation, and her commentary on the poems frequently alludes to links between the Anglican lectionary and Keble's religious thought—links that are by no means obvious today.

24. Landow, *Victorian Types, Victorian Shadows*, discusses the application of types to the individual believer in his first chapter, "Typological Interpretation in the Victorian Period," particularly pp. 67–69.

25. Secor believes that January 1869 is probably the more accurate date for the composition of the poem, as a fair copy made in May 1869 bears the January date. Even if George Eliot wrote the poem a month after Christmas, however, her dating of the gift copy "Christmas, 1868" would seem to demonstrate her association of it with Christmas ("The Poems of George Eliot," p. 172).

26. Browning, *Poems of Robert Browning*, p. 259.

27. Joyce, "Music's Principle of Retrograde Motion," p. 469. Joyce points out that "Transcendentalism," which appears near the end of the 1855 edition of *Men and Women*, was placed at the beginning of the 1863 and 1868 editions, where it serves as an "introduction and guide" to the following poems. His argument that these later editions of *Men and Women* were actually organized on a musical principle ("retrograde motion"), as well as utilizing the structuring metaphor of soul as "song," suggests another poetic model for George Eliot.

28. A second and interesting point of comparison between *Aurora Leigh* and *The Legend of Jubal* is that the plot of *Aurora Leigh* constitutes, as Cora Kaplan comments, "an overlapping sequence of dialogues with other texts, other writers" (*Aurora Leigh and Other Poems*, p. 16). Although the correspondence to Keble's *Christian Year* seems to be the most consistent such "dialogue" in *Jubal*, I have pointed to examples of responses to a number of other writers as well.

29. Prickett, *Romanticism and Religion*, p. 110. G. B. Tennyson refutes this interpretation of Keble's poetics, previously proposed by Alba H. Warren in *English Poetic Theory, 1828–1865*, and M. H. Abrams in *The Mirror and the Lamp*. According to Tennyson, Keble is not speaking of repressed emotion but of yearning for God and that "even when Keble speaks of poetry as preserving the poet from mental disease, we must be careful not to read such an expression [sic] in twentieth-century terms. The mental disease is here a sickness of spirit to which one is liable when the yearning for God is stifled" (*Victorian Devotional Poetry*, p. 60). George Eliot, however, clearly interpreted Keble as referring to repression of emotion rather than theological yearnings.

30. Eliot, *Daniel Deronda*, p. 694.

31. Blake, "*Armgart*—George Eliot on the Woman Artist," p. 79.

32. In *The Madwoman in the Attic* Gilbert and Gubar take Armgart as a prime example of their thesis that George Eliot associated the female artist with a satanic Eve, or the "female gothic" (p. 453).

33. Robertson and Stevens, eds., *Pelican History of Music*, p. 36.

34. In an early letter to Sophia Hennell, George Eliot describes what was evidently her first experience of Gluck's opera, heard in Berlin in 1855: "The voices—except in the choruses—are all women's voices, and there are only three characters—Orpheus, Amor and Euridice. One wonders that Pluto does not come as a Basso, and one would prefer Mercury as a tenor to Amor in the shape of an ugly German soprano—but Gluck willed it otherwise and the music is delightful" (*GEL*, 2:191). George Eliot's description strongly suggests that she was unaware, at this time, of Gluck's reason for "willing" the part of Amor as a soprano and for the absence of vocal parts written for the "male," or lower ranges. She could not, however, have continued so naive by the time of the writing of "Armgart." Not only were she and George Henry Lewes avid operagoers both in England and on the Continent, but in preparation for *Middlemarch*, George Eliot read Charles Burney's *General History of Music*. Burney devotes considerable space to discussion of the *castrati* singers—both deploring the parental motives that led to the creation of this peculiar mode and defending the voices and talent of individual singers (vol. 4, especially pp. 40–43). Burney details the English operas in which parts were written specifically for individual *castrato* singers. Burney also refers to *Orfeo* as Gluck's first opera on the "reformed plan" (ibid., 4:579).

35. "Armgart," as I have explicated it, substantiates Zelda Austen's thesis in "Why Feminist Critics Are Angry with George Eliot." Austen proposes that George Eliot's novels, especially *Middlemarch*, refuse to exalt the woman with superior gifts above the common lot and instead show "the attractions of the conventional life for the extraordinary girl, and thus her sisterhood with all other women" (p. 558).

36. Keats, *Selected Poems and Letters*, pp. 141–56.

37. "Isabella" is based on Boccaccio's *Decameron*, Day 4, story 5. "Lisa" is based on Day 10, story 7.

38. Eliot, *Middlemarch*, p. 575.

39. Ford, *Keats and the Victorians*, pp. 77–78.

40. See Rosenberg, "The Two Kingdoms in *In Memoriam*," p. 240, and Landow, *Victorian Types, Victorian Shadows*, pp. 10–12, for discussion of Tennyson's concept of type as part of a divine evolutionary scheme.

41. On August 7, 1878, William Blackwood wrote to George Eliot that the "other volume" of poetry for the Cabinet edition "will take some planning and scheming to swell it out to the required length unless you have any other poems you wish to insert in it. Will you kindly let me know as to this at your early convenience?" (*GEL*, 7:51). On August 9, 1878, George Eliot replied, "as to the 'Jubal' volume, there will, I hope[,] be added matter enough to save you from difficulty as to the size. I *should* like to see the proofs" (*GEL*, 7:55). On August 15, 1878, George Eliot again commented, "For the volume of miscellaneous poems, there will be (retaining

the present page of 20 lines) enough additional matter to make the volume about 300 pages. . . . Pray tell me as nearly as you can when you shall want the additional pages for the Jubal volume" (*GEL*, 7:58). The poems added were printed as follows: (1) "A College Breakfast-Party," placed between "Stradivarius" and "Two Lovers"; (2) "Self and Life," " 'Sweet Evenings Come and Go, Love,' " and "The Death of Moses," placed between "Two Lovers" and "Arion."

42. Interestingly, concern for social relations is considered characteristic of women in some present-day feminist theory as well as in Victorian Positivist theory. Carol Gilligan, for example, states that "women not only define themselves in a context of human relationships, but judge themselves in terms of their ability to care. Woman's place in man's life cycle has been that of nurturer, caretaker, and helpmate, the weaver of those networks of relationships on which she, in turn, relies" ("Why Should a Woman Be More Like a Man?" in *Psychology Today* [June 1982], p. 68). The article is excerpted from Gilligan's book, *In a Different Voice*.

43. In his chapter "The Smitten Rock" in *Victorian Types, Victorian Shadows*, Landow describes and analyzes Moses' rod as a biblical type that appeared frequently in Victorian literature (pp. 88–127). Among other examples, he comments on two uses of the type in Keble's poems for *The Christian Year* (ibid., pp. 110–14).

44. Thompson, "*The Temple* and the *Christian Year*," pp. 1018–25, considers Keble's debt to Herbert in general but does not mention the many echoes from Herbert's "Easter" in Keble's poem for Palm Sunday, "The Children in the Temple." Compare, for example, Herbert's "Rise heart, thy Lord is Risen. Sing his praise / Without delays. . . . Awake, my Lute, and struggle for thy part / With all thy art," with Keble's "Ye whose hearts are beating high / With the pulse of Poesy. . . . Know ye, who hath set your parts? / He who gave you breath to sing." Keble adopts Herbert's entire metaphor of childlike song as the "best" because it is the most humble praise. Martin, *John Keble, Priest, Professor and Poet*, pp. 156–57, also considers a few individual examples of Keble's indebtedness to Herbert but does not mention this one. Martin notes that "the parallel in ideas and imagery between Keble's poetry and Herbert's is obvious, although Keble's poems lack the energy and dexterity of Herbert's" (ibid., p. 157).

45. Prickett, *Romanticism and Religion*, p. 104.

46. Secor, "The Poems of George Eliot," p. 337.

Bibliography

PRIMARY SOURCES

George Eliot

Baker, William, ed. *Some George Eliot Notebooks: An Edition of the Carl H. Pforzheimer Library's George Eliot Holograph Notebooks, MSS 707, 708, 709, 710, 711.* Vol. 1, MS 707. Salzburg Studies in Literature. Salzburg, Austria: Universität Salzburg, 1976.
Eliot, George. *Adam Bede.* Edited by Stephen Gill. Harmondsworth: Penguin Books, 1972.
―――. *Complete Poems.* Boston: Dana Estes & Co., n.d. [1878].
―――. *Daniel Deronda.* Edited by Barbara Hardy. Harmondsworth: Penguin Books, 1967.
―――. *Felix Holt, the Radical.* Edited by Peter Coveney. Harmondsworth: Penguin Books, 1972.
―――. George Eliot's Notes for Romola. MS #40768. British Library, London. Microfilm.
―――. Journal. Yale MS IV.3. Beinecke Library, Yale University, New Haven, Conn.
―――. *The Legend of Jubal and Other Poems.* Boston: James R. Osgood and Co., 1874.
―――. *The Legend of Jubal and Other Poems.* London: William Blackwood and Sons, 1874.
―――. *Middlemarch.* Norton Critical Edition. Edited by Bert G. Hornback. New York: W. W. Norton & Co., 1977.
―――. *The Mill on the Floss.* Edited by Gordon S. Haight. Boston: Riverside Edition, Houghton Mifflin Co., 1961.
―――. Notebooks. Pforzheimer MS 711. Carl H. Pforzheimer Library, New York, N.Y. Microfilm.
―――. "Oriental Memoranda" [notebook]. Pforzheimer MS 710. Carl H. Pforzheimer Library, New York, N.Y. Microfilm.
―――. *Romola.* Edited by Andrew Sanders. Harmondsworth: Penguin Books, 1980.
―――. *Scenes of Clerical Life.* Edited by David Lodge. Harmondsworth: Penguin Books, 1973.

Haight, Gordon S., ed. *The George Eliot Letters.* New Haven: Yale University Press, 1954.
Paris, Bernard J. "George Eliot's Unpublished Poetry." *Studies in Philology* 56 (1959): 535–58.
Pinney, Thomas, ed. *Essays of George Eliot.* New York: Columbia University Press, 1963.
Pratt, John Clark, and Victor A. Neufeldt, eds. *George Eliot's Middlemarch Notebooks.* Berkeley: University of California Press, 1979.
Secor, Cynthia Ann. "The Poems of George Eliot: A Critical Edition with Introduction and Notes." Ph.D. diss., Cornell University, 1969.
Wiesenfarth, Joseph, ed. *George Eliot: A Writer's Notebook, 1854–1879; and Uncollected Writings.* Charlottesville: Published for the Bibliographical Society of the University of Virginia by the University Press of Virginia, 1981.

British Apocalyptic Exposition, 1600–1875:
A Selective Bibliography

Note: Since my intention in compiling this bibliography has been to outline apocalyptic controversy in nineteenth-century England and Scotland, I have included works that were either published, reprinted, translated, or widely quoted in Great Britain. I have not aimed at completeness so much as at identification of the most influential and prolific expositors of the different schools, their chief concerns in exposition, the extent of their interreaction as an intellectual community, and the chronological period during which they flourished. My emphasis falls on exposition of the "continuous historical" school during the Romantic and Victorian eras, from the years immediately following the French Revolution to 1875. For this period, I have listed not only published books but important articles on apocalyptics published in English journals. For the seventeenth and eighteenth centuries, by contrast, I have listed only those works on apocalyptics that were frequently cited by "continuous historical" expositors in the nineteenth century.

Alford, Henry. *The Greek Testament.* 4 vols. London, 1849–61.
Allwood, Philip. *Twelve Lectures on the Prophecies Relating to the Christian Church, and Especially to the Apostacy of Papal Rome.* Warburtonian Lectures. 2 vols. London, 1815.
Armstrong, Amzi. *A Syllabus of Lectures on the Visions of the Revelation.* Morristown, N.J., 1815.
Bale, John. *Select Works of John Bale . . . Containing . . . the Image of Both Churches.* Edited by Rev. Henry Christmas. Cambridge, England, 1849.

Barnes, Albert. *Notes, Explanatory and Practical, on the Book of Revelation.* New York, 1858.

Baxter, Michael P. *The Coming Battle, and the Appalling National Convulsions Foreshown in Prophecy Immediately to Occur during the Period of 1861–67....* London, 1860.

———. *Louis Napoleon, the Destined Monarch of the World.* 4th ed. Philadelphia, 1863.

Bicheno, James. *The Destiny of the German Empire; or An Attempt to Ascertain the Apocalyptic Dragon.* London, 1801.

———. *Explanation of Scripture Prophecy—the Signs of the Times.* West Springfield, Mass., 1796.

———. *A Friendly Address to the Jews . . . to Which Is Added a Letter to Mr. D. Levi....* London, [1787].

———. *A Glance at the History of Christianity and of English Nonconformity*, 4th ed., with . . . *a Postscript on the Present Movement in the East*. [Newbury, England, 1799.]

———. *Preparation for the Coming of Christ.* London, 1803.

———. *The Restoration of the Jews....* London, 1800.

———. *The Signs of the Times: or, The Overthrow of the Papal Tyranny in France.* 2 vols. Vol. 1, 4th ed.; Vol. 2, 2d ed. Edinburgh, 1794.

———. *Supplement to the Signs of the Times, Containing a Reply to the Objections of Rev. G. S. Faber.* London, n.d.

Bickersteth, Edward. *Practical Guide to the Prophecies.* From the 6th London ed. As published in *The Literalist*, vol. 4. Philadelphia, 1841.

———. *Scripture Help.* The Christian's Family Library. London, 1834? First published 1816.

Birchmore, John W. *Prophecy Interpreted by History; Including Present Events. Being a Brief and Popular Explanation of Daniel and of St. John.* New York, 1871.

Birks, T. R. *The Four Prophetic Empires and the Kingdom of Messiah: Being an Exposition of the First Two Visions of Daniel.* 2d ed. The Christian's Family Library, ed. Edward Bickersteth. London, 1845.

Bleek, Friedrich. *Lectures on the Apocalypse.* Edited by Samuel Davidson. London, 1875.

Book of Common Prayer. London: Barritt and Co., 1837.

Bosanquet, James Whatman. *Messiah the Prince; or, The Inspiration of the Prophecies of Daniel....* 2d ed. London, 1869.

Boyle, William Robert Augustus. *The Inspiration of the Book of Daniel.* London, 1863.

Brown, John. *The Harmony of Scripture Prophecies....* Edinburgh, 1800.

Brown, John Aquila. *The Jew, the Master-Key of the Apocalypse; in Answer to Mr. Frere's "General Structure," and the Dissertations of the Rev. Edward Irving, and Other Commentators.* London, 1827.

Call, W. M. W. "The Apocalypse." *Westminster Review*, o.s. 76, n.s. 20 (Octo-

ber 1861): 448–87.
Cowles, Henry. *The Revelation of John.* . . . New York, 1872.
Cumming, John. *Apocalyptic Sketches; Lectures on the Book of Revelation.* First Series. Philadelphia, 1855.
———. *Apocalyptic Sketches; Lectures on the Book of Revelation.* Second Series. Philadelphia, 1855.
———. *The End; or the Proximate Signs of the Close of the Dispensation.* Boston, 1855.
———. *The Great Tribulation, or the Things Coming on the Earth.* 2 vols. New York, 1860.
———. *Prophetic Studies; Lectures on the Book of Daniel.* Philadelphia, 1854.
Cuninghame, William. *A Critical Examination of Some of the Fundamental Principles of the Rev. George Stanley Faber's Sacred Calendar of Prophecy.* Glasgow, 1829.
———. *A Dissertation on the Seals and Trumpets of the Apocalypse, and the Prophetical Period of 1260 years.* 4th ed. London, 1843.
———. *The Pre-Millennial Advent of Messiah Demonstrated from the Scriptures.* 3d ed. 1828; London, 1836.
Darby, John Nelson. *Notes on the Book of Revelations.* . . . London, 1839.
———. *Studies in the Book of Daniel.* 3d ed. London, 1864.
Daubuz, Charles. *A Perpetual Commentary on the Revelation of St. John.* London, 1720.
Davidson, Samuel. "The Apocalypse of St. John." *National Review* 18 (April 1864): 311–55.
Davison, John. *Discourses on Prophecy . . . Its Structure, Use and Inspiration.* . . . 5th ed. London, 1845.
Desprez, Philip S. *Daniel; or, The Apocalypse of the Old Testament.* London, 1865.
———. *John, or, The Apocalypse of the New Testament.* London, 1870.
De Wette, Wilhelm M. L. *A Critical ana Historical Introduction to the Canonical Scriptures of the Old Testament.* 3d ed. 2 vols. Boston, 1859. First published in English in 1843.
———. *An Historico-Critical Introduction to the Canonical Books of the New Testament.* Translated from the 5th edition by Frederick Frothingham. Boston, 1858.
Döllinger, Johann. *Prophecies and the Prophetic Spirit in the Christian Era.* London, 1873.
Drummond, Henry. "A Popular Introduction to the Study of the Apocalypse." *Christian Observer* (1830): 129–42.
Elliott, Edward Bishop. *Horae Apocalypticae.* 5th ed. 4 vols. London, 1862.
Ewald, Heinrich. *History of Israel.* Translated from the German. 8 vols. London, 1871–86.
Faber, George Stanley. *An Answer to the Reply and Strictures Contained in Mr. Bicheno's Supplement to the Signs of the Times.* London, 1807.

———. *A Dissertation on the Prophecies . . . Relative to the Great Period of the 1260 Years.* 1st American ed. from 2d London ed. 2 vols. in 1. Boston, 1808.

———. *A Dissertation on the Prophecy Contained in Daniel IX. 24–27; Generally Denominated the Prophecy of the 70 Weeks.* London, 1811.

———. *Eight Dissertations on Certain Connected Prophetical Passages. . . .* 2 vols. London, 1845.

———. *A General and Connected View of the Prophecies. . . .* Boston, 1809.

———. *Napoleon III, the Man of Prophecy. . . .* 1st American from 2d English ed. New York, 1859.

———. *The Origin of Pagan Idolatry.* 3 vols. London, 1816.

———. *Remarks on the Effusion of the 5th Apocalyptic Vial. . . .* London, 1815.

———. *The Sacred Calendar of Prophecy.* 3 vols. London, 1828.

———. *The 70 Weeks of Daniel (Dan. 9). . . .* 2d ed. London, 1861.

———. *A Supplement to the Dissertation on the 1260 Years: Containing a Full Reply to . . . the Rev. E. W. Whitaker. . . .* Stockton, England, 1806.

———. *View of the Prophesies Relating to Israel.* 2 vols. London, 1809.

Fairbairn, Patrick. *Prophecy Viewed in Respect to Its Distinctive Nature. . . .* Edinburgh and Philadelphia, 1856. 2d ed. Edinburgh, 1865.

———. *The Typology of Scripture.* From the 3d Edinburgh ed. [Vol. 1, 1845; Vol. 2, 1847]. 2 vols. in 1. Philadelphia, 1859.

Frere, James Hatley. *A Combined View of the Prophecies of Daniel, Esdras, and St. John.* 2d ed. London, 1815.

———. "On the Expectation of an Individual Antichrist." *Christian Observer* (November 1835): 658–61.

———. *On the General Structure of the Apocalypse.* London, 1826.

Fuller, John Mee. *An Essay on the Authenticity of the Book of Daniel.* Cambridge, England, 1864.

Gaussen, Louis. *Geneva and Rome: Rome Papal as Portrayed by Prophecy and History.* With an Introduction by E. Bickersteth. New York, 1844.

Gifford, Edwin Hamilton. *Voices of the Prophets.* Warburtonian Lectures, 1870–74. London, 1874.

Goode, William. *Fulfilled Prophecy a Proof of the Truth of Revealed Religion . . . Including a Full Investigation of Daniel's Prophecy of the Seventy Weeks.* Warburtonian Lectures, 1854–58. London, 1863.

Greg, William Rathbone. *The Creed of Christendom.* London, 1851.

Hedge, Frederic H., ed. *Recent Inquiries in Theology, by Eminent English Churchmen, Being "Essays and Reviews."* 2d American from 2d London ed. Boston, 1861.

Hengstenberg, Ernst Wilhelm. *The Revelation of St. John. . . .* Translated by Patrick Fairbairn. 2 vols. New York, 1852–53.

Hennell, Charles Christian. *An Inquiry Concerning the Origin of Christianity.* London, 1838.

Hennell, Sara Sophia. *The Early Christian Anticipation of an Approaching End*

of the World. . . . London, 1860.
Irving, Edward. *Babylon and Infidelity Foredoomed of God: A Discourse on the Prophecies of Daniel and the Apocalypse*. 2 vols. Glasgow, 1826.
———. *The Coming of the Messiah* . . . by Ben-Ezra [i.e., Manuel Lacunza]. 2 vols. London, 1827.
———. *The Prophetical Works of Edward Irving*. Edited by Gavin Carlyle. 2 vols. London, 1867–70.
Johnston, Bryce. *A Commentary on the Revelation of St. John*. 2 vols. London, 1807.
Keble, John. *The Christian Year*. 1827. Boston, 1867.
Keith, Alexander. *The Evidence of Prophecy*. . . . New York, [1833].
———. *The Harmony of Prophecy; or, Scriptural Illustrations of the Apocalypse*. New York, [1855?].
Kelly, William. *Lectures on the Book of Revelation*. London, 1861. New and rev. ed. Glasgow, 1869.
———. *Notes on the Book of Daniel*. London, [1875?].
———. *The Revelation of John*. . . . London, 1860.
Kuenen, Abraham. *Religion of Israel*. Translated by Alfred Heath May. 3 vols. London, 1875.
Lange, Johann Peter. *The Revelation of John*. Translated by Evelina Moore. New York, 1874. Also in *Lange's Commentary*, ed. Johann Peter Lange. New York, 1868–80.
Lee, Samuel. *Six Sermons on the Study of the Holy Scriptures . . . to Which Are Annexed Two Dissertations . . . the Second on the Interpretation of Prophecy*. London, 1830.
Levi, David. *Dissertations on the Prophecies*. 3 vols. London, 1796–1800.
Lord, David Nevins. *An Exposition of the Apocalypse*. New York, 1847.
Lowman, Moses. *A Paraphrase and Notes on the Revelation of St. John*. 2d ed. London, 1745.
Lowth, Robert. *Lectures on the Sacred Poetry of the Hebrews*. Boston, 1815.
Mackay, Robert William. *The Progress of the Intellect*. 2 vols. London, 1850.
McLeod, Alexander. *Lectures upon the Principal Prophecies of the Revelation*. New York, 1814.
Maitland, Charles. *The Apostles' School of Prophetic Interpretation*. . . . London, 1849.
Mann, Joel. *An Exposition of the Revelation of John*. . . . New York, 1851.
Maurice, F. D. *Lectures on the Apocalypse*. London, 1861.
Mede, Joseph. *The Apostasy of the Latter Times*. 1642. London, 1836, 1845.
———. *Clavis Apocalyptica, or The Key to the Apocalypse*. Translated by a clergyman of the established church. 1632. Dublin, 1831.
———. *Commentary on the Revelation of St. John . . . by a Follower of the Learned Joseph Mede*. Translated by Robert Bronsby Cooper. London, 1833. [Contains a translation of Mede's *Clavis Apocalyptica*.]
———. *The Key of the Revelation*. London, 1643.

———. *Paraphrase and Exposition of the Prophesie of Saint Peter.* London, 1642.
Milman, Henry Hart. *History of the Jews.* 2d ed. New York, 1864.
Muggleton, Ludowick. *A True Interpretation of the Eleventh Chapter of the Revelation of St. John.* 1622. London, 1833.
Newman, J. H. *Lectures on the Prophetical Office of the Church.* . . . London, 1837.
Newton, Isaac. *Observations upon the Prophecies of Daniel, and the Apocalypse of St. John.* London, 1733.
Newton, Thomas, Bp. *Dissertations on the Prophecies.* 1754. London, 1832.
Nolan, Frederick. *The Chronological Prophecies.* London, 1837.
"On the General Scheme and Structure of the Apocalypse." *Jewish Expositor* 12 (1827): 244–50.
Orobio, Balthasar de. *Israel Defended, or The Jewish Exposition of the Hebrew Prophecies Applied by the Christians to Their Messiah.* . . . Trans. from the French, and Printed Exclusively for the Use of Young Persons of the Jewish Faith. London, 1838.
Payne-Smith, Robert. *Prophecy a Preparation for Christ.* Bampton Lectures. London, 1869.
Pearson, Abel. *An Analysis of the Principles of Divine Government . . . and a Dissertation on the Prophecies.* Athens, Tenn. 1833.
"The Prophetic Sentence Denounced against the Serpent." *Christian Observer* (December 1840): 711–15.
Pusey, E. B. *Daniel the Prophet.* London, 1864.
Review of Alexander Keith's *Evidence of the Truth of the Christian Religion, Derived from the Fulfilment of Prophecy. Jewish Expositor* 2 (1826): 290–91.
Review of Works on Prophecy and the Millennium. *Christian Observer* (July and August 1825): 422–35, 489–520.
Richards, George. *The Divine Origin of Prophecy Illustrated and Defended.* Bampton Lectures. Oxford, 1800.
Sawyer, Leicester Ambrose. *Daniel, with Its Apocryphal Additions.* Boston, 1864.
"The School of the Prophets." *The Times*, November 7, 1859.
Southcott, Joanna. *Sound an Alarm in My Holy Mountain.* 3d ed. London, 1806.
Stanley, Arthur Penrhyn. *Lectures on the History of the Jewish Church.* 2 vols. London, 1863–65. A third volume was published in 1876.
Stewart, John. *The Revelation of Nature.* . . . 1790. Reprint. Middletown, N.J., 1835.
Stuart, Moses. *Commentary on the Apocalypse.* 2 vols. Andover, Mass., 1845.
———. *A Commentary on the Book of Daniel.* Boston, 1850.
———. *Hints on the Interpretation of Prophecy.* Andover, Mass., 1842.
Thurman, William Carr. *Our Bible Chronology Established, the Sealed Book of Daniel Opened.* 5th ed. Boston, 1867.

"The Time of the End": . . . Respecting the Prophecies and Periods That Foretell the End. . . . By a Congregationalist. Boston, 1856.
Trench, Richard Chenevix, Archbishop of Dublin. *Commentary on the Epistles to the Seven Churches in Asia.* New York, 1861.
Waldegrave, Samuel. *New Testament Millenarianism.* Bampton Lectures. London, 1855.
Whitaker, Edward William. *Commentary on the Revelation of St. John.* London, 1802.
Williams, Isaac. *The Apocalypse, with Notes and Reflections.* London, 1852.
Winchester, Elhanan. *A Course of Lectures on the Prophecies That Remain to Be Fulfilled.* Walpole, Mass., 1800.
Woodhouse, John Chappel. *The Apocalypse.* London, 1805.
Wordsworth, Christopher. *The Apocalypse.* London, 1849.
Zöckler, Otto. *The Book of the Prophet Daniel. . . .* Translated by James Strong. New York, 1876. In *Lange's Commentary,* ed. Johann Peter Lange. New York, 1868–80.

SECONDARY SOURCES

George Eliot and Victorian Literature

Abel, Elizabeth; Marianne Hirsch; and Elizabeth Langland, eds. *The Voyage In: Fictions of Female Development.* Hanover, N.H.: University Press of New England, 1983.
Abrams, M. H. "English Romanticism: The Spirit of the Age." In *Romanticism Reconsidered,* edited by Northrop Frye, pp. 53–73. New York: Columbia University Press, 1963.
⸻. *The Mirror and the Lamp: Romantic Theory and the Critical Tradition.* London: Oxford University Press, 1953.
⸻. *Natural Supernaturalism: Tradition and Revolution in Romantic Literature.* New York: W. W. Norton & Co., 1971.
Adam, Ian, ed. *This Particular Web: Essays on "Middlemarch."* Toronto: University of Toronto Press, 1975.
Alley, Henry. "New Year's at the Abbey: Point of View in the Pivotal Chapters of *Daniel Deronda.*" *Journal of Narrative Technique* 9 (1979): 147–49.
Austen, Zelda. "Why Feminist Critics Are Angry with George Eliot." *College English* 37 (1976): 549–61.
Baker, Houston A., Jr. "The Poet's Progress: Rossetti's *The House of Life.*" *Victorian Poetry* 8 (1970): 1–14.
Baker, William. *George Eliot and Judaism.* In *Romantic Reassessment,* no. 45, edited by James Hogg. Salzburg, Austria, 1975.
⸻, ed. *The George Eliot–George Henry Lewes Library.* New York: Garland Publishing Co., 1977.

Barricelli, Jean-Pierre. "Romantic Writers and Music: The Case of Mazzini." *Studies in Romanticism* 14 (1975): 95–117.
Beaty, Jerome. "*Daniel Deronda* and the Question of Unity in Fiction." *Victorian Newsletter* 15 (1959): 16–19.
———. "*Middlemarch*" *from Notebook to Novel*. Urbana: University of Illinois Press, 1960.
Beebe, Maurice. "'Visions Are Creators': The Unity of *Daniel Deronda*." *Boston University Studies in English* 1 (1955): 166–77.
Beer, Gillian. *Darwin's Plots: Evolutionary Narrative in Darwin, George Eliot and Nineteenth-Century Fiction*. London: Routledge & Kegan Paul, 1983.
Blake, Kathleen. "*Armgart*—George Eliot on the Woman Artist." *Victorian Poetry* 18 (1980): 75–80.
Bonaparte, Felicia. *The Triptych and the Cross: The Central Myths of George Eliot's Poetic Imagination*. New York: New York University Press, 1979.
———. *Will and Destiny: Morality and Tragedy in George Eliot's Novels*. New York: New York University Press, 1975.
Bright, Michael H. "English Literary Romanticism and the Oxford Movement." *Journal of the History of Ideas* 40 (1979): 385–404.
Brinkley, Roberta Florence. *Coleridge on the Seventeenth Century*. Durham, N.C.: Duke University Press, 1955.
Browne, Thomas. *The Works of Sir Thomas Browne*. Edited by Simon Wilkin. 3 vols. London, 1852.
Browning, Elizabeth Barrett. *Aurora Leigh and Other Poems*. Edited by Cora Kaplan. London: The Women's Press, 1978.
Browning, Robert. *Poems of Robert Browning*. Edited by David Smalley. Boston: Houghton Mifflin Co., Riverside Edition, 1956.
Buckley, Jerome, ed. *The Worlds of Victorian Fiction*. Cambridge, Mass.: Harvard University Press, 1975.
Bullen, J. B. "George Eliot's *Romola* as a Positivist Allegory." *Review of English Studies* 26 (1975): 425–35.
Bullet, Gerald. *George Eliot: Her Life and Books*. London: Collins, 1947.
Burney, Dr. Charles. *General History of Music*. 4 vols. London, 1776–79.
Carroll, David R. "The Unity of *Daniel Deronda*." *Essays in Criticism* 9 (1959): 360–80.
Chase, Cynthia. "The Decomposition of the Elephants: Double-Reading *Daniel Deronda*." *PMLA* 93 (1978): 215–27.
Childs, Herbert E. "Emily Dickinson and Sir Thomas Browne." *American Literature* 22 (1955): 455–65.
Clayton, Jay. "Visionary Power and Narrative Form: Wordsworth and *Adam Bede*." *ELH* 46 (1978): 646–72.
Coleridge, Samuel Taylor. *Selected Poetry and Prose*. Edited by Donald A. Stauffer. New York: Modern Library, 1951.
De Jong, Mary Gosselink. "*Romola*—A *Bildungsroman* for Feminists?" *South Atlantic Review* 49 (1984): 75–90.

Fleishman, Avrom. *The English Historical Novel*. Baltimore: Johns Hopkins University Press, 1971.
———. *Fiction and the Ways of Knowing*. Austin: University of Texas Press, 1978.
———. *Figures of Autobiography: The Language of Self-Writing in Victorian and Modern England*. Berkeley: University of California Press, 1983.
Ford, George H. *Keats and the Victorians*. New Haven: Yale University Press, 1944.
Fraistat, Neil. *The Poem and the Book: Interpreting Collections of Romantic Poetry*. Chapel Hill: University of North Carolina Press, 1985.
Gallagher, Catherine. "The Failure of Realism: *Felix Holt*." *Nineteenth-Century Fiction* 35 (1980): 372–84.
Gangulee, N., ed. *Giuseppe Mazzini: Selected Writings*. 1945. Reprint. Westport, Conn.: Greenwood Press, 1974.
Garrett, Peter K. *The Victorian Multiplot Novel: Studies in Dialogical Form*. New Haven: Yale University Press, 1980.
Gezari, Janet K. "*Romola* and the Myth of the Apocalypse." In *George Eliot: Centenary Essays and an Unpublished Fragment*, edited by Anne Smith, pp. 77–182. Totowa, N.J.: Barnes & Noble, 1980.
Gilbert, Sandra M., and Susan Gubar. *The Madwoman in the Attic: A Study of Women and the Literary Imagination in the Nineteenth Century*. New Haven: Yale University Press, 1979.
Gilligan, Carol. *In a Different Voice: Psychological Theory and Women's Development*. Cambridge, Mass.: Harvard University Press, 1982.
Graver, Suzanne. *George Eliot and Community: A Study in Social Theory and Fictional Form*. Berkeley: University of California Press, 1984.
Greenberg, Robert A. "Plexuses and Ganglia: Scientific Allusions in *Middlemarch*." *Nineteenth-Century Fiction* 30 (1975): 33–52.
Haight, Gordon S. *George Eliot, A Biography*. Oxford: Oxford University Press, 1968.
Hallam, Henry. *Introduction to the Literature of Europe in the 15th, 16th and 17th Centuries*. London, 1839–40.
Hardy, Barbara. *The Novels of George Eliot*. New York: Oxford University Press, 1959.
———, ed. *Critical Essays on George Eliot*. London: Routledge & Kegan Paul, 1970.
———. *Middlemarch: Critical Approaches to the Novel*. London: Routledge & Kegan Paul, 1967.
Harvey, William J. *The Art of George Eliot*. 1969. Reprint. Westport, Conn.: Greenwood Press, 1978.
Henkle, Roger B. *Comedy and Culture: England 1820–1900*. Princeton: Princeton University Press, 1980.
Hertz, Neil. "Recognizing Casaubon." *Glyph* 6 (1979): 24–41.

Hirsch, Marianne. "Spiritual *Bildung*: The Beautiful Soul as Paradigm." In *The Voyage In: Fictions of Female Development*, edited by Elizabeth Abel, Marianne Hirsch, and Elizabeth Langland, pp. 23–48. Hanover, N.H.: University Press of New England, 1983.

Homans, Margaret. *Women Writers and Poetic Identity*. Princeton: Princeton University Press, 1980.

Jacobus, Mary. "The Law of/and Gender: Genre Theory and *The Prelude*." *Diacritics* 14 (1984): 47–57.

Jay, Elisabeth. *The Religion of the Heart*. Oxford: Clarendon Press, 1979.

Joyce, John J. "Music's Principle of Retrograde Motion as a Structuring Element for Browning's Men and Women (1863, 1868)." *Texas Studies in Language and Literature* 22 (1980): 468–83.

Keats, John. *Selected Poems and Letters*. Edited by Douglas Bush. Boston: Houghton Mifflin Co., Riverside Edition, 1959.

Kent, David A. "Sequence and Meaning in Christina Rossetti's Verses (1893)." *Victorian Poetry* 17 (1979): 259–64.

Kermode, Frank. *The Sense of an Ending: Studies in the Theory of Fiction*. Oxford: Oxford University Press, 1966.

Kieft, Ruth Vande. "'When Big Hearts Strike Together': The Concussion of Melville and Sir Thomas Browne." *Papers on Language and Literature* 5 (1969): 39–50.

Kilroy, James. "The Chiastic Structure of *In Memoriam, A. H. H.*" *Philological Quarterly* 56 (1977): 358–73.

Kincaid, James R. "Coherent Readers, Incoherent Texts." *Critical Inquiry* 3 (1977): 781–802.

Knoepflmacher, U. C. *George Eliot's Early Novels: The Limits of Realism*. Berkeley: University of California Press, 1968.

———. "*Middlemarch*: An Avuncular View." *Nineteenth-Century Fiction* 30 (1975): 53–81.

———. *Religious Humanism in the Victorian Novel*. Princeton: Princeton University Press, 1965.

Kriefall, Luther Harry. "A Victorian Apocalypse: A Study of George Eliot's *Daniel Deronda* and Its Relation to David F. Strauss' *Das Leben Jesu*." Ph.D. diss., University of Michigan, 1966.

Landow, George P. *The Aesthetic and Critical Theories of John Ruskin*. Princeton: Princeton University Press, 1971.

———. *Victorian Types, Victorian Shadows: Biblical Typology in Victorian Literature, Art, and Thought*. London: Routledge & Kegan Paul, 1981.

———. *William Holman Hunt and Typological Symbolism*. New Haven: Yale University Press, 1979.

Lang, Paul Henry, ed. *The Creative World of Beethoven*. New York: W. W. Norton & Co., 1970.

Leavis, F. R. *The Great Tradition: George Eliot, Henry James, Joseph Conrad*.

New York: G. W. Stewart, 1949.

Levine, Herbert J. "The Marriage of Allegory and Realism." *Genre* 15 (1982): 421–46.

Lewes, George Henry. "A Word about *Tom Jones*." *Blackwood's* 87 (March 1860): 331–41.

Longyear, Rey M. "Beethoven and Romantic Irony." In *The Creative World of Beethoven*, edited by Paul Henry Lang, pp. 145–62. New York: W. W. Norton & Co., 1970.

McCaffery, Larry. "Robert Coover on His Own and Other Fictions: An Interview." *Genre* 14 (1981): 45–63.

McDonnell, Jane. "'A Little Spirit of Independence'": Sexual Politics and the *Bildungsroman* in *Mansfield Park*." *Novel* 17 (1984): 197–214.

―――. "'Perfect Goodness' or 'The Wider Life': *The Mill on the Floss* as *Bildungsroman*." *Genre* 15 (1982): 379–402.

McGowan, John P. "The Turn of George Eliot's Realism." *Nineteenth-Century Fiction* 35 (1980): 171–92.

Mann, Karen B. "George Eliot and Wordsworth: The Power of Sound and the Power of Mind." *Studies in English Literature* 20 (1980): 675–94.

Martin, Brian W. *John Keble, Priest, Professor and Poet*. London: Croom Helm, 1976.

Martin, Carol A. "George Eliot: Feminist Critic." *Victorian Newsletter* 65 (1984): 22–25.

Mellor, Anne K. *English Romantic Irony*. Cambridge, Mass.: Harvard University Press, 1980.

Miller, J. Hillis. "Narrative and History." *ELH* 41 (1974): 455–73.

―――. "Optic and Semiotic in *Middlemarch*." In *The Worlds of Victorian Fiction*, edited by Jerome Buckley, pp. 125–45. Cambridge, Mass.: Harvard University Press, 1975.

Miller, Nancy. "Emphasis Added: Plots and Plausibilities in Women's Fiction." *PMLA* 96 (1981): 36–48.

Moers, Ellen. *Literary Women*. New York: Oxford University Press, 1963.

Newsome, David. *Two Classes of Men: Platonism and English Romantic Thought*. London: John Murray, 1972.

Newton, K. M. *George Eliot, Romantic Humanist*. Totowa, N.J.: Barnes & Noble, 1981.

―――. "*Daniel Deronda* and Circumcision." *Essays in Criticism* 31 (1981): 313–27.

Paden, W. D. *Tennyson in Egypt: A Study of the Imagery in His Earlier Work*. Lawrence: University of Kansas Publications, 1942.

Palliser, Charles. "*Adam Bede* and 'The Story of the Past.'" In *George Eliot: Centenary Essays and an Unpublished Fragment*, edited by Anne Smith, pp. 55–76. Totowa, N.J.: Barnes & Noble, 1980.

Paris, Bernard J. *Experiments in Life*. Detroit: Wayne State University Press, 1965.

Patrides, C. A., ed. *Approaches to Sir Thomas Browne*. Columbia: University of Missouri Press, 1982.
Peterson, Virgil A. "*Romola*: A Victorian Quest for Values." *Philological Papers* 16 (1967): 49–62.
Poston, Lawrence. "Setting and Theme in *Romola*." *Nineteenth-Century Fiction* 20 (1966): 355–66.
Prickett, Stephen. *Romanticism and Religion*. Cambridge, England: Cambridge University Press, 1979.
Robertson, Alec, and Denis Stevens, eds. *Pelican History of Music: Classical and Romantic*. Harmondsworth: Penguin Books, 1968.
Robinson, Carole. "*Romola*: A Reading of the Novel." *Victorian Studies* 6 (1962): 29–42.
Rosenberg, John. "The Two Kingdoms in *In Memoriam*." *Journal of English and Germanic Philology* 58 (1959): 228–40.
Sadoff, Diane F. *Monsters of Affection: Dickens, Eliot and Bronte on Fatherhood*. Baltimore: Johns Hopkins University Press, 1982.
―――. "Nature's Language: Metaphor in the Text of *Adam Bede*." *Genre* 11 (1978): 411–26.
Sedgwick, Eve Kosofsky. *Between Men: English Literature and Male Homosocial Desire*. New York: Columbia University Press, 1985.
Shaffer, E. S. *"Kubla Khan" and the Fall of Jerusalem: The Mythological School in Biblical Criticism and Secular Literature 1770–1880*. Cambridge, England: Cambridge University Press, 1975.
Showalter, Elaine. *A Literature of Their Own: British Women Novelists from Brontë to Lessing*. Princeton: Princeton University Press, 1977.
―――. "Towards a Feminist Poetics." In *Women Writing and Writing about Women*, edited by Mary Jacobus, pp. 22–41. London: Croom Helm, 1979.
Stange, G. Robert. "The Voices of the Essayist." *Nineteenth-Century Fiction* 35 (1980): 312–30.
Stump, Reva. *Movement and Vision in George Eliot's Novels*. Seattle: University of Washington Press, 1959.
Sudrann, Jean. "*Daniel Deronda* and the Landscape of Exile." *ELH* 37 (1970): 433–55.
Sullivan, W. J. "The Sketch of the Three Masks in *Romola*." *Victorian Newsletter* 41 (1972): 9–13.
Sussman, Herbert L. *Fact into Figure: Typology in Carlyle, Ruskin, and the Pre-Raphaelite Brotherhood*. Columbus: Ohio University Press, 1979.
Swann, Brian. "Eyes in the Mirror: Imagery and Symbolism in *Daniel Deronda*." *Nineteenth-Century Fiction* 23 (1969): 434–45.
―――. "George Eliot's Ecumenical Jew, or the Novel as Outdoor Temple." *Novel* 8 (1974–75): 39–50.
Tennyson, Alfred Tennyson, Baron. *The Poetry of Tennyson*. Edited by A. Dwight Culler. New Haven: Yale University Press, 1977.

Tennyson, G. B. *Victorian Devotional Poetry*. Cambridge, Mass.: Harvard University Press, 1981.
Thompson, Elbert N. S. "*The Temple* and the *Christian Year*." *PMLA* 54 (1939): 1018–25.
Warren, Alba H. *English Poetic Theory, 1828–1865*. Princeton: Princeton University Press, 1950.
Wiesenfarth, Joseph. *George Eliot's Mythmaking*. Heidelberg: Carl Winter, Universitätsverlag, 1977.
Willey, Basil. *Nineteenth-Century Studies: Coleridge to Matthew Arnold*. London: Chatto & Windus, 1949.
Wilson, Katharina M. "The Key to All Mythologies—A Possible Source of Inspiration." *Victorian Newsletter* 61 (1982): 27–28.
Witemeyer, Hugh. *George Eliot and the Visual Arts*. New Haven: Yale University Press, 1979.
Wordsworth, William. *Selected Poems and Prefaces*. Edited by Jack Stillinger. Boston: Riverside Edition, Houghton Mifflin Co., 1965.
Yonge, Charlotte. *Musings Over the Christian Year*. 2d ed. London, 1872.

Nineteenth-Century British Millenarianism and the Idea of History

Arnold, Matthew. *Culture and Anarchy*. Edited by J. Dover Wilson. Cambridge, England: Cambridge University Press, 1969.
Bauckham, Richard. *Tudor Apocalypse*. Oxford: Sutton Courtenoy Press, 1978.
Bercovitch, Sacvan, ed. *Typology and Early American Literature*. Amherst: University of Massachusetts Press, 1972.
Birks, T. R. *Memoir of the Rev. Edward Bickersteth*. 2 vols. New York: Harper & Brothers, 1851.
Browne, Thomas. *Sir Thomas Browne: The Major Works*. Edited by C. A. Patrides. New York: Penguin Books, 1977.
Buckley, Jerome H. *The Triumph of Time—A Study of Victorian Concepts of Time, History, Progress and Decadence*. Oxford: Oxford University Press, 1967.
Call, W. M. W. "The Religion of Positivism." *Westminster Review*, o.s. 69, n.s. 13 (April 1858): 305–50.
Chadwick, Owen. *The Victorian Church*. 2 vols. New York: Oxford University Press, 1966.
Charles, R. H. *Studies in the Apocalypse*. Edinburgh: T. & T. Clark, 1913.
Christianson, Paul. *Reformers and Babylon: English Apocalyptic Visions from the Reformation to the Eve of the Civil War*. Toronto: Toronto University Press, 1979.
Clements, Ronald Ernest. *One Hundred Years of Old Testament Interpretation*. Philadelphia: Westminster Press, 1976.

Cohn, Norman. *The Pursuit of the Millennium: Revolutionary and Mystical Anarchists of the Middle Ages*. New York: Oxford University Press, 1970.
Collingwood, R. G. *The Idea of History*. Oxford: Clarendon Press, 1946.
Court, John. *Myth and History in the Book of Revelation*. London: SPCK, 1979.
Dale, Peter Allen. *The Victorian Critic and the Idea of History: Carlyle, Arnold and Pater*. Cambridge, Mass.: Harvard University Press, 1977.
Dudley, Guilford. *The Recovery of Christian Myth*. Philadelphia: Westminster Press, 1967.
Eliade, Mircea. *The Myth of the Eternal Return*. New York: Pantheon Books, 1954.
Elliott-Binns, L. E. *Religion in the Victorian Era*. Greenwich, Conn.: Seabury Press, 1953.
Evans, Arthur William. *Warburton and the Warburtonians: A Study in Some Eighteenth-Century Controversies*. London: Oxford University Press and H. Milford, 1932.
Fairfield, Leslie P. *John Bale, Mythmaker for the English Reformation*. West Lafayette, Ind.: Purdue University Press, 1976.
Farrer, Austin Marsden. *A Rebirth of Images: The Making of St. John's Apocalypse*. Glasgow: Glasgow University Press, 1949.
Firth, Katharine R. *The Apocalyptic Tradition in Reformation Britain, 1530–1645*. Oxford: Oxford University Press, 1979.
Fisch, Harold. *Jerusalem and Albion: The Hebraic Factor in Seventeenth-Century Literature*. New York: Schocken Books, 1964.
Fixler, Michael. *Milton and the Kingdoms of God*. Evanston, Ill.: Northwestern University Press, 1964.
Forbes, Duncan. *The Liberal Anglican Idea of History*. Cambridge, England: Cambridge University Press, 1952.
Ford, Massyngberde J. "Revelation." In *The Anchor Bible*. New York: Doubleday and Co., 1975.
Fowler, Alastair. *Silent Poetry: Essays in Numerological Analysis*. New York: Barnes & Noble, 1970.
Frei, Hans W. *The Eclipse of Biblical Narrative*. New Haven: Yale University Press, 1974.
Froom, Le Roy Edwin. *The Prophetic Faith of Our Fathers: The Historical Development of Prophetic Interpretation*. 4 vols. Washington, D.C.: Review and Herald, 1946.
Garrett, Clarke. *Respectable Folly: Millenarians and the French Revolution in France and England*. Baltimore: Johns Hopkins University Press, 1975.
Handlin, Oscar. *Truth in History*. Cambridge, Mass.: Belknap Press, Harvard University Press, 1979.
Harrison, Frederick. "Neo-Christianity." *Westminster Review*, o.s. 74, n.s. 18 (October 1860): 293–332.
Harrison, J. F. C. *The Second Coming: Popular Millenarianism, 1780–1850*.

New Brunswick, N.J.: Rutgers University Press, 1979.
Hartman, Louis F., and Alexander A. Di Lella. "The Book of Daniel." In *The Anchor Bible*. New York: Doubleday & Co., 1978.
Heideman, Margaret A. "*Hydriotaphia* and *The Garden of Cyrus*: A Paradox and a Cosmic Vision." *University of Toronto Quarterly* 19 (1950): 235–46.
Heninger, S. K., Jr. *The Cosmographical Glass: Renaissance Diagrams of the Universe*. San Marino, Calif.: Huntington Library, 1977.
Heschel, Abraham. *The Prophets*. 1962. Reprint. New York: Harper and Row, 1969.
Hill, Christopher. *Antichrist in Seventeenth-Century England*. London: Oxford University Press, 1971.
Holloway, John. *The Victorian Sage*. London: Macmillan and Co., 1953.
Houghton, Walter. *The Victorian Frame of Mind, 1830–1870*. New Haven: Yale University Press, 1957.
Huntley, Frank Livingstone. "*The Garden of Cyrus* as Prophecy." In *Approaches to Sir Thomas Browne*, ed. C. A. Patrides, pp. 132–42. Columbia: University of Missouri Press, 1982.
———. *Sir Thomas Browne: A Biographical and Critical Study*. Ann Arbor: University of Michigan Press, 1962.
Jay, Elisabeth. *The Religion of the Heart*. Oxford: Clarendon Press, 1979.
Kermode, Frank. *The Genesis of Secrecy; On the Interpretation of Narrative*. Cambridge, Mass.: Harvard University Press, 1979.
———. *The Sense of an Ending*. London: Oxford University Press, 1966.
Kerrigan, William. *The Prophetic Milton*. Charlottesville: University Press of Virginia, 1974.
Kozicki, Henry. *Tennyson and Clio: History in the Major Poems*. Baltimore: Johns Hopkins University Press, 1980.
Lacocque, Andrew. *The Book of Daniel*. Atlanta: John Knox Press, 1979.
Landow, George P. "Bruising the Serpent's Head: Typological Symbol in Victorian Poetry." *Victorian Newsletter* 55 (Spring 1979): 11–14.
LaValley, Albert J. *Carlyle and the Idea of the Modern: Studies in Carlyle's Prophetic Literature and Its Relation to Blake, Nietzsche, Marx, and Others*. New Haven: Yale University Press, 1968.
Lawrence, D. H. *Apocalypse*. Florence: G. Orioli, 1931.
Lewalski, Barbara Kiefer. *Protestant Poetics and the Seventeenth-Century Religious Lyric*. Princeton: Princeton University Press, 1979.
———. "*Samson Agonistes* and the Tragedy of the Apocalypse." *PMLA* 85 (1970): 1050–62.
Lindsey, Hal. *The Late Great Planet Earth*. New York: Bantam Books, 1970.
McGinn, Bernard. *Visions of the End: Apocalyptic Traditions in the Middle Ages*. New York: Columbia University Press, 1979.
Mackay, Robert. *The Rise and Progress of Christianity*. London, 1854.
Manuel, Frank E. *Shapes of Philosophical History*. Stanford: Stanford University Press, 1965.

Martin, William. "Waiting for the End." *Atlantic Monthly* (June 1982): 31–37.
Martineau, James. "Early History of Messianic Ideas." *National Review* 18 (April 1864): 554–79.
Mill, John Stuart. *The Spirit of the Age*. 1831. Chicago: University of Chicago Press, 1942.
Milman, H. H. "Savonarola." *Quarterly Review* 99 (June 1856): 1–60.
Miner, Earl Roy, ed. *Literary Uses of Typology*. Princeton: Princeton University Press, 1977.
Mirandola, Pico Della. *Heptaplus*. Translated by Douglas Carmichael. Indianapolis: Bobbs-Merrill Co., 1940.
Morris, David. *The Religious Sublime: Christian Poetry and Critical Tradition in Eighteenth-Century England*. Lexington: University of Kentucky Press, 1972.
Nolan, Barbara. *The Gothic Visionary Perspective*. Princeton: Princeton University Press, 1977.
Patrides, C. A. *The Grand Design of God*. London: Routledge & Kegan Paul, 1972.
——, and Joseph A. Wittreich, Jr., eds. *The Apocalypse in English Renaissance Thought and Literature*. Manchester, England: Manchester University Press, 1984.
Preus, James. *From Shadow to Promise: Old Testament Interpretation from Augustine to the Youth Luther*. Cambridge, Mass.: Belknap Press, Harvard University Press, 1969.
Reeves, Marjorie. *The Influence of Prophecy in the Later Middle Ages: A Study of Joachimism*. Oxford: Clarendon Press, 1969.
Roston, Murray. *Prophet and Poet*. Evanston, Ill.: Northwestern University Press, 1965.
Sandeen, Ernest R. *The Roots of Fundamentalism: British and American Millenarianism, 1800–1932*. Chicago: University of Chicago Press, 1970.
Tuveson, Ernest Lee. *Redeemer Nation: The Idea of America's Millennial Role*. Chicago: University of Chicago Press, 1968.
Villari, Pasquale. *The History of Girolamo Savonarola and of His Times*. Translated by Leonard Horner. London, 1863.
Weinstein, Donald. *Savonarola and Florence, Prophecy and Patriotism in the Renaissance*. Princeton: Princeton University Press, 1970.
Williams, Carolyn. "Typology as Narrative Form: The Temporal Logic of *Marius*." *English Literature in Transition* 27 (1984): 11–30.
Wittreich, Joseph A., Jr. *Visionary Poetics: Milton's Tradition and His Legacy*. San Marino, Calif.: Huntington Library, 1979.
Yost, George. "Sir Thomas Browne and Aristotle." In *Studies in Sir Thomas Browne*, by Robert Ralston Cawley and George Yost. Eugene: University of Oregon, 1965.

Index

Acts of the Apostles, 44
Ages of time, seven, 81, 83, 92; of Abraham, 58, 96; of Babylonian Exile or Captivity, 59, 98; of Christianity, 60, 99; of Creation, 85; of David, 58, 97; of Flood, 94, 98
Albury Park, 10
Alford, Henry, 21
Angel Gabriel, 139, 146, 164
Apocalypse, The, 3, 4, 6, 9, 11, 18, 23, 24, 25, 27, 28, 61, 63, 74, 76, 81, 82, 83, 96, 100, 122, 140. *See also* Revelation, Book of
Apocalypse of history, 30, 54, 60, 101, 103

Bale, John, 18
Baptism, 33, 46, 47, 48, 51, 98, 101; baptismal rite, 19
Basilicus. *See* Way, Lewis
Bede, the Venerable, 32, 50
Beethoven, Ludwig, 120, 170
Berlioz, Hector, 169
Bicheno, James: *Signs of the Times*, 8
Bickersteth, Edward, 14, 73, 81, 84, 99, 137; *Practical Guide to the Prophecies*, 10, 12; *Practical Remarks on the Prophecies*, 12; *Scripture Help*, 7, 10
Bildungsroman, 62
Binary apocalyptic structure, 30, 64, 67; "continuous historical" structure, 117; division, 39, 64, 66. *See also* Midpoint division
Birks, T. R.: *The Four Prophetic Empires*, 134
Blackwood, John, 156
Boccaccio, Giovanni, 156, 172
Boniface, third Bishop of Rome, 10
Book of Common Prayer, 157
Book of Origins, 147, 148, 153
Browne, Sir Thomas, 105, 107, 110, 112, 113, 118, 120, 127; *Brampton Urns*, 110; *Garden of Cyrus*, 105, 106, 108, 109, 111, 112; *Pseudodoxia Epidemica*, 105, 107, 118; *Urn Burial*, 109, 110, 111; *Works*, ed. Simon Wilkin, 107
Browning, Elizabeth Barrett: *Aurora Leigh*, 166
Browning, Robert, 155, 156, 165, 185
Bullinger, Henry, 18
Burgh, William, 22

Calendar, 38, 44; Anglican, 41, 51, 157; Christian, 156; church, 32
Call, W. M. W., 26, 27, 28, 29, 103, 155, 174
Casaubon, Isaac, 110
Casaubon, Meric, 110, 111
Catholic Apostolic church, 13
Catholic Emancipation Bill (Act), 3, 13
Cave of Hera, 8
Christian Observer, 11–14, 16, 82

Index

Christian's Family Library, 7, 10, 134
Chronology, 30–32, 35, 38, 51, 55, 61, 82
Columbus, Christopher, 81
Communion, 47; eucharist, 72
Comte, Auguste: *Catechism of Positive Religion*, 26
Comtean age of fiction, 85; banner, 27; conception, 61; doctrine, 102; interpretation, 26, 74, 155; New Jerusalem, 101; sense, 160; stages, 63
Constantine, 11, 13
Continuous historical apocalyptics, 23, 47, 63, 73, 80; exegesis, x, 17, 24, 61, 137; exegetes, 76, 81; exposition, xi, 3, 21, 22, 73; expositors, 4, 8, 9; hermeneutics, 5; interpretation, ix, 8, 11, 13, 66, 69, 134, 136, 138
Corinthians, First Epistle to, 181
Cumming, John, 17, 19, 21–23, 27, 62, 114–15, 122–24; *Apocalyptic Sketches: Lectures on the Book of Revelation*, 20, 115
Cuninghame, William, 10

Daniel, Book of, ix, 21, 24, 27, 64, 67, 75–80, 134, 137; "Ancient of Days," 142; "Apocalypse of the Old Testament," 131–53; Four Empires, 24, 64, 75–80, 121; "little horn," 8; Nebuchadnezzar's Dream, 134; Seventy Weeks, 101, 118, 136–42; "Son of man," 142
Daubuz, Charles: *Perpetual Commentary on the Revelation of St. John*, 18
Davidson, Samuel, 21, 28
Davison, John: *Discourses on Prophecy*, 12, 15, 134, 136
Days of creation, seven, 83, 96–98
Defoe, Daniel: *History of the Devil*, 57–58

Desprez, Philip S.: *Daniel; or, the Apocalypse of the Old Testament*, 22
DeWette, Wilhelm M. L., 21; *Commentary on the Old Testament*, 22
Drummond, Henry: "Popular Introduction to the Study of the Apocalypse," 13

Ecclesiastical chart, 7, 11, 15; history, 4, 8, 30, 32, 53, 189
Ecclesiasticus, 123
Eliot, George: *Adam Bede*, 5, 29, 30–53, 55, 59, 63, 72, 95, 116, 139, 144; "Agatha," 163–65, 171, 185; "Arion," 186–87; "Armgart," 165–71; "Brother and Sister," 178–83; *Daniel Deronda*, 4, 77, 118, 119, 131–53; "Erinna," 162–63, 167; "Evangelical Teaching: Dr. Cumming," 20; *Felix Holt, The Radical*, ix, 133; "How Lisa Loved the King," 171–74; "In the South," 156; "Janet's Repentance," 30, 66; "Knowing That Shortly I Must Put Off This Tabernacle," 14, 16; *Legend of Jubal*, 154–90; "The Legend of Jubal," 158–64, 179; "The Lifted Veil," 68; *Middlemarch*, 104–29, 133, 136, 139, 145, 158, 164, 166, 172, 177, 179, 185; *Middlemarch Miscellany*, 108, 123; *Mill on the Floss*, 54–60, 69, 71, 97, 98, 100, 101, 102, 117, 179; "A Minor Prophet," 174–78; "My Vegetarian Friend," 175; "O May I Join The Choir Invisible," 187–89; "Oriental Memoranda," 132, 147; "The Progress of the Intellect," 70; *Romola*, 4, 25, 29, 30, 33, 47, 54–103, 116, 117, 121, 129, 131, 133, 136, 139, 155, 189; *Scenes of Clerical Life*, 4, 30; "Stradivarius," 183–86; "Two

Lovers," 185–86
Elliott, Edward Bishop, 17–20, 22, 23, 96; *Horae Apocalypticae,* 17, 18, 20, 24; "Sketch of the History of Apocalyptic Interpretation," 24
Enoch, Book of, 27
Esdras, Fourth Book of, 27
Essays and Reviews, 4, 77, 78, 133
Esther, Book of, 133, 138
Ewald, Heinrich, 21
Exodus, Book of, 148
Ezekiel, Book of, 38

Faber, George Stanley, 10, 12, 24; *Dissertation on . . . 1260 Years,* 8, 24; *Sacred Calendar of Prophecy,* 10, 24, 96, 136, 137
Fairbairn, Patrick, x
Fathers of the Church, 55
Flashback, 95, 96
Foxe, John, 18
French Revolution, 3, 6, 8, 9, 10, 13, 17, 18, 22, 23, 28
Frere, James Hatley, 10, 13
Futurist expositors, 22; school, 21

Galatians, Epistle to, 40
Genesis, Book of, 53, 82, 158, 182
Gluck, C. W.: *Orfeo and Eurydice,* 165, 169
Golden Age, 75, 78, 85
Guest, Edwin: *A History of English Rhythms,* 109

Harrison, Frederick, 78
Hennell, Charles: *An Inquiry Concerning the Origin of Christianity,* 15
Hennell, Sarah: *End of the World,* 25–28
Herbert, George: "Easter," 184
Hesiod, Four Ages of, 77, 78; Hesiodic cycle, 81

Irenaeus, 27
Irving, Edward, 10, 13; Irvingites, 5
Isaiah, Book of, 33, 35, 173; "Good Shepherd," 34, 36, 47, 50

Jackson, Martha, 11
Jeremiah, Book of, 37, 137
Jewish Civil Disabilities Bill, 3, 14
Jewish Expositor, 9, 12
Jewish Sibyl, 27
Jews, London Society for the Conversion of, 9, 12
Jews, prophetic history of, 135–53
Joachim of Fiore, 6, 27; Joachimite, 63; myth of Fra Angelico, 81
Joel, Book of, 44, 52
John the Baptist, 84. *See also* Liturgical year: John the Baptist, Feast of
John the Evangelist, 166
Juda, Leo, 18
Justinian, 8, 10; Justinian Code, 10, 17

Keats, John: *Lamia, Isabella, The Eve of St. Agnes and Other Poems,* 156, 157, 171
Keble, John: *The Christian Year,* 41, 73, 85, 121, 151, 152, 154–90
Kempis, Thomas à, 58, 59, 69, 71
Kuenen, Abraham, 132, 149; *Religion of Israel,* 142, 143, 147

Lectionary, Anglican, 32, 38, 48, 49
Leviticus, Book of, 148
Lewes, George Henry, 64–65; *Problems of Life and Mind,* 142
Lewis, Maria, 5, 7, 11
Liturgical year, 83, 154, 155, 157; Advent, 84, 94, 95, 157, 158, 163; Advent, Fourth Sunday in, 159; Advent Sunday, 159; All

Saints' Day, 73, 84; Ascension, 157, 188; Ash Wednesday, 44, 51, 52; Christmas, 84, 95, 97, 150, 157, 163, 165, 166, 174, 178; Christmas, First Sunday after, 171; Circumcision, Feast of, 150, 151, 152; Easter, 101, 118, 178; Easter, Monday before, 186; Epiphany, 174; Epiphany, Sixth Sunday after, 174, 177; Good Friday, 157, 186; Holy Innocents, 166; Holy Week, 156, 178; John the Baptist, Feast of, 33, 34, 37, 45, 47, 48, 84, 85; Lent, 178; Lent, Second Sunday in, 53; New Year's Day, 150, 151, 152; Palm Sunday, 100, 121, 183, 186; Pre-Lenten Sundays, 178, 181; Quinquagesima, 178, 181; Saint Stephen's Day, 166; Septuagesima, 178; Sexagesima, 178, 181; Trinity, Twentieth Sunday after, 51; Trinity, Twenty-fourth Sunday after, 41, 52
London Society for the Conversion of the Jews, 9, 12
Louis Napoleon, 94
Luke, Gospel of, 35, 48; evangelist, 123
Luther, Martin, 73
Lydgate, John, 109, 110

Mackay, Robert, 20, 82, 99; *Progress of the Intellect*, 15, 24, 70, 77, 85, 97; *Rise and Progress of Christianity*, 20, 71
Mahommedanism, 7, 8; "Mahomet," 8, 10, 13
Maitland, S. R., 22
Malachi, Book of, 85
Matthew, Gospel of, 50
Maurice, F. D., 26–28, 74; *Lectures on the Apocalypse*, 25

Mazzini, Giuseppe: *Filosophia della Musica*, 126–29
Mede, Joseph, 10–12, 15, 18, 23, 67, 74, 95, 136, 137
Meier, Karl, 70
Messiah, 137, 144
Methodist women preachers, 31, 35, 50
Midpoint division, 59, 150. *See also* Binary apocalyptic structure
Midsummer, 85
Mill, John Stuart, 3
Millenarianism, 6, 14, 17
Milton, 111, 158; "L'Allegro" and "Il Penseroso," 109; "Lycidas," 184; Milton's Christ, 144; *Paradise Lost*, 57, 182; *Paradise Regained*, 144
Monotheism (Comtean stage), 63

Napoleonic Wars, 3
Neoplatonism, 185; Neoplatonic, 108, 112, 113, 121, 124, 129, 184
Newton, Isaac, 18
Newton, Thomas (bishop), 9, 18, 67, 69
Numbers, Book of, 148
Numerological implications, 139; symbolism, xi, 96; web, 113, 121
Numerology, 26, 34, 117, 118, 129

Ottoman Empire, 19

Passover, 41
Peter, Second Epistle, 14
Philo, 118
Philosophy of history, 61
Phocas, 7, 8, 10, 17
Plato, 118
Platonist, 84, 112
Plymouth Brethren, 22
Polytheism (Comtean stage), 63
Positivism (Comtean stage), 63, 165

Praeterist, 21
Prophecy and history, x, 48–49
Prophecy "fulfilled and unfulfilled," 3, 11
Prophecy of the Seventy Weeks, 101, 118, 136–42. *See also* Daniel, Book of
Prophetess, 39, 43, 48, 49, 50
Protestantism, 10, 58, 59, 62, 63, 66, 70, 71, 101
Proverbs, Book of, 41
Pusey, E. B.: *Daniel the Prophet*, 133, 134
Puseyites, 19
Pythagoras, 118; Pythagorean, 113, 119; Pythagorean-Platonic, 106

Realism, 31, 62, 106
Reform Act (Bill), 3, 117
Reformation (Protestant), 3, 6, 7, 13, 18, 19, 23, 64, 66, 67, 70, 71, 74, 80, 81, 116
Reform Movement, 13
Revelation, Book of, ix, 3, 6, 7, 8, 9, 10, 13, 15, 17, 18, 21, 61, 62, 66, 67, 73, 74, 100, 103, 122, 137, 139, 145; angel, rainbow-crowned, 67; Antichrist, 19, 94; Armageddon, 19; beast, 8, 9, 10, 27, 83, 100, 119; false prophet, 100, 119; harvest of the Church, 73; harvest of the earth, 11; little book opened, 67; little open book, 66, 98; seal(s), 13, 63, 64, 66, 67; sealed book, 66; sealed nation, 10, 62; septenary, 3, 63; structuring, 54; trumpets, 13, 21, 63, 67; vials, 3, 12, 13, 18, 19, 21, 63; witnesses, two, 18, 33, 47, 69, 73, 145; Whore of Babylon, 100; woman clothed with the sun, 26, 27, 54, 67, 74, 82, 97, 100, 104, 119, 145, 155. *See also* Apocalypse, The
Revolution of 1848, 3, 19, 20
Ritter, Charles (translator), 187
Roman Catholicism, 19, 70
Romans, Epistle to, 159
Romantic poets, 23
Rossetti, Christina, 155
Rossetti, Dante Gabriel, 155

Savonarola, Girolamo, 4, 27, 29, 62–64, 66, 69–71, 73–77, 79, 83, 84, 94, 95, 97–101, 115, 150
Scheme of the Apocalypse, 7, 54–103, 104
School of the prophets, 4, 21, 32
Scott, Thomas, 7
Second Advent, 3, 11, 18, 19, 55, 94, 174
Second Coming, 160
Seeley and Burnside, 11
Septenary structure, 33, 54, 55, 64, 81, 83, 84; symbolism, 98, 113; unit, 50, 74, 101
Southcott (Southcote), Joanna, 5, 6
Spenser, Edmund, 176
Spinoza, Baruch: *Tractatus Theologico-Politicus*, 15
Stoicism, 69, 75, 76; Stoical philosophy, 72
Strauss, David: *Das Leben Jesu*, 15
Stuart, Moses, 21, 133; *Commentary on the Apocalypse*, 21
Synchronization, 96, 100

Tabernacles, Feast of, 11, 73. *See also* Revelation, Book of: harvest of the Church; Revelation, Book of: harvest of the earth
Talmud, 147
Temple, Frederick: "The Education of the World," 77, 78, 98
Tennyson, Alfred, Lord: *In Memoriam*, 155, 158, 177

Tertiary apocalyptic configuration, 64; scheme, 63
Timothy, First Epistle to, 40
Todd, J. H., 22
Tractarians, 22
Turkish Empire, 12, 19, 20
1260 Days, 8, 10
Typological interpretation, 73, 82, 136, 138, 141, 163, 165
Typology, x

Universalgeschichte, 15, 70, 78
Universal history, 15, 32

Villari, Pasquale: *History of Girolamo Savonarola*, 70, 84

Waldenses, 18
Warburtonian Lectures, 134
Warton, Thomas: *The History of English Poetry*, 109, 121
Way, Lewis [pseud. Basilicus], 12
Westminster Review, 20, 25, 27, 70, 78, 127
Wilkin, Simon, ed.: *The Works of Sir Thomas Browne*, 107, 109
Williams, Rowland, 134
Women preachers, Methodist, 31, 35, 50
Woodhouse, John: *The Apocalypse*, 8
Wordsworth, William, 156, 159, 160, 179

Year-day principle, 8
Yonge, Charlotte: *Musings Over the Christian Year*, 163, 171, 174, 178, 180, 181

www.ingramcontent.com/pod-product-compliance
Lightning Source LLC
Chambersburg PA
CBHW021359290426
44108CB00010B/302